CLAIRE MONTGOMERIE'S

COMPLETE GUIDE TO GRANNY SQUARES

100 mix-and-match designs, with charts, written patterns and 8 stunning projects

CLAIRE MONTGOMERIE'S

COMPLETE GUIDE TO GRANNY SQUARES

100 mix-and-match designs, with charts, written patterns and 8 stunning projects

SEARCH PRESS

CONTENTS

page 54

page 56

page 58

page 60

page 62

page 64

page 66

page 68

page 70

page 72

page 74

page 76

page 78

page 80

page 82

page 84

page 86

page 88

page 90

page 92

page 94

page 96

page 98

page 100

page 102

page 104

page 106

page 108

page 110

page 112

page 114

page 116

page 118

page 120

page 122

page 124

page 126

page 128

page 130

page 132

page 134

page 136

page 138

page 140

page 142

page 144

page 146

page 148

page 150

page 152

page 154

page 156

page 158

page 160

page 162

page 164

page 166

page 168

page 170

page 172

page 174

page 176

page 178

page 180

page 182

page 184

page 186

page 188

page 190

page 192

page 194

page 196

page 198

page 200

page 202

page 204

page 206

page 208

page 210

page 212

page 214

page 216

page 218

page 220

page 222

page 224

page 226

page 228

page 230

page 232

page 234

page 236

page 238

page 240

page 242

page 244

page 246

page 248

page 250

page 252

INTRODUCTION

I have been blown away by the overwhelmingly positive reception to *The Granny Square Card Deck™* series. The card decks have been translated into 13 languages and I regularly receive lovely messages about them from around the world, sharing with me what people have been inspired to make using the building blocks of the card motifs. I am so pleased that people have been so inspired by the patterns and so many crocheters, both experienced and newbies, have been able to learn how to read charts by following them. These are precisely the ways I had hoped that the decks would be used – as a tool of inspiration for creating your own individual projects and as a teaching tool.

However, I do sometimes get requests for the written patterns to accompany the charts, and if I have any projects that demonstrate how to use the squares, so I have created this book as a handy information pack that can be used alongside the card decks or on its own to create beautiful motifs and projects. I've combined all the content from two of the decks, along with a step-by-step guide to everything you need to use them, including the written patterns for the charted motifs, in case you prefer to follow written instructions or if you wish to use those instructions alongside the cards to help you read the charts.

Within this book you'll find 100 granny-square designs to choose from. Every stunning design is shown with both a full written pattern and a crochet chart. If you need some help reading crochet charts, a complete guide, along with two step-by-step examples, is given on pages 34–41.

With this colorful book I hope to demonstrate that you can produce stunning patterns and joyful fabrics either by simply repeating one of the squares or by combining multiple motifs. I want to encourage you to play with color and your hook size to literally think outside of the box and the original 4 x 4in (10 x 10cm) format to crochet motifs of many different sizes. Just one simple change can generate totally unexpected results, such as the delightfully bold and wonderfully cozy oversized scarf on page 276 which is made on such a large hook that it will work up in no time at all.

I hope you enjoy using this book as much as I have enjoyed creating both it and *The Granny Square Card Deck™* series, and don't forget to show me what you make!

Please note, **US crochet terms** are used throughout; you can find US to UK conversion guides on pages 30–31 and on the book's flaps.

Happy crocheting!

Claire Montgomerie

GETTING STARTED

The way you use this book will depend on many things; whether you are learning to crochet granny squares, are recreating one of the projects in the book or are wanting to create your own bespoke project. In fact, you might want to use the book as a guide to do all of these things eventually! All you need to know is that there is a motif library of 100 squares of varying complexity that you can use as samplers to perfect your technique or as building blocks to a final project.

If you want to hook any of the projects shown in this book, you can create them exactly as I have, using the same motifs, the same hook and the same colors, or you can play with all of these elements. As all of the motifs are designed to fit together, you can interchange any of the squares you love from the library for different effects. This means that although there are technically only eight projects shown in this book, you can make infinite varieties of these projects. You can also play with the yarn and hook for each motif, so long as you don't mix multiple weights of yarn and hook sizes within a project, as then they will not fit together evenly.

If you are inspired to create your own projects, then simply select any of your favorite motifs from the stitch library and play with how they fit together. Each of the squares will fit neatly next to any of the others from the library, so you needn't worry about the construction, only think about the colors and textures next to each other. If you also have the cards from *The Granny Square Card Deck™* series, you can physically use these to play with the different combinations of motifs to see how they sit next to each other.

ABOUT THE GRANNY SQUARES

Each of the 100 squares in the motif library has been made using the same hook and yarn type – 4mm (G/6, UK 8) hook and light worsted (DK/8-ply) yarn – and they all have the same finished dimensions – 4in (10cm) – so that you can choose any of the designs and be confident that they will fit together perfectly; you have a couple of different options for joining all your wonderful squares together (see pages 48–50). Of course, if your squares come out a little bigger or smaller than mine, it doesn't really matter – the most important thing is that your gauge (tension) is consistent across all your blocks, so that they all fit together at the end.

CREATING THE PROJECTS

The book contains eight gorgeous granny-square projects to inspire you to put your squares to good use (see pages 254–287). Recreate the same colorways as I have or follow my advice for picking out colors that really speak to you (see pages 256–257).

ADAPTING THE GRANNY SQUARES

You can also alter the look and size of your granny squares by going up or down a hook size and yarn weight. Why not try a lovely chunky yarn (as shown in the scarf project on page 276), which gives a completely different finished look to the original squares. You'll follow the instructions in exactly the same way... your resulting square will just be larger than 4in (10cm).

For the blanket opposite, I mixed and matched a selection of really textural floral squares with some very simple 'neutral' squares for a harmonious finished blanket. See pages 269–271 for instructions.

YARN

As mentioned on page 12, you can change your yarn weight to make granny squares in different sizes and for different purposes, provided you adjust your hook size accordingly. If you want to make a 4 x 4in (10 x 10cm) granny square, use a light worsted (DK/8-ply) yarn; the shades I used to make the 100 granny square motifs are given opposite.

The other important consideration is the fiber content of your yarn. Here is a quick guide to different types of yarn to help you, particularly when you are thinking about making up the projects on pages 260–287:

Fibers

Traditional crochet yarn is a very fine cotton, mercerized and tightly spun to give a strong and unyielding thread. However, many other yarns can be much more comfortable on your hands and easier to use. Elastic, warm and comfortable wool and wool-mix yarns are just as good as cotton, if not better, if you are just starting out. Wool and cotton are beautiful natural fibers, which in addition to having a lovely handle have great benefits as well.

Wool regulates your temperature – it has fabulous insulating properties and while keeping you toasty in the cold will also help keep you cool in the heat! Wool is anti-bacterial and it also draws away moisture from the body. All of these properties make it perfect for garments and snuggly blankets.

Cotton is usually spun with a smooth finish and it is durable, making it perfect for hooking traditional crochet homewares such as dishcloths, doilies and pillow edgings. It is also cool and breathable, which makes it perfect for summer-weight garments and accessories. Cotton can be quite stiff if hooked tightly and it takes dye well, meaning it is available in an array of bright, strong shades. These properties make the fiber great for working baskets, bags and fun three-dimensional items like the small, cute crochet toys called amigurumi.

Man-made yarns were developed to imitate natural fibers, without replicating any of their weaknesses. Therefore, they are generally strong, cheap, lightweight, colorfast and moth resistant. However, they usually don't feel as soft and tactile as natural fibers and aren't as breathable. A mix of both man-made and natural can be the best compromise, taking the best from both worlds and meaning a yarn can be both beautiful and incredibly durable.

The best yarns for beginners are smooth, to produce clearer stitch definition, and have no fancy nubs, loops or slubs, which are all bumps or loops of extra fiber in the length of the yarn that can snag on the hook and create messy stitches. Mohair yarns and others that are overly hairy should also be avoided if you are just starting out, as the stitches will be hard to make and mistakes are tricky to see and to pull out.

YARN SUBS

Substitute yarn of the same weight for a 4in (10cm) block. I used Scheepjes Merino Soft light worsted (8-ply/DK) yarn, 115yd/105m/1¾oz/50g (50% merino, 25% acrylic, 25% microfiber) in shades:

- 602 Raphael (cream)
- 612 Vermeer (mid-blue)
- 620 Munch (orange)
- 621 Picasso (bright red)
- 627 Manet (moss green)
- 628 Botticelli (turquoise)
- 629 Constable (spring green)
- 632 Degas (coral pink)
- 634 Copley (lilac)
- 635 Matisse (bright pink)
- 636 Carney (violet)
- 638 Hockney (purple)
- 639 Monet (lilac)
- 642 Caravaggio (peach)
- 644 Dürer (bright yellow)
- 645 van Eyck (orange)
- 647 Titian (pale pink)
- 648 de Goya (lemon)
- 649 Waterhouse (light pink)
- 652 Modigliani (burgundy)
- 653 Ernst (light teal)
- 655 Chagall (purple)

HOOKS

Hook sizes are determined by the thickness of their shaft – the hook narrows as it merges with the head, but it is the diameter of the thickest part that is measured in millimeters, usually increasing in increments of a millimeter or fractions of a millimeter.

As a yarn increases in thickness, increase the size of the hook you use with it; your yarn label will give you a recommended hook size, or you can look it up online. If you want a firmer finish or a more hard-wearing fabric, choose a slightly smaller hook than suggested on the yarn label. If you want a softer fabric with a flowing drape or a more open, lacy finish, try using a larger hook than suggested. However, a pattern will always suggest the hook size to use for your particular project.

Traditional hooks are usually made from a thin steel, but now they come in many shapes, sizes and materials and the type of hook you choose will ultimately come down to personal preference. Try out a few different types and, as you become more experienced, you will have a preferred type or even brand of hooks you like to use. Here is a rundown of some of the most common types of hooks.

1. BAMBOO/WOODEN HOOKS

Bamboo or wooden hooks come in many shapes and sizes, some with ornate or ergonomic handles. Sometimes, unless they are lacquered or varnished, bamboo or wooden hooks can mean a less smooth hooking action. Keep an eye out for a sharp tip and deep hook, as shallow hooks can make grabbing the yarn harder.

2. METAL HOOKS

Any hooks with metal shafts are perfect for quick, smooth and easy hooking as there are fewer snags. Thinner hooks are usually made from steel for strength, due to the stress that these hooks are subjected to. Aluminum hooks are similar to the traditional steel hooks, but lighter and not as cold to the touch.

3. PLASTIC HOOKS

Larger sized hooks are usually plastic so they are light and easy to work with. They are often color coordinated so you can see the correct size at a glance.

4. HANDLED HOOKS

Many modern hooks have some kind of grip along the shaft for comfort. The best of these have metal tips for smooth hooking action, but are paired with a handle made of plastic, silicone, wood or other material. This gives the crocheter more bulk to hold, which allows for more comfortable crocheting and puts less stress on the hands.

All 100 granny squares in this book were made using a 4mm (G/6, UK 8) hook and light worsted (8-ply/DK) yarn.

N/P 10.0 mm
10.0 mm
1
2
4
3
1

OTHER EQUIPMENT

1. SCISSORS

Scissors are a must-have for cutting yarn when a project is finished and snipping yarn ends. Small, sharp embroidery or sewing scissors are best for ensuring a quick, clean cut and are handily sized to fit in your kit bag or roll.

2. STITCH MARKERS

When working in a spiral, stitch markers are essential for marking the beginning of a round, but they can also be used for marking a specific row or stitch that you will need to refer to later, or to mark the right side of your work. The markers generally come in two versions, a split ring or a lockable marker. Split rings are handy for the occasions when you need to move a marker frequently, while lockable ones are great for ensuring the marker does not fall out. There are a myriad of fancy markers on the market, made in plastic or metal or embellished with beads and fancy decorations. However, if you don't want to buy expensive markers, a small safety pin works perfectly.

3. TAPE MEASURE

Always keep a tape measure close by for checking the gauge (tension) of your crochet and measuring your work.

4. NEEDLES

A blunt tapestry or yarn needle is essential for sewing in your ends neatly. The blunt end ensures that the needle passes just through the stitches and not the yarn to create a neat and professional finish. These needles come in different sizes, with variously sized eyes for diverse weights of yarn.

Sewing needles will also be handy for attaching buttons, clasps, beads and other embellishments, as well as for sewing in linings.

5. PINS

Marking pins are useful for holding two pieces of crochet together while sewing them up, or for pinning the crochet to shape when blocking (see pages 28–29). Make sure the pins have a large head to prevent them slipping between the stitches.

1
5
3
4
2

BASIC STITCHES

SLIP KNOT

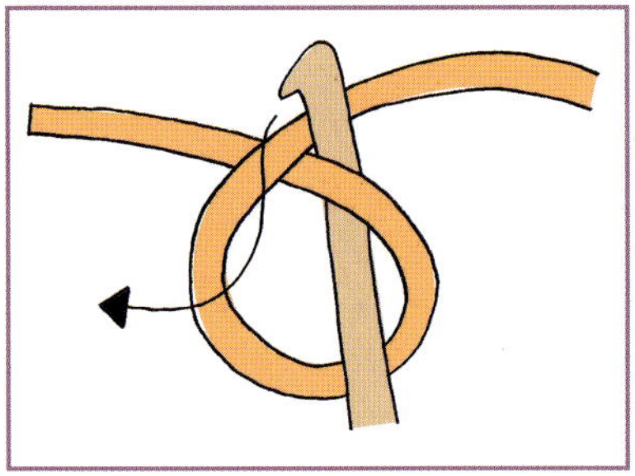

1. Make a loop in the yarn, about 6in (15cm) from the end. Insert the hook through the loop, then pull the yarn through.

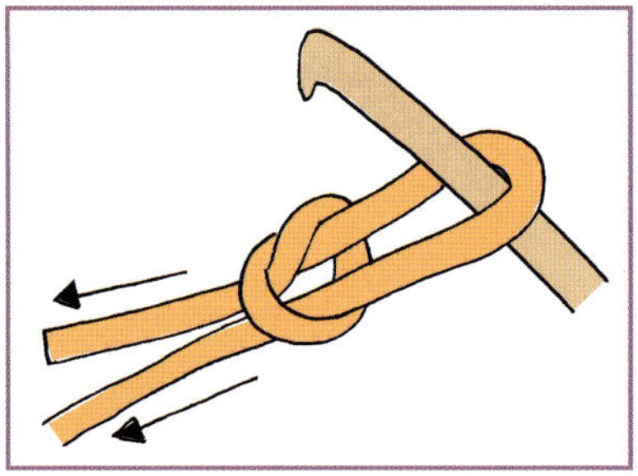

2. Pull on both ends of the yarn to loosely tighten the knot.

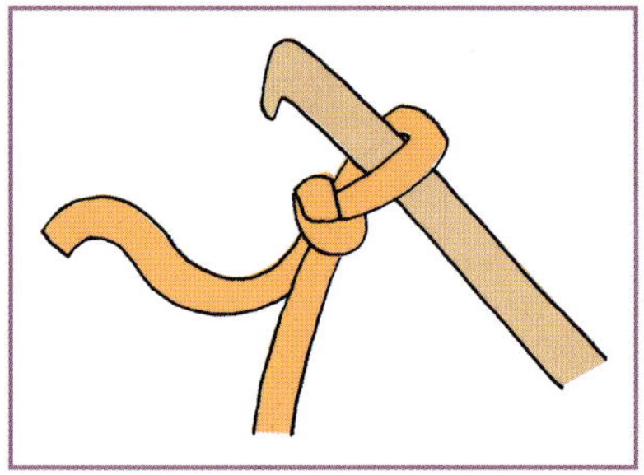

3. Your slip knot is complete.

○ CHAIN STITCH (CH)

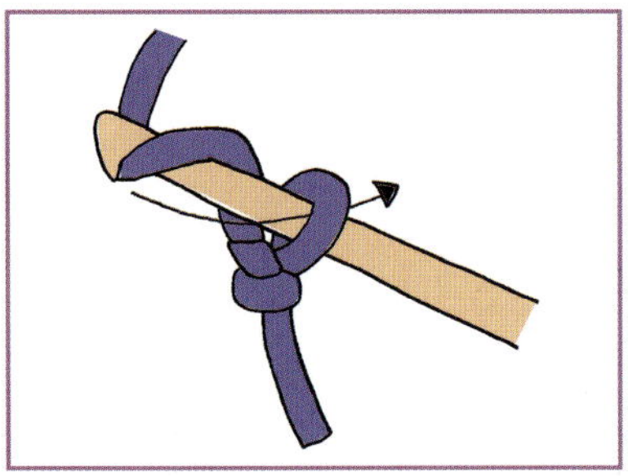

1. Start with a slip knot on your hook. Wrap the working yarn over the hook (known as 'yarn round hook' or 'yarn over'), then pull it through the loop on the hook.

2. One chain made.

3. Repeat step 1 to create the required number of chains.

COUNTING CHAINS

The right side of your chain is the one that looks like a little plait of 'v' shapes. Each 'v' is a stitch and must be counted. When you are working the chain, you do not count the slip knot, but begin to count your chain when you pull through the first loop.

The back of the chain has little 'bumps'. Each bump is a stitch and should only be worked through if specifically indicated.

MAKING A RING

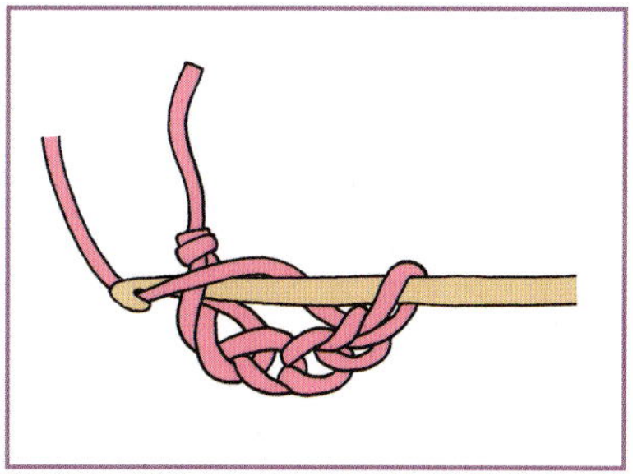

Make a length of chain as required, then instead of working back along the chain, insert the hook into the first chain stitch made. Yarn round hook and work a slip stitch to join, by drawing the yarn through everything on the hook.

• SLIP STITCH (SL ST)

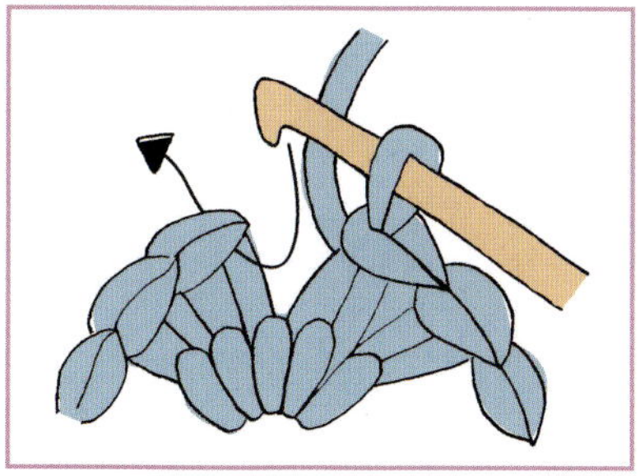

1. Insert the hook through the chain or stitch indicated in your pattern.

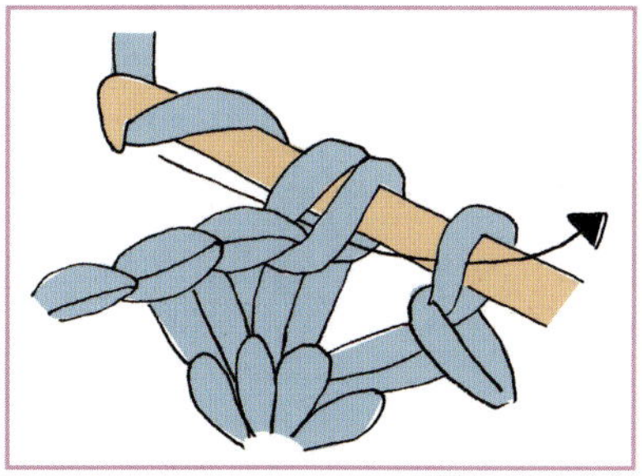

2. Take the yarn over and pull it through the loops on the hook...

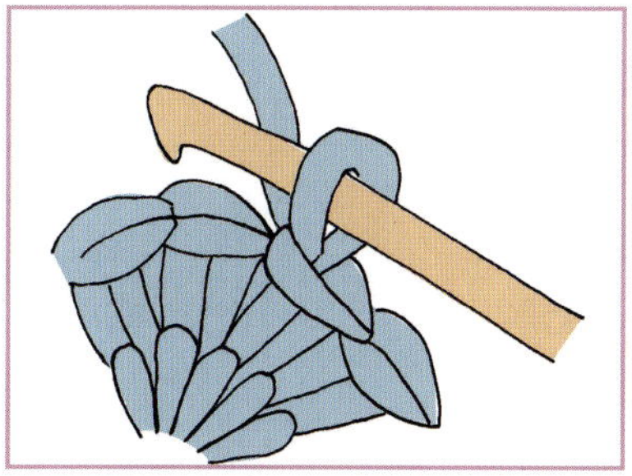

3. ... to complete the slip stitch.

+ SINGLE CROCHET (SC)
(UK DOUBLE CROCHET (DC))

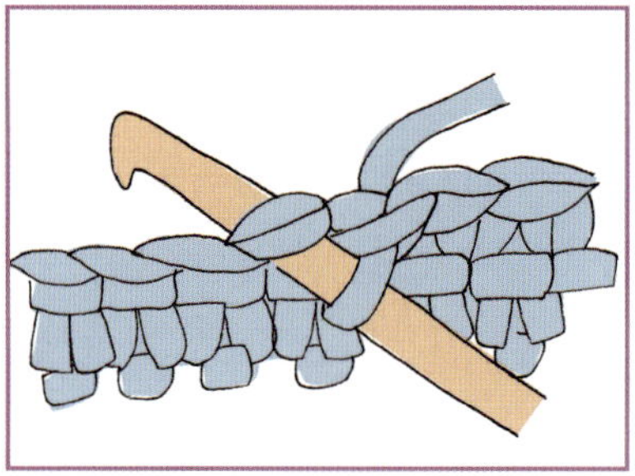

1. Insert the hook through the chain or stitch required.

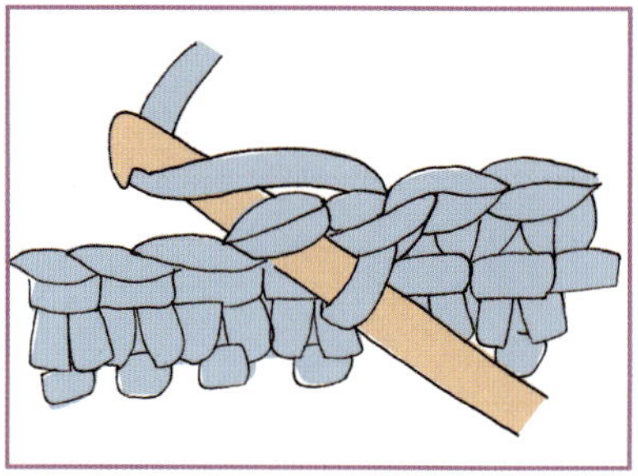

2. Yarn over...

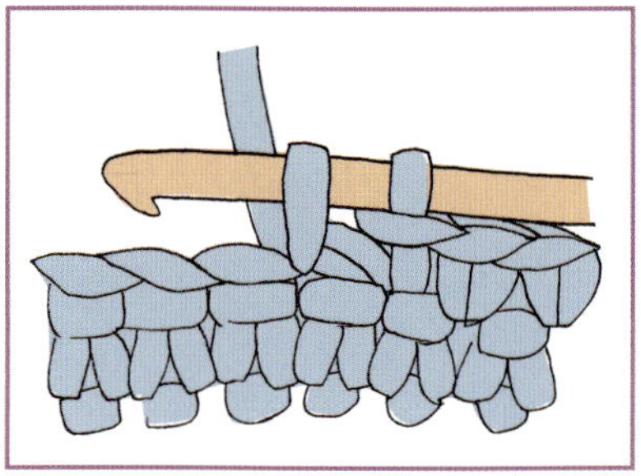

3. ... pull through the stitch (two loops on the hook).

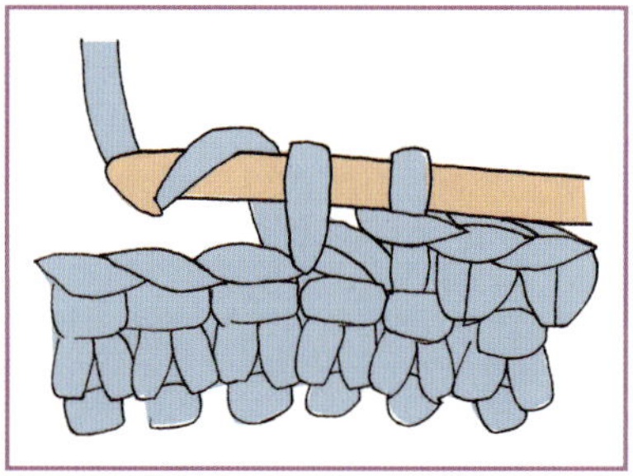

4. Yarn over again...

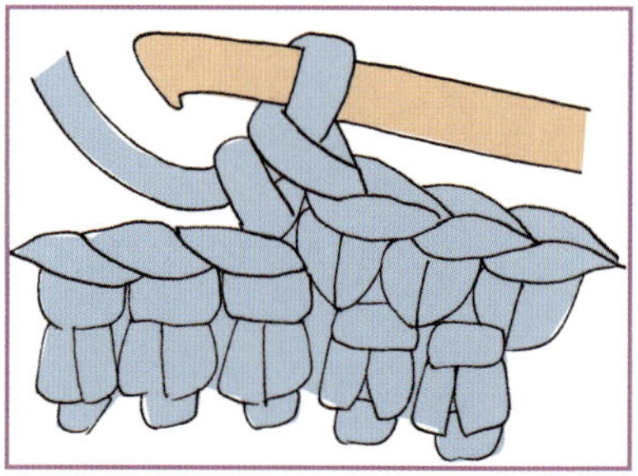

5. ... pull through, completing the stitch (one loop remaining on the hook).

HALF DOUBLE CROCHET (HDC)
(UK HALF TREBLE CROCHET (HTR))

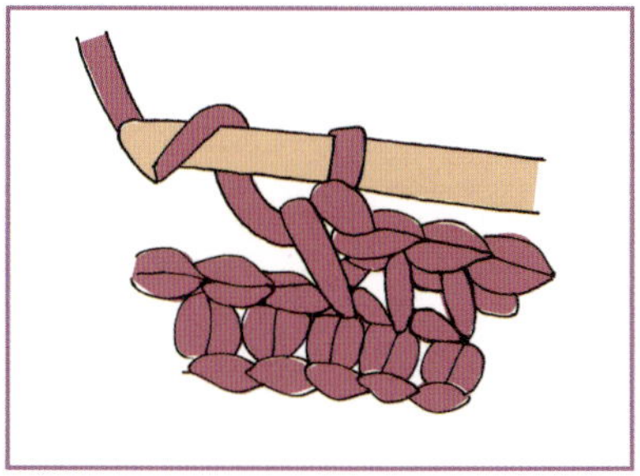

1. Take the yarn over the hook...

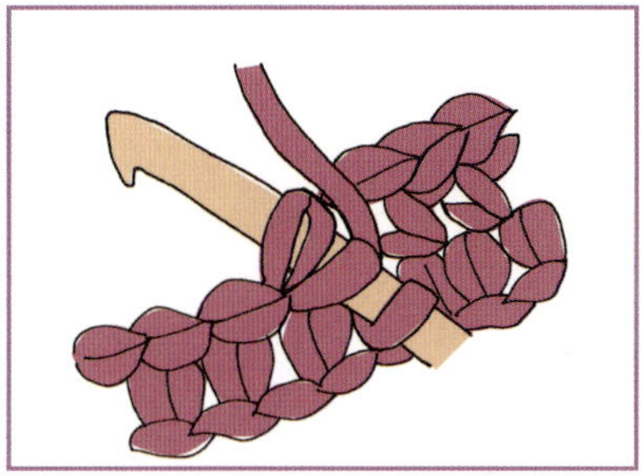

2. ... then insert the hook through the chain or stitch required.

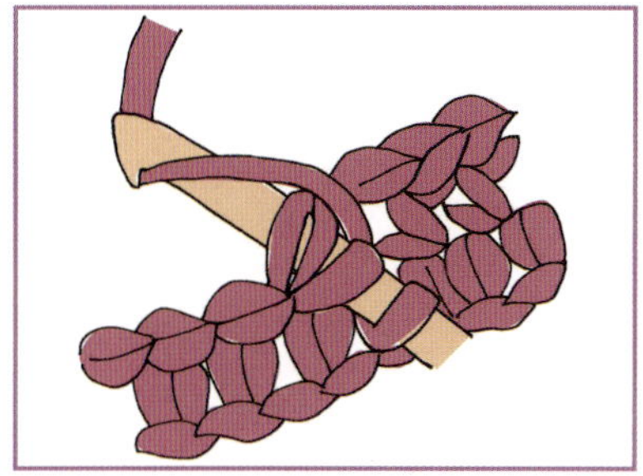

3. Yarn over again...

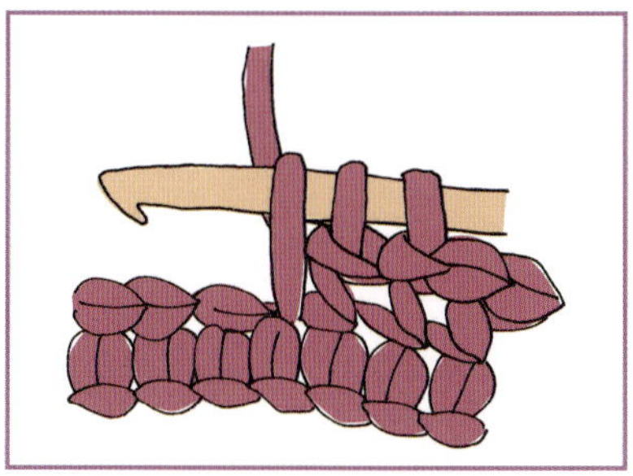

4. ... and pull it through the first loop only (three loops on the hook).

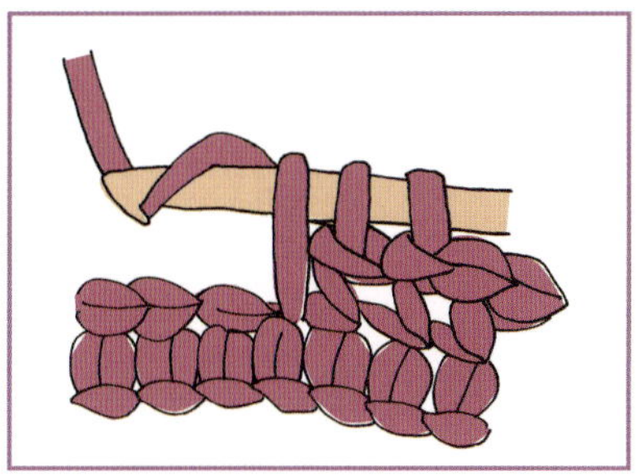

5. Yarn over once again...

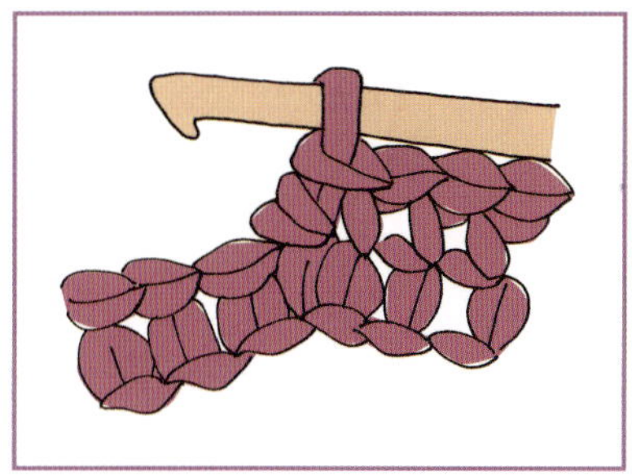

6. ... then pull it through all three loops on the hook to complete the stitch.

DOUBLE CROCHET
(UK TREBLE CROCHET (TR))

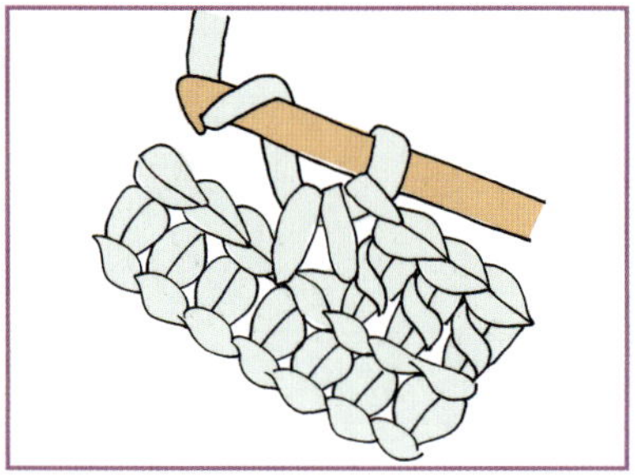

1. Take the yarn over the hook...

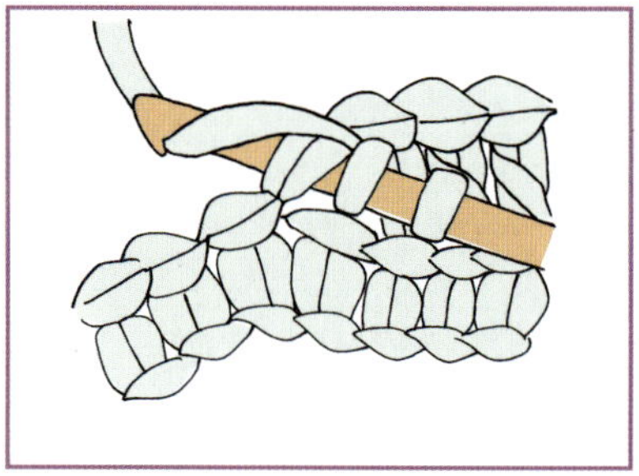

2. ... then insert the hook through the chain or stitch required. Yarn over again...

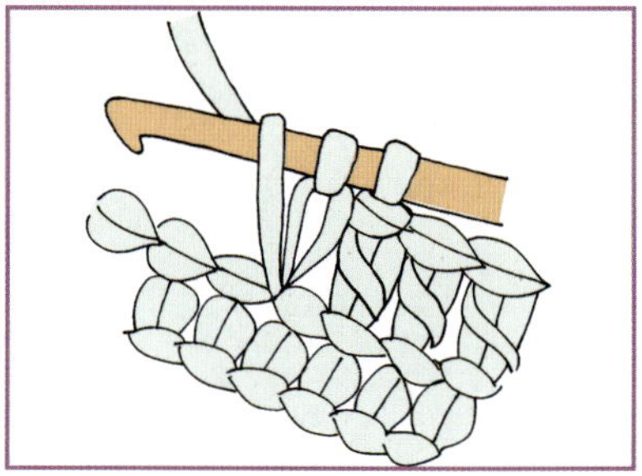

3. ... and pull it through the first loop only (three loops on the hook).

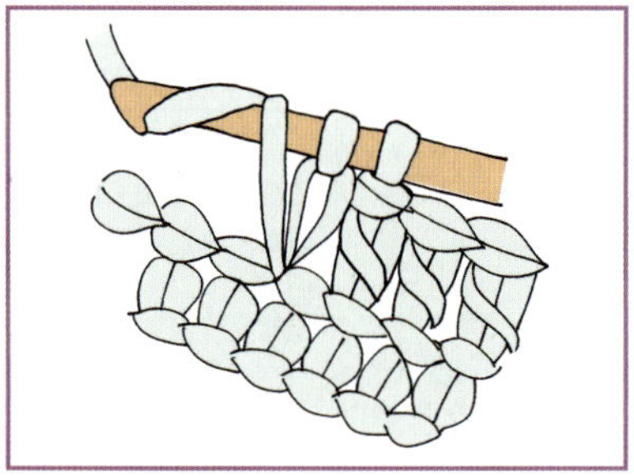

4. Yarn over again...

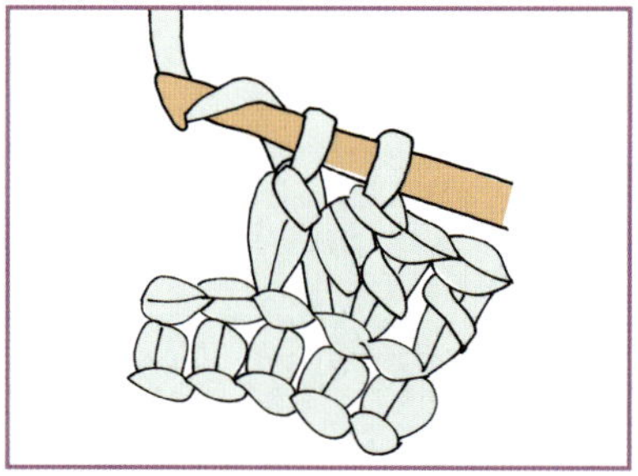

5. ... and pull it through two of the loops (two loops on the hook). Yarn over the hook for the final time...

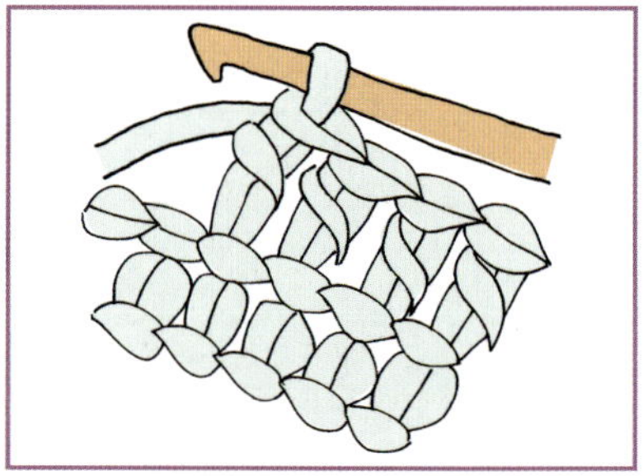

6. ... then pull it through the remaining two loops to complete the stitch.

TREBLE CROCHET (TR)
(UK DOUBLE TREBLE CROCHET (DTR))

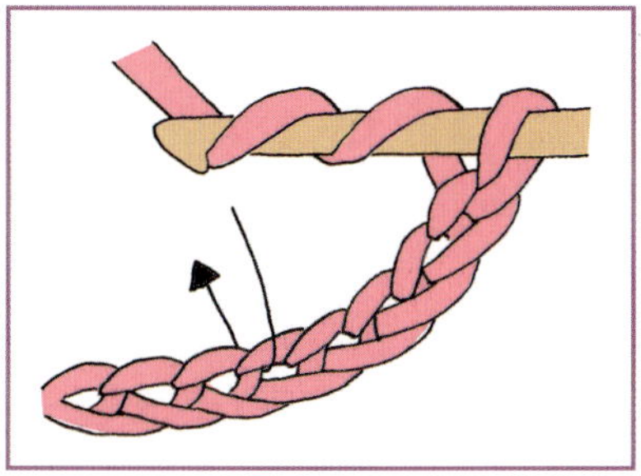

1. Take the yarn over the hook twice...

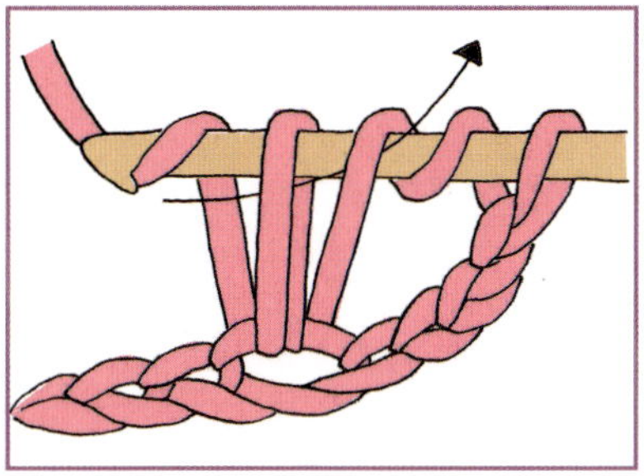

2. ... then insert the hook through the chain or stitch required. Take the yarn over the hook again and pull it through the stitch only (four loops on the hook). Yarn over and pull through two loops on the hook (three loops on the hook).

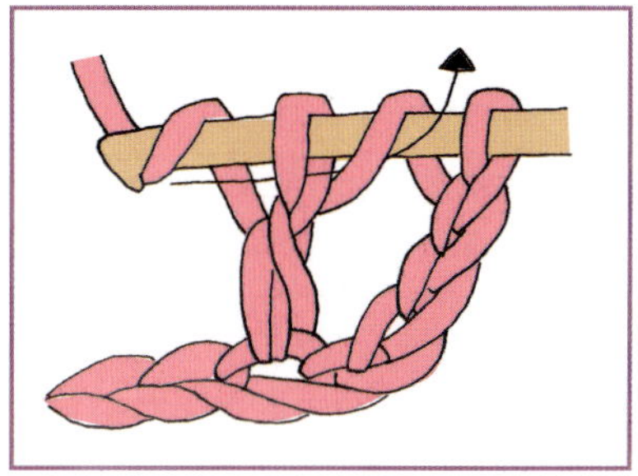

3. Yarn over and pull through two loops on the hook (two loops on the hook).

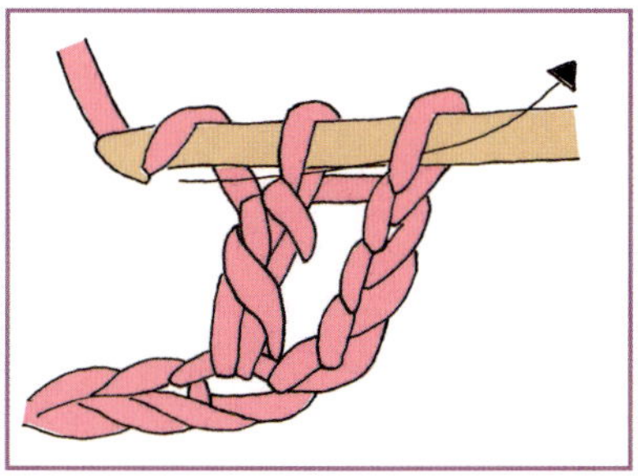

4. Yarn over once more and pull through the remaining two loops...

5. ... to complete the stitch.

⊼ DECREASING: SC2TOG
(UK DC2TOG)

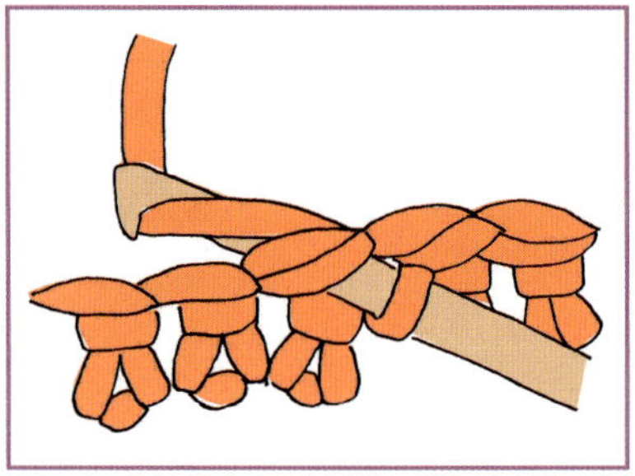

1. Insert the hook through the chain or stitch required. Yarn over...

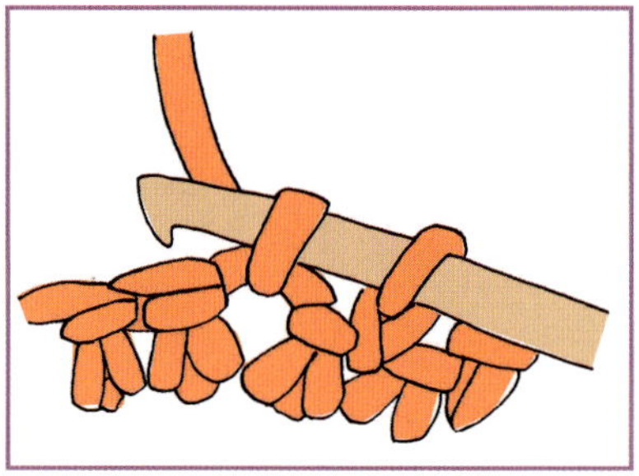

2. ... pull through (two loops on the hook).

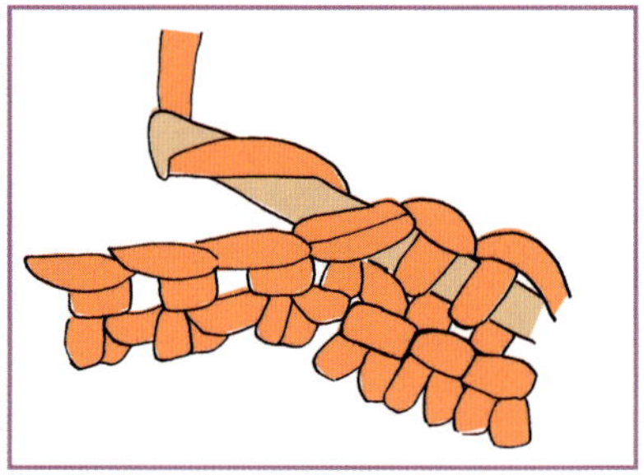

3. Now insert your hook into the next stitch and yarn over again...

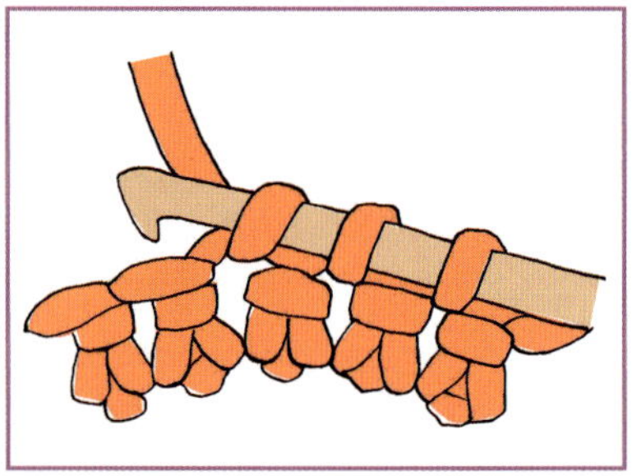

4. ... pull through (three loops on the hook).

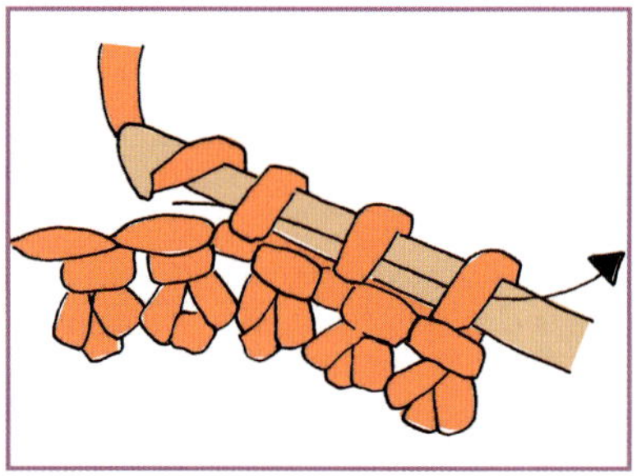

5. Yarn over for the final time and pull through all the loops on the hook.

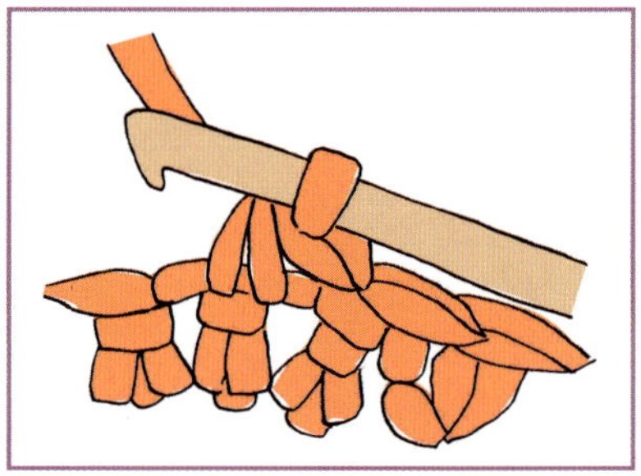

6. One completed sc2tog (*UK dc2tog*).

WORKING FRONT POST OR BACK POST

Raised treble front (RtrF) *(UK raised double treble front (RdtrF))*

Yrh twice, wrap hook around next stitch from right to left, inserting hook into the space to the right of the stitch from front of fabric, around the back and out to the front again into the space to the left of the stitch, yrh, draw a loop around the back of the stitch to the front, (4 loops on hook), finish off treble (*UK dtr*) as normal.

Raised Treble Back (RtrB) *(UK raised double treble back (RdtrB))*

Yrh twice, wrap hook around next stitch from right to left, inserting hook into the space to the right of the stitch from back of fabric, around the front and out to the back again into the space to the left of the stitch, yrh, draw a loop around the front of the stitch to the back, (4 loops on hook), finish off treble (*UK dtr*) as normal.

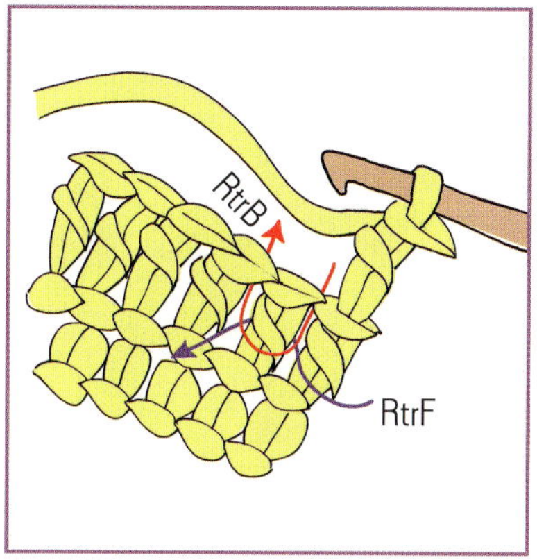

WORKING BACK LOOP ONLY (BLO) AND FRONT LOOP ONLY (FLO)

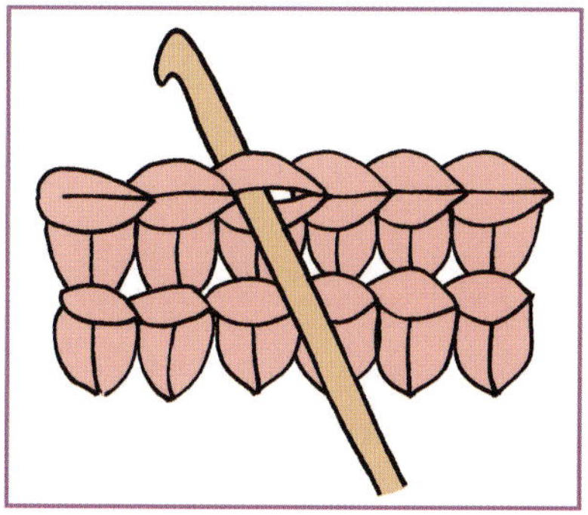

To work through the back loop only (blo), insert hook through center of stitch, under the back loop to the back, then complete stitch as normal.

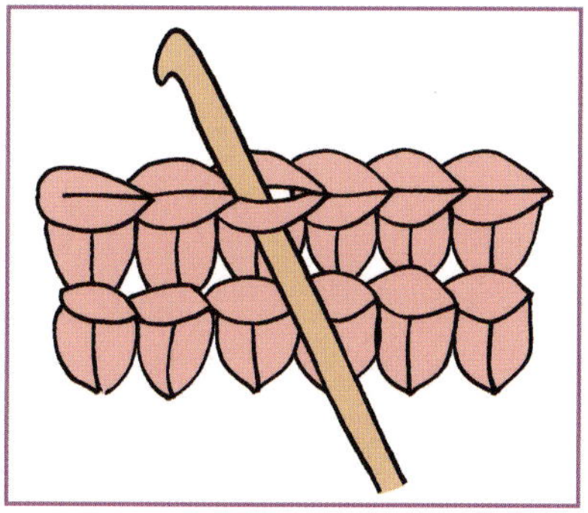

To work through the front loop only (flo), insert hook under the front loop of next stitch, from the front to the center of the stitch, then complete stitch as normal.

FASTENING OFF AND WEAVING IN YARN ENDS

Simply work one chain, then, leaving at least a 4in (10cm) tail, cut the yarn then pull the tail through the chain.

Thread your 4in (10cm) tail of yarn into a yarn needle, then work the yarn back and forth through one or two stitches to secure it. Trim off the excess yarn tail.

BLOCKING

Handmade items can vary a little in size and shape, even when we follow the pattern and use the right gauge (tension), but a little light blocking of your motifs before you join them will ensure that you get them all to the correct size and shape.

The blocking of crochet is the action of setting the stitches, evening out any lumps and bumps and achieving the ideal size and drape of your fabric.

This manipulation can be achieved using a few different techniques, depending on the project.

Consider investing in a blocking board: you will be able to fit multiple granny squares on at one time.

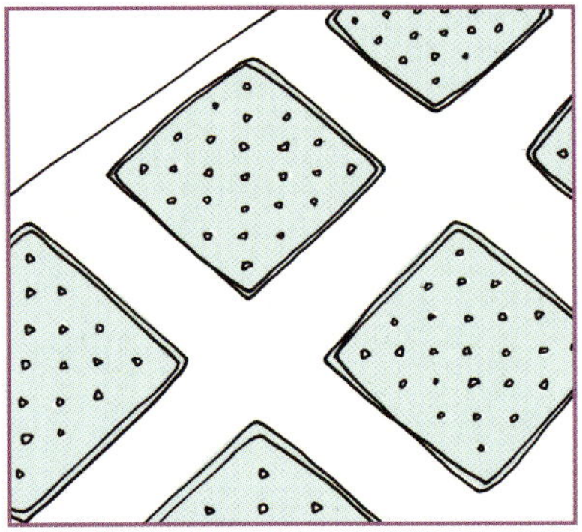

1. Small, simple pieces can sometimes be manipulated into shape carefully and then lightly steamed with an iron to set the stitches. A word of warning: do not press down with the iron, as this will flatten the stitches; simply hover it over the fabric and allow the steam to work its magic.

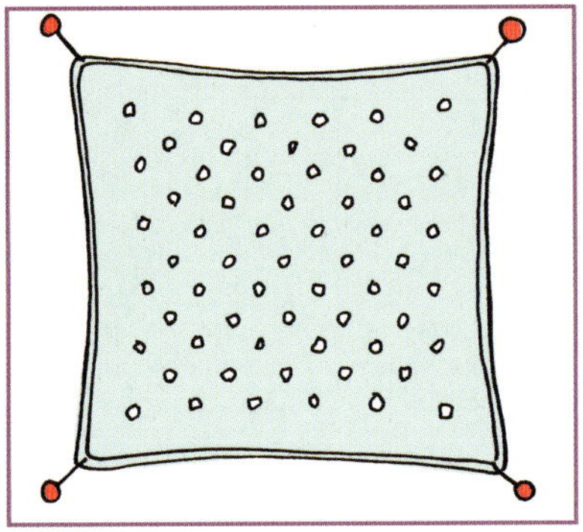

2. If you want straight, even edges or to pull your motif into shape a little more strongly, pin it before steaming. Start in each corner.

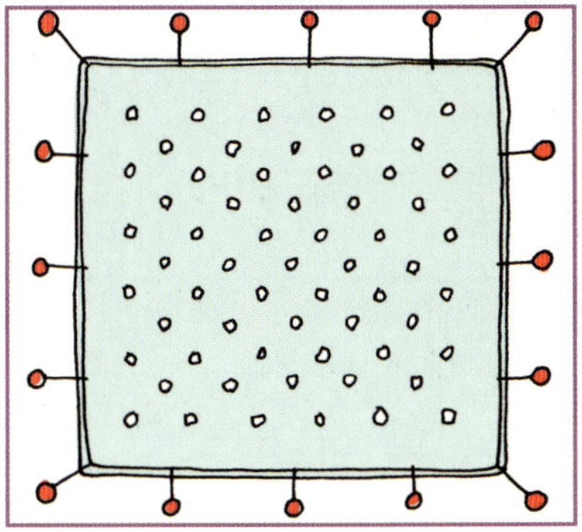

3. Be careful not to overstretch, and use plenty of pins to prevent uneven, scalloped edges.

4. If steam alone doesn't work, try spritzing a little water over the piece, or alternatively lay a slightly damp cloth over the crochet before steaming (still remembering not to press down with the iron) which will encourage more steam. If using a cloth, remove it once you have steamed the piece but do not unpin until the piece is completely cooled and dry.

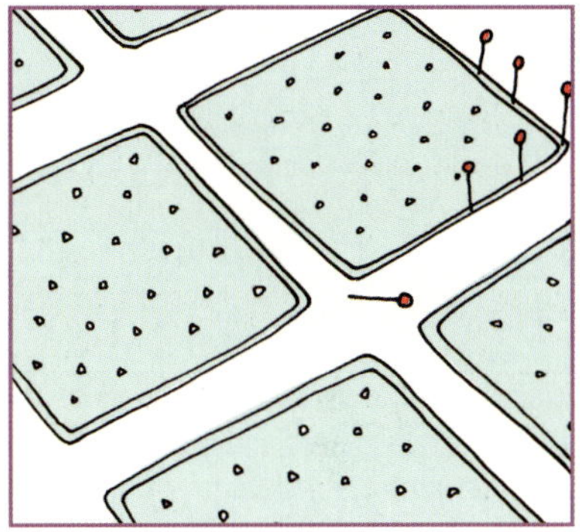

5. Unpin when cool and dry.

STITCH CHART SYMBOLS

US and UK crochet conversions

US crochet terms are used in the motif and project patterns in this book. To make life simpler for those who follow the UK system you will find complete conversion tables here and on the book's flaps, which can be opened out for easy reference and visibility as you follow the patterns.

Back loop only (blo) and front loop only (flo)

I have given examples, right, for single crochet in the back and front loops – any stitches are interchangeable with the addition of the blo/flo symbols.

US TERM	SYMBOL	UK TERM
chain (ch)		chain (ch)
slip stitch (sl st)	•	slip stitch (sl st)
sc (single crochet)	+	dc (double crochet)
hdc (half double crochet)		htr (half treble crochet)
dc (double crochet)		tr (treble crochet)
tr (treble crochet)		dtr (double treble crochet)
V stitch (V)	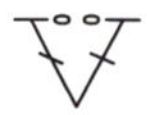	V stitch (V)
picot		picot
raised treble crochet front (RtrF)		raised double treble crochet front (RdtrF)
raised single crochet back (RscB)		raised double crochet back (RdcB)
used to denote working in the opposite direction to usual, or to show where to insert your hook if it is in an unusual place	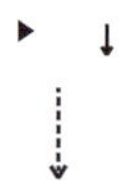	used to denote working in the opposite direction to usual, or to show where to insert your hook if it is in an unusual place
BACK LOOP ONLY (BLO) AND FRONT LOOP ONLY (FLO)		
single crochet back loop only (scblo)		double crochet back loop only (dcblo)
single crochet front loop only (scflo)		double crochet front loop only (dcflo)

US TERM	SYMBOL	UK TERM
CLUSTERS		
2 dc cluster (cl2)		2 tr cluster (cl2)
3 dc cluster (cl3)		3 tr cluster (cl3)
2 tr cluster (trcl2)		2 dtr cluster (dtrcl2)
3 tr cluster (trcl3)		3 dtr cluster (dtrcl3)
puff stitch (puff)		puff stitch (puff)
split cluster (splcl)		split cluster (splcl)
puff2 stitch (puff2)		puff2 stitch (puff2)
large puff stitch (large puff)		large puff stitch (large puff)
popcorn stitch (pop)		popcorn stitch (pop)
INCREASES AND DECREASES		
3 dc increase		3 tr increase
3 tr increase		3 dtr increase
2 dc increase		2 tr increase
2 sc increase		2 dc increase
dc 3 together (dc3tog)		tr 3 together (tr3tog)
dc 2 together (dc2tog)		tr 2 together (tr2tog)
2 sc decrease (sc2tog)		2 dc decrease (dc2tog)

Clusters

Clusters are denoted by more than one stitch converging at the top and bottom. Some examples are given, left, but other combinations are used throughout. Simply count the posts of the sts in the symbol to see how many sts make up the cluster.

Increases and decreases

Increases and decreases are denoted by more than one stitch converging at a single point; if the stitches converge at the bottom it indicates an increase, if they are converging at the top it indicates a decrease. A selection of examples are given, left, but other combinations are used.

OTHER ABBREVIATIONS	
repeat	rep
round	rnd
right side	RS
space	sp
wrong side	WS
yarn round hook/yarn over	yrh/yo

SPECIAL STITCHES

PUFF

* Yarn round hook (yrh), insert into stitch and draw a loop through, pulling it up to the height of 1 hdc (*UK htr*); rep from * three times more into the same stitch, 9 loops on hook, yrh and carefully draw a loop through all 9 loops, make 1 ch to complete.

LARGE PUFF

* Yrh, insert into st and draw a loop through, pulling it up to the height of a hdc (*UK htr*); rep from * seven times in total into the same st, 15 loops on hook, yrh and carefully draw a loop through all 15 loops, make 1 ch to complete.

PUFF2

* Yrh, insert into st and draw a loop through, pulling it up to the height of a hdc (*UK htr*); rep from * once more into the same st, 5 loops on hook, yrh and carefully draw a loop through all 5 loops, make 1 ch to complete.

POPCORN (POP)

5 dc (*UK tr*) in next st, make loop on hook slightly bigger, remove hook, then insert hook back into the top of the first of the 5 dc (*UK tr*) and pop loop back on the hook too, tighten elongated loop, then yrh and draw through everything on hook, make 1 ch to complete.

2 DC CLUSTER (CL2)

(UK 2 TR CLUSTER)

* Yrh and insert in st, pull up a loop, yrh and draw through 2 loops; rep from * once more into the same st, 3 loops on hook, yrh and draw through all 3 loops to complete.

3 (4, 5) DC CLUSTER (CL3 (CL4, CL5))

(UK 3 (4, 5) TR CLUSTER)

* Yrh and insert in st, pull up a loop, yrh and draw through 2 loops; rep from * three (four, five) times in total into the same st, 4 (5, 6) loops on hook, yrh and draw through all 4 (5, 6) loops to complete.

2 TR CLUSTER (TRCL2)

(UK 2 TR CLUSTER)

* Yrh twice and insert in st, pull up a loop, (yrh and draw through 2 loops) twice; rep from * once more into the same st, 3 loops on hook, yrh and draw through all 3 loops to complete.

3 (4, 5) TR CLUSTER (TRCL3 (TRCL4, TRCL5))

(UK 3 (4, 5) DTR CLUSTER)

* Yrh twice and insert in st, pull up a loop, (yrh and draw through 2 loops) twice; rep from * three (four, five) times in total into the same st, 4 (5, 6) loops on hook, yrh and draw through all 4 (5, 6) loops to complete.

V STITCH (V ST)

(1 dc, 2 ch, 1 dc) in next stitch or space (*UK 1 tr, 2 ch, 1 tr*).

SC 2 STITCHES TOGETHER (SC2TOG)

(UK DC2TOG)

Insert hook into next st, draw up a loop, insert hook into following st, draw up a loop, 3 loops on hook, yrh and draw through all 3 loops to complete sc2tog (*UK dc2tog*), 1 st decreased.

DC 2 STITCHES TOGETHER (DC2TOG)

(UK TR2TOG)

* Yrh and insert into next st, draw up a loop, yrh and draw through 2 loops; rep from * once more, working into the next st – 3 loops on hook, yrh and draw through all 3 loops to complete dc2tog (*UK tr2tog*), 1 st decreased.

DC 3 STITCHES TOGETHER (DC3TOG)

(UK TR3TOG)

* Yrh and insert into next st, draw up a loop, yrh and draw through 2 loops; rep from * twice more, working into the next 2 consecutive sts – 4 loops on hook, yrh and draw through all 4 loops to complete dc3tog (*UK tr3tog*), 2 sts decreased.

SPLIT CLUSTER (SPLCL)/WORK TWO CL2 TOGETHER

* Yrh and insert hook into next st, draw up a loop, yrh and draw through 2 loops; rep from * twice in total into same st, 3 loops on hook, rep from * twice into the following st, 5 loops on hook, yrh and draw through all 5 loops to complete splcl.

RAISED TREBLE FRONT (RTRF)

(UK RDTRF)

Yrh twice, wrap hook around next stitch from right to left, inserting hook into the space to the right of the stitch from front of fabric, around the back and out to the front again into the space to the left of the stitch, yrh, draw a loop around the back of the stitch to the front – 4 loops on hook. Finish off tr (*UK dtr*) as normal.

RAISED SINGLE CROCHET BACK (RSCB)

(UK RDCB)

Wrap hook around next st from right to left, inserting hook into the space to the right of the st from the back of the work, around the front of the st and out to the back again into the space to the left of the st, yrh, draw a loop around the st to the back again, 2 loops on hook, yrh and draw through 2 loops to complete RscB (*UK RdcB*).

SPIKED SINGLE CROCHET (SPSC)

(UK SPDC)

Insert hook into indicated st or space from one or more rows below next st or space, draw up a loop to the height of the current row, 2 loops on hook, yrh and draw through both loops to complete.

SPIKED DOUBLE CROCHET (SPDC)

(UK SPTR)

Yrh, insert hook into indicated st or space from one or more rows below next st or space, draw up a loop to the height of the current row, 3 loops on hook, (yrh and draw through 2 loops) twice to complete.

SPIKED TREBLE CROCHET (SPTR)

(UK SPDTR)

Yrh twice, insert hook into indicated st or space from one or more rows below next st or space, draw up a loop to the height of the current row, 4 loops on hook, (yrh and draw through 2 loops) three times to complete.

PICOT

3 ch, slip stitch (sl st) back down into bottom of chain.

READING A STITCH CHART

A stitch chart is simply a visual representation of a written pattern. Each round is drawn in the color used in the granny square, which both shows when to change color and also makes the chart easier to read. Familiarize yourself with a chart before you start it, so that you know how the rounds or rows will be worked, and what stitches you will be using.

The full list of stitch symbols is given on pages 30–31 and on the book flaps; any special stitches are given on pages 32–33. I've included two complete step-by-step examples to get you started.

EXAMPLE 1

Commonly you will start in the center of the chart and work outwards (though not always). The beginning of each round is indicated by the number of that round. Here you have a starting ring, then four rounds.

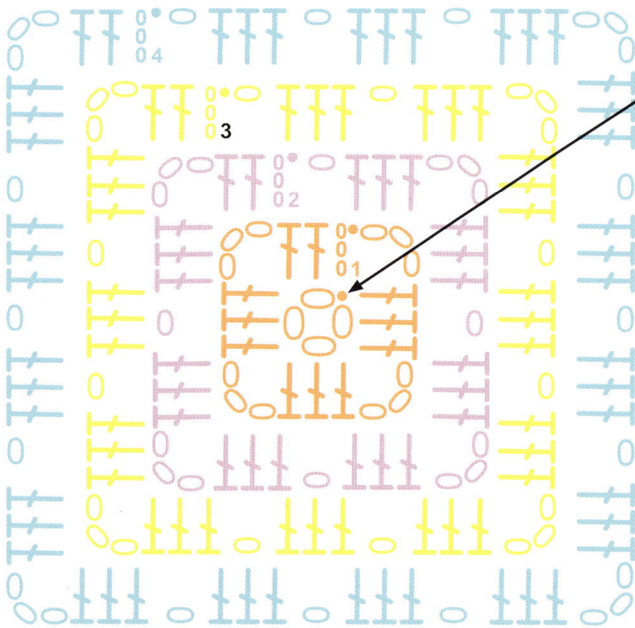

The crochet chart (above), with the finished square made up in yarn (right). This is granny square no. 1, Traditional.

Step 1: Your starting ring

At the center of the chart you can see four chains, joined together with a slip stitch. This is the starting ring for many of the granny-square patterns.

Step 2: Round 1

Here you can see that we have carried on with the same orange yarn from the starting ring. To move from the starting ring into round 1, you will create three chains (in this example) to achieve the correct height for the following stitches. These three chains count as your first stitch. You make them at point 1, as indicated on the chart.

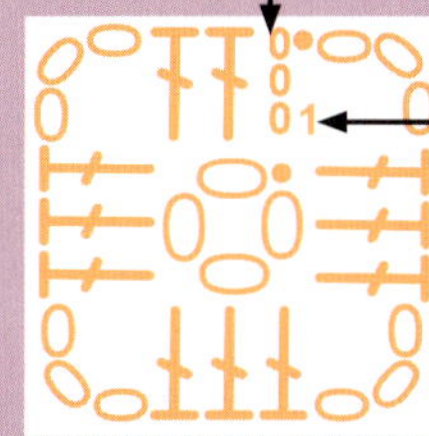

Step 3: Round 1 continued

After your three chains (which counts as your first dc) you will follow the chart in a counterclockwise direction (if you're right-handed; clockwise if you're left-handed), working round in a circle until you get back to where you started.

Make 2 dc stitches into the starting ring. Then make three chains, which will form the corner space.

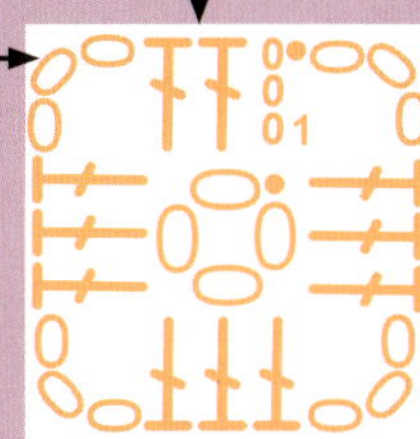

Step 4: Round 1 continued

Continue on, working into the starting ring. Make 3 dc, 3 ch, 3 dc, 3 ch, 3 dc, 3 ch, and complete the first round (rnd) by joining the yarn with a slip stitch to the third chain of your starting set of chains.

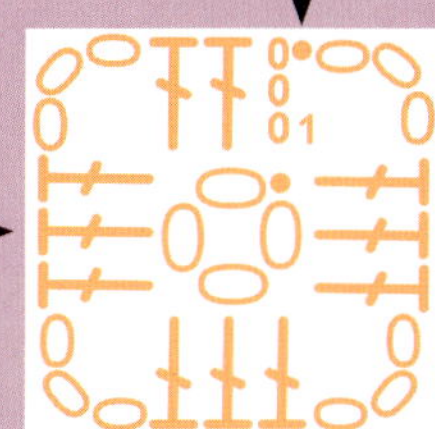

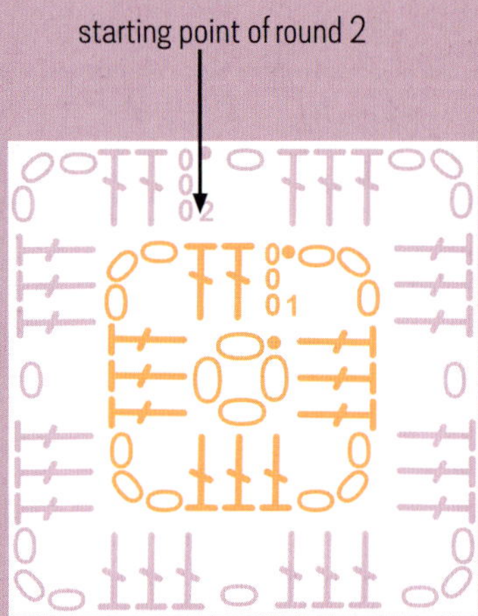

Step 5: Round 2

Your pattern will tell you where to join in your new color: here, in a 3-chain corner space, indicated by the number 2. You will start by creating three chains (which counts as your first dc). The following stitches (2 dc, 3 ch, 3 dc), should all be worked into the same corner space.

The chart will visually indicate where each stitch should be placed. Within this particular pattern, all stitches are worked into chain spaces of the previous round, so the bottom of each symbol directly corresponds with where it should be made.

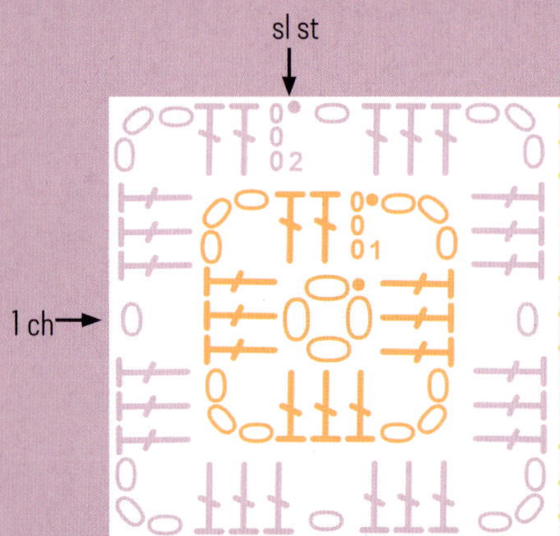

Step 6: Round 2 continued

Continuing counterclockwise, work 1 ch, then work the following into the next 3-chain corner space: 3 dc, 3 ch, 3 dc, 1 ch. Repeat this twice more to get back to your starting point, then complete the second round by joining to the third chain of your starting chain with a slip stitch.

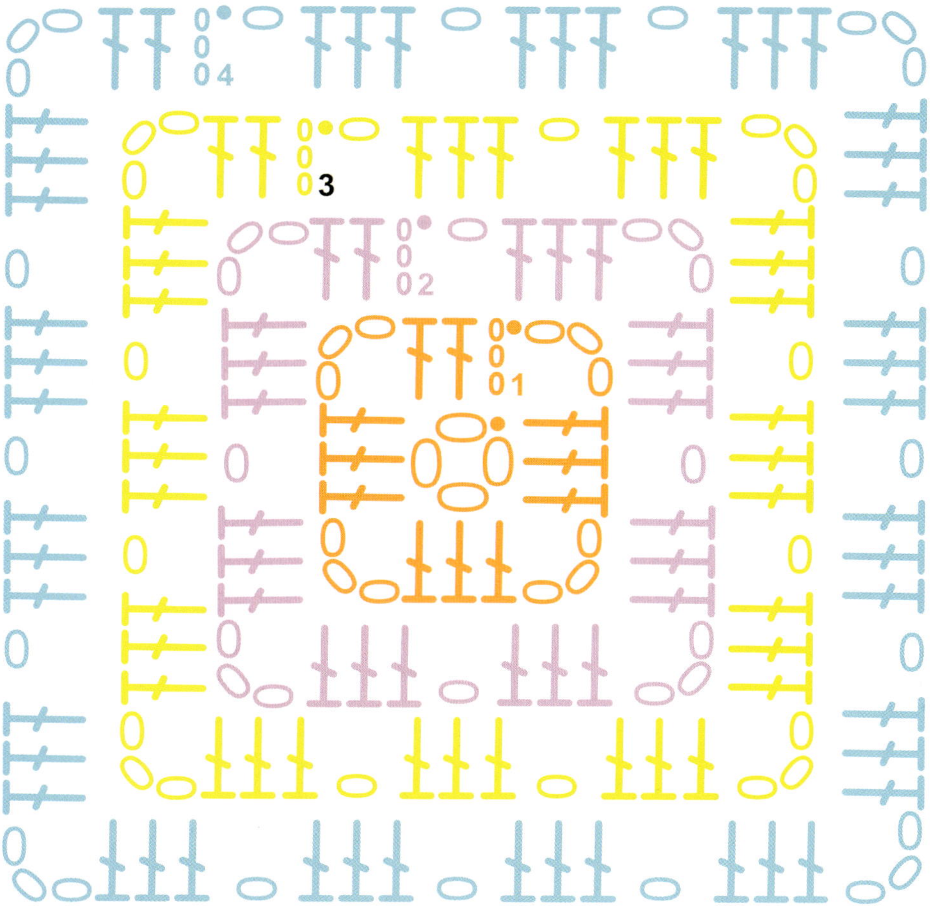

Step 7: Rounds 3 and 4

To complete the granny square, continue on in the same way, paying attention to where you start and finish each round, the color changes, and where your stitches need to be positioned. You will need to fasten off whenever there is a color change, unless specified otherwise in the notes.

EXAMPLE 2

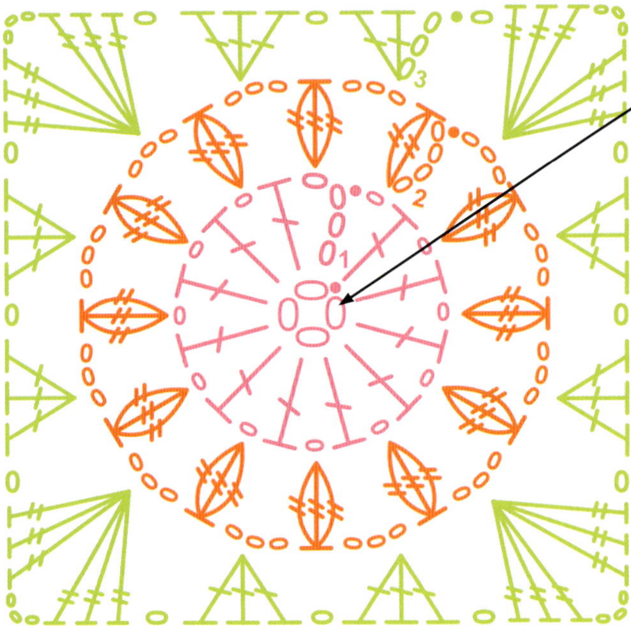

You will start in the center of this chart and work outwards. The beginning of each round is indicated by the number of that round. Here you have a starting ring, then three rounds.

The crochet chart (above), with the finished square made up in yarn (right). This is granny square no. 51, Calendula.

Step 1: your starting ring

At the center of the chart you can see four chains, joined together with a slip stitch.

Step 2: Round 1

Here you can see that we have carried on with the same pink yarn from the starting ring. To move from the starting ring into round 1, you will create three chains (in this example) to achieve the correct height for the following stitches. These three chains count as your first stitch. You make them at point 1, as indicated on the chart.

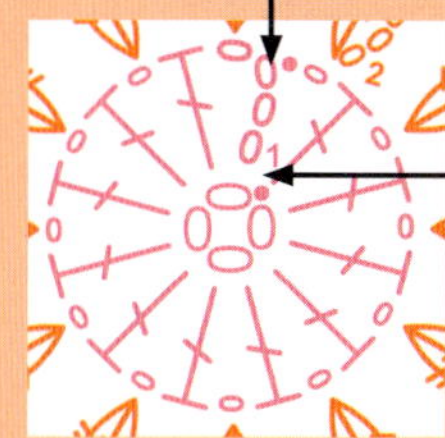

Step 3: Round 1 continued

After your three chains (which count as your first dc) you will follow the chart in a counter-clockwise direction (if you're right-handed; clockwise if you're left-handed), working round in a circle until you get back to where you started.

To work round 1 in this example, make one chain, then one dc stitch into the starting ring, then repeat until you have made 11 dc stitches. Make one final chain and then complete the first round (rnd) by joining the yarn with a slip stitch to the third chain of your starting set of chains. 12 dc and 12 chain spaces made in total.

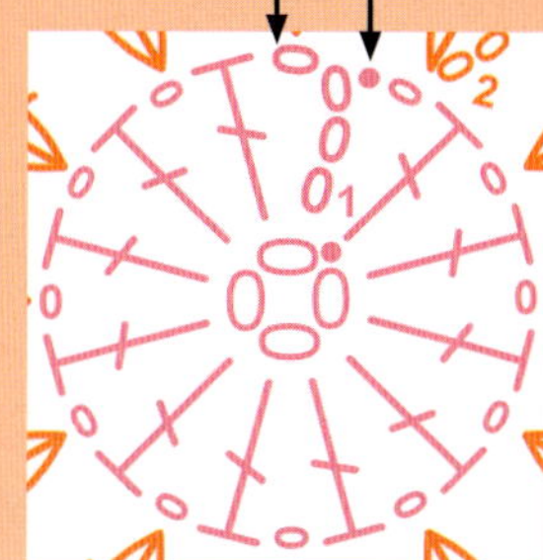

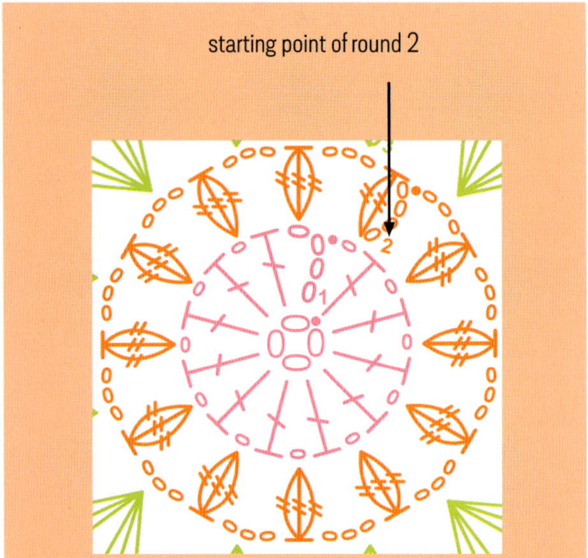

Step 4: Round 2

Your pattern will tell you where to join in your new color: here, in a chain space, indicated by the number 2. You will start by creating four chains (which count as your first tr). The adjoined 2 trebles indicate a trcl2 worked into the same space, which together with the first 4 ch, counts as the first trcl3 of the round (see page 32 for how to work a trcl2 and trcl3).

The chart will visually indicate where each stitch should be placed. Within this particular round, all clusters are worked into chain spaces of the previous round, so the bottom of each symbol directly corresponds with where it should be made.

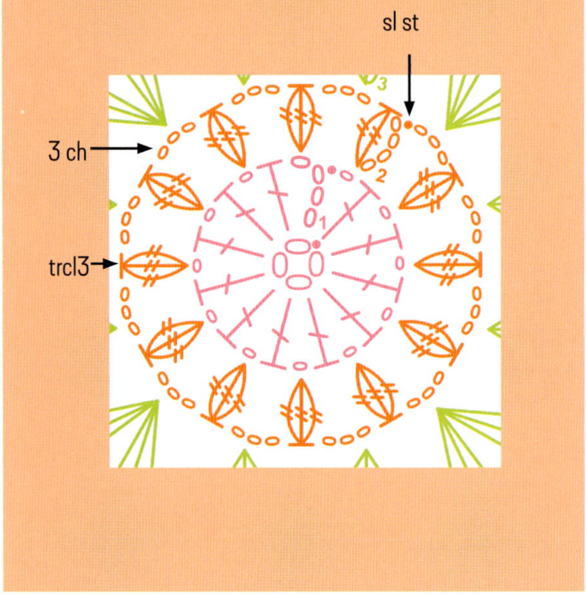

Step 5: Round 2 continued

Continuing counter-clockwise (or clockwise if you are left-handed), work 3 ch, then work a 3-treble cluster (trcl3) into the next chain space. Repeat this ten more times, then ch 3, to get back to your starting point. Complete the second round by joining to the fourth chain of your starting chain with a slip stitch.

Step 6: Round 3

To complete the granny square, continue to pay attention to where you start and finish each round, the color changes, and where your stitches need to be positioned. You will need to fasten off whenever there is a color change.

Join in your new color in a 3 ch sp. 3 ch (which counts as your first dc), then make 2 further dc stitches into the same 3 ch sp. Ch 1, then make 3 dc sts into the next 3 ch sp.

At each corner you will work all the sts into one 3 ch sp: 3 tr, 3 ch, 3 tr. (To see the instructions for this round in full, see page 155.)

When you get back to your starting point, complete the round by joining to the third chain of your starting chain with a slip stitch.

DIFFERENT WORKING DIRECTIONS

Some granny squares are worked in different ways, so check your chart before you start. Here, the chart begins with round 1, but from then on is worked in rows around only two of the four sides. You know that you always start on the right-hand edge, as this is denoted by the number of the round, and you always work with the right side facing you.

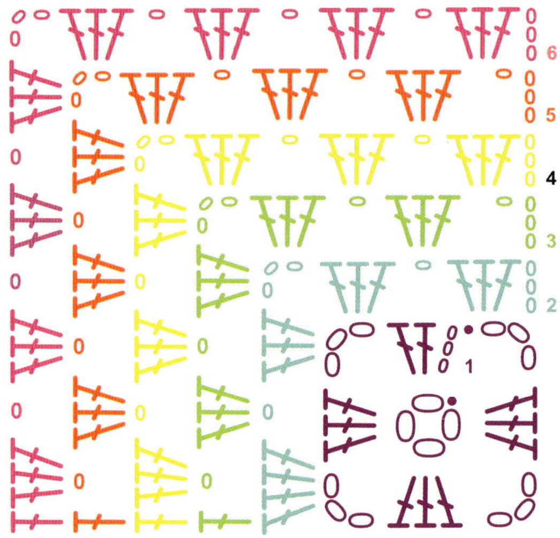

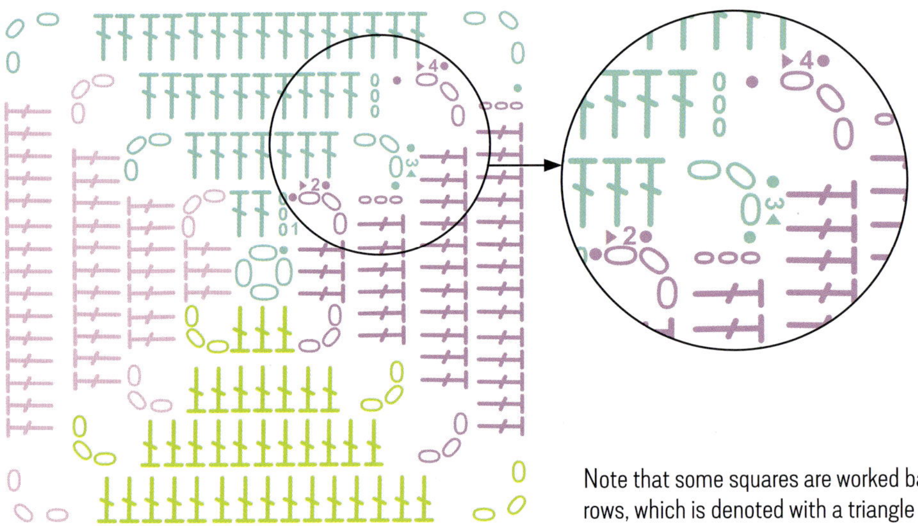

Note that some squares are worked back and forth in turned rows, which is denoted with a triangle pointing in the direction it should be worked.

WORKING OVER OR UNDER EXISTING STITCHES

Some of the motifs in this book are three-dimensional, with the petals layered over each other to look like real flowers. This layering is hard to show in chart form without obscuring some of the symbols. So, for ease of reading, when a round overlays another, the chart will show the rounds in order from the center outwards without overlapping, but there will be arrows to indicate which stitches you should work into, going either behind or in front of the symbols in the previous round(s), depending on how the motif is created.

For example, in the Forget-Me-Not chart shown above, rounds 3 and 4 (in green) are made by working behind the petals in round 2 (though note that they are drawn outside round 2). The arrows on round 3 demonstrate where this round's stitches should be worked. Here, they go behind round 2, pointing directly at the stitches that need to be used from round 1.

USING SEGMENTED CHARTS

Some of the patterns in this book are too complicated to show the whole motif in the given chart and still be legible, so a few of the most complicated motifs have just a section of the chart drawn.

If this is the case, then you know that the pattern is symmetrical, and so will repeat around the motif in the same way as is laid out in the segment shown. The chart will have an arrow to show how many times you must repeat the petals around the motif. Where possible, we have shown more than one petal in the segment so you know how to start and finish your round, so the number given by the arrow will always be the number of repeats to work in total, not in addition to the ones shown.

Here, for example, you can see that 16 repeats in total are needed for this Chrysanthemum's petals, but if all of these were shown, the chart would be unreadable. Therefore, only 4 of these repeats have been shown: each repeat is separated with a chain space every round. This repeat needs to be worked into every single crochet stitch from round 2. The start and ends of rounds 3, 4 and 5 are shown so that you know how to begin and end each one – simply work the stitch repeat around in between.

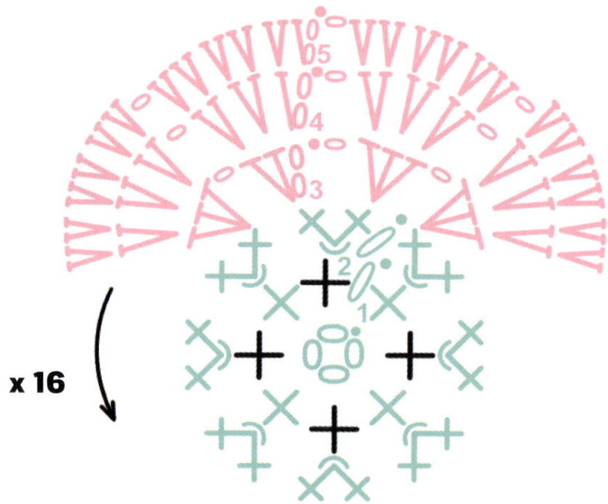

The chart (top) showing one complete petal section; the finished square (right), with all 16 petals, which naturally fold into each other to make the full three-dimensional flower.

WORKING 3D FLOWERS

You can sew your 3D flower motifs onto crochet squares or you can make them an integral part of a granny square by crocheting a background square around them.

The two background squares shown on pages 46 and 47 can be used with any of the 3D flower motifs. You will work the central flower first, then, once the flower is complete, use one of the background charts to complete the square.

The first round of the background will be worked in the same first round as the center of your floral motif. Simply attach your yarn to the back loop only of any of the stitches marked in black in the first round of the flower chart (as shown right).

Once the yarn is attached, work into each of the four indicated (black) stitches as given in the pattern, picking up the back loops only, and with the yarn and hook at the back of your flower, working behind the petals made.

The chart (top); the front view (below left); the back view (below right). This flower has been worked on the background square shown on page 47.

GRANNY BACKGROUND CHART

NOTE

This design can form the background of any of the 3D flower motifs: come back to this chart once the central 3D flower has been completed and refer to the instructions on page 45 to complete the square. If you'd like written instructions for this square, refer to page 57, working round 1 into the back of your flower.

JOINING

Use the slip stitch method or join as you go (pages 48–50).

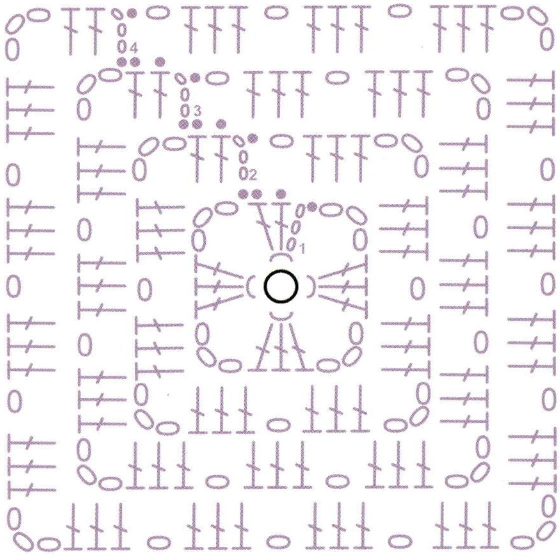

The black circle at the center here, and opposite, represents the first round of the flower you have already made. Hook round 1 of the background as shown here, but work into the back loops only of the four stitches indicated in black on round 1 of the chart for your chosen flower motif.

SOLID GRANNY BACKGROUND CHART

NOTE

This design can form the background of any of the 3D flower motifs: come back to this chart once the central 3D flower has been completed and refer to the instructions on page 45 to complete the square. If you'd like written instructions for this square, refer to page 61, working round 1 into the back of your flower.

JOINING

Use the slip stitch method (page 48).

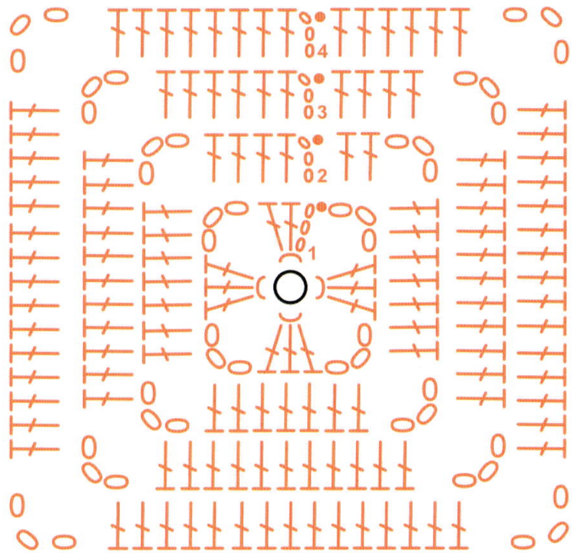

JOINING YOUR GRANNY SQUARES

Here are two of the most effective ways to join your squares together. Method 1 can be used for all the squares, Method 2 only for those with a 'traditional' granny-square final round; if in doubt, each pattern details which method(s) can be used.

METHOD 1: SLIP STITCH JOIN

This join fastens together completed squares with a solid, flat, neat seam, as is used to create the blanket (shown left and on page 267). Every square has been made with the same number of stitches along each edge, so you will be able to match them up perfectly whichever squares you choose.

Simply hold your pieces with right sides together, then attach your yarn to the right-hand end of the edge to be joined (or left-hand end if you are left-handed). Work a row of slip stitch all along the top edge, working each slip stitch through adjoining stitches of both squares at the same time; you can either work through the whole stitch of each square or through part of each adjoining stitch. I worked through the outer loops only: I inserted the hook through the front loop of the stitch on the front square and through the back loop of the stitch on the back square, then worked a slip stitch into both these loops at the same time. This creates a flatter seam on the reverse of the fabric and leaves a neat edge around each square at the front of the fabric.

METHOD 2: JOIN AS YOU GO

Granny squares are perfect for the join-as-you-go method, where you attach each new square to previous ones while you are still working the final round; it allows you to continue the open nature of the groups of stitches into the join, creating an almost seamless join and a fabric in which the squares look less patchworked and more integrated.

To join squares as you go, you must work the first square completely, to the last round, then all following squares to the penultimate round. You will join each to the last square on this final round with a seamless, neat and practically invisible seam. Simply attach the square you are working to the previous square by slip stitching to it at regular intervals.

You can work this join on any of the squares that have a traditional granny-square final round, which has four 3-chain corner spaces, with three 1-chain spaces along each side (as demonstrated in granny square no. 1).

1 Work around one edge of the square in the regular granny-square pattern from the final round until you reach the corner chain space. Work the first group of stitches of the corner (in the steps shown it is a 3 dc group) then make 1 ch.

2 After one chain of the corner has been worked, join to the corresponding corner ch sp of the first square with a slip stitch in place of the second chain.

3 Complete the corner stitch of the second motif by working one further chain, then work the second group of stitches of the corner (here, we are working 3 dc).

1

2

3

4

5

4 Now work a slip stitch into the next 1 ch sp of the first square.

5 Complete the next 3 dc group.

6 Continue in this manner along the edge being joined, slip stitching to the first square at each chain space and corner.

7 Finish the remaining edges of the second square without joining. For future squares, after the first row of squares, you will need to join along two edges in the same way.

6

7

THE GRANNY SQUARES

1. TRADITIONAL

NOTE

To increase the size, repeat round 4 until the desired size is reached, changing color every round.

WRITTEN PATTERN

Using yarn A, make 4 ch, join with a sl st to form a ring.

Round 1: 3 ch (counts as first dc here and throughout), 2 dc in ring, 3 ch, (3 dc in ring, 3 ch) three times. Join rnd with sl st to top of first 3 ch. Fasten off yarn. Attach yarn B to any corner sp of round 1.

Round 2: 3 ch, (2 dc, 3 ch, 3 dc) in same sp, 1 ch, *(3 dc, 3 ch, 3 dc) in next 3 ch sp, 1 ch; rep from * twice more. Join rnd with sl st to top of first 3 ch. Fasten off yarn.
Attach yarn C to any corner sp of round 2.

Round 3: 3 ch, (2 dc, 3 ch, 3 dc) in same sp, 1 ch, 3 dc in next 1 ch sp, 1 ch, *(3 dc, 3 ch, 3 dc) in next 3 ch sp for corner, 1 ch, 3 dc in next 1 ch sp, 1 ch; rep from * twice more. Join rnd with a sl st to top of first 3 ch. Fasten off yarn.
Attach yarn D to any corner sp of round 3.

Round 4: 3 ch, (2 dc, 3 ch, 3 dc) all in same 3 ch sp, 1 ch, (3 dc in next 1 ch sp, 1 ch) to next corner, *(3 dc, 3 ch, 3 dc) in corner ch sp, 1 ch, (3 dc in next 1 ch sp, 1 ch) to next corner; repeat from * around. Join rnd with sl st to top of first ch. Fasten off yarn.

CHART PATTERN

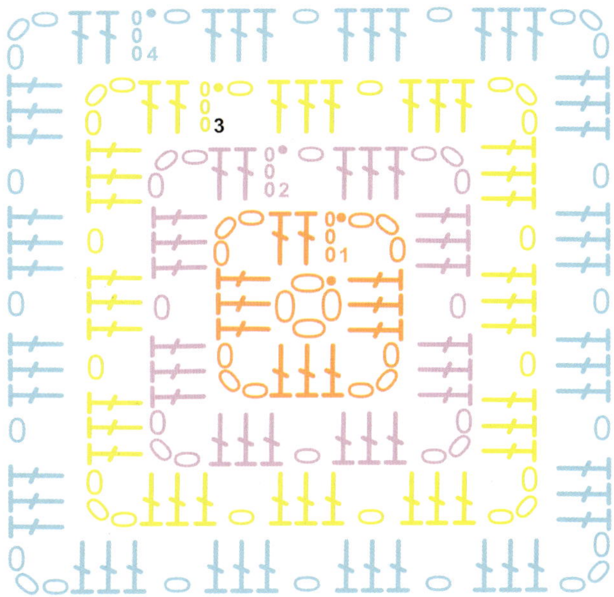

JOINING

Use the slip stitch method (see page 48) or join as you go (see pages 49–50).

2. SINGLE COLOR

NOTE

To increase the size, repeat round 4 until the desired size is reached.

WRITTEN PATTERN

Using yarn A, make 4 ch, join with a sl st to form a ring.

Round 1: 3 ch (counts as first dc here and throughout), 2 dc in ring, 3 ch, (3 dc in ring, 3 ch) three times. Join rnd with sl st to top of first 3 ch.

Round 2: sl st across each dc to next 3 ch sp, sl st in 3 ch sp, 3 ch, (2 dc, 3 ch, 3 dc) in same sp, 1 ch, *(3 dc, 3 ch, 3 dc) in next 3 ch sp, 1 ch; rep from * twice more. Join rnd with sl st to top of first 3 ch.

Round 3: sl st across each dc to next 3 ch sp, sl st in 3 ch sp, 3 ch, (2 dc, 3 ch, 3 dc) in same sp, 1 ch, 3 dc in next 1 ch sp, 1 ch, *(3 dc, 3 ch, 3 dc) in next 3 ch sp for corner, 1 ch, 3 dc in next 1 ch sp, 1 ch; rep from * twice more. Join rnd with a sl st to top of first 3 ch.

Round 4: sl st across each dc to next 3 ch sp, sl st in 3 ch sp, 3 ch, (2 dc, 3 ch, 3 dc) all in same 3 ch sp, 1 ch, (3 dc in next 1 ch sp, 1 ch) to next corner, *(3 dc, 3 ch, 3 dc) in corner ch sp, 1 ch, (3 dc in next 1 ch sp, 1 ch) to next corner; rep from * twice more. Join rnd with sl st to top of first 3 ch. Fasten off yarn.

CHART PATTERN

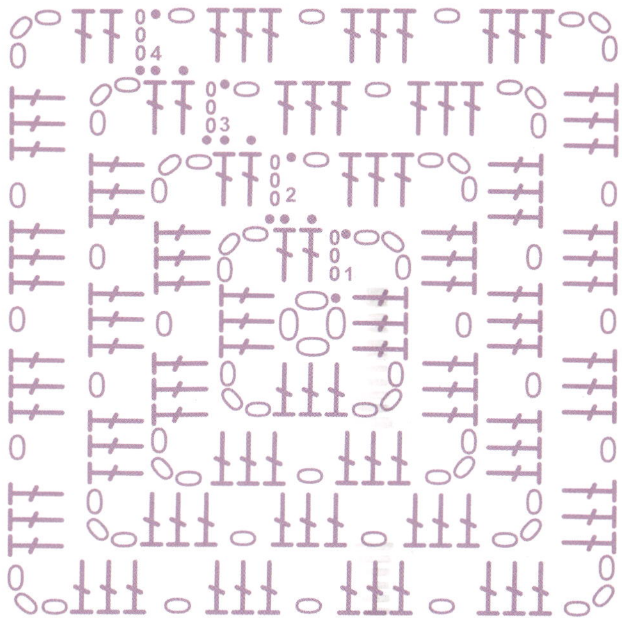

JOINING

Use the slip stitch method (see page 48) or join as you go (see pages 49–50).

3. SOLID STRIPED

NOTE

To increase the size, repeat round 3 until the desired size is reached, changing color every round.

WRITTEN PATTERN

Using yarn A, make 4 ch, join with a sl st to form a ring.

Round 1: 3 ch (counts as first dc here and throughout), 2 dc in ring, 3 ch, (3 dc in ring, 3 ch) three times. Join rnd with sl st to top of first 3 ch. Fasten off yarn.
Attach yarn B to any corner sp of round 1.

Round 2: 3 ch, (1 dc, 3 ch, 2 dc) in same sp, 3 dc, *(2 dc, 3 ch, 2 dc) in next corner sp, 3 dc; rep from * twice more. Join rnd with sl st to top of first 3 ch. Fasten off yarn.
Attach yarn C to any corner sp of round 2.

Round 3: 3 ch, (1 dc, 3 ch, 2 dc) in same sp, 1 dc in each dc to next corner sp, *(2 dc, 3 ch, 2 dc) into next corner sp, 1 dc in each dc to next corner sp; rep from * twice more. Join rnd with sl st to top of first 3 ch. Fasten off yarn.
Attach yarn D to any corner sp of round 3.

Round 4: as round 3. Fasten off yarn.

CHART PATTERN

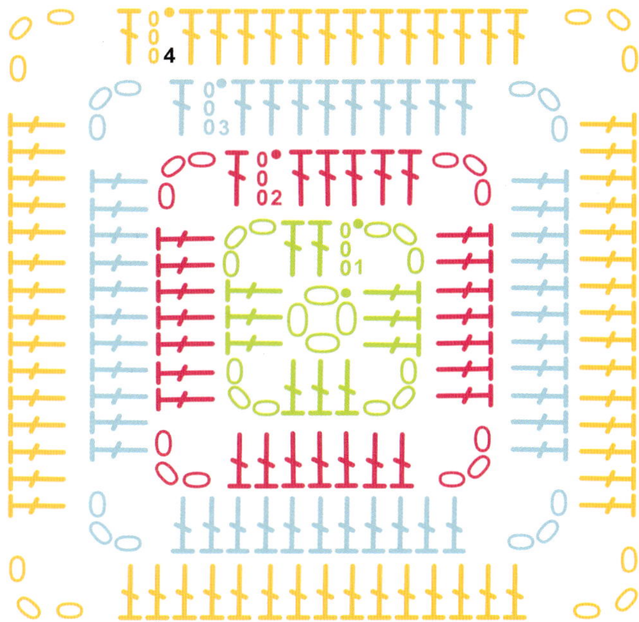

JOINING

Use the slip stitch method (see page 48).

4. SOLID

NOTE

To increase the size, repeat round 3 until the desired size is reached.

WRITTEN PATTERN

Using yarn A, make 4 ch, join with a sl st to form a ring.

Round 1: 3 ch (counts as first dc here and throughout), 2 dc in ring, 3 ch, (3 dc in ring, 3 ch) three times. Join rnd with sl st to top of first 3 ch.

Round 2: 3 ch, 1 dc in each of the next 2 dc, (2 dc, 3 ch, 2 dc) in 3 ch sp, *3 dc, (2 dc, 3 ch, 2 dc) in next corner sp; rep from * twice more. Join rnd with sl st to top of first 3 ch.

Round 3: 3 ch, *1 dc in each dc to next corner sp, (2 dc, 3 ch, 2 dc) into next corner sp; rep from * three times more, 1 dc in each dc to end of rnd. Join rnd with sl st to top of first 3 ch.

Round 4: as round 3. Fasten off yarn.

CHART PATTERN

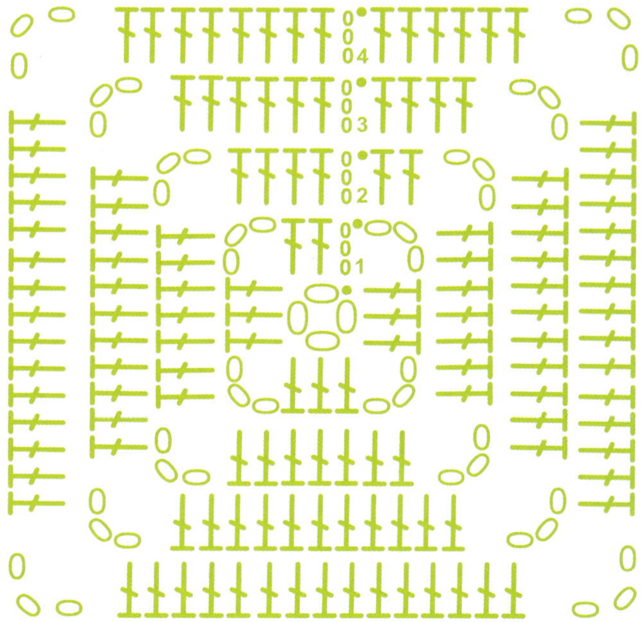

JOINING

Use the slip stitch method (see page 48).

5. TWO-COLOR

NOTE

To increase the size, repeat round 4 until the desired size is reached.

WRITTEN PATTERN

Using yarn A, make 4 ch, join with a sl st to form a ring.

Round 1: 3 ch (counts as first dc here and throughout), 2 dc in ring, 3 ch, (3 dc in ring, 3 ch) three times. Join rnd with sl st to top of first 3 ch. Fasten off yarn A.
Attach yarn B to any corner sp of round 1.

Round 2: 3 ch, (2 dc, 3 ch, 3 dc) in same sp, 1 ch, *(3 dc, 3 ch, 3 dc) in next 3 ch sp, 1 ch; rep from * twice more. Join rnd with sl st to top of first 3 ch.

Round 3: sl st across each dc to next 3 ch sp, sl st in 3 ch sp, 3 ch, (2 dc, 3 ch, 3 dc) in same sp, 1 ch, 3 dc in next 1 ch sp, 1 ch, *(3 dc, 3 ch, 3 dc) in next 3 ch sp for corner, 1 ch, 3 dc in next 1 ch sp, 1 ch; rep from * twice more. Join rnd with sl st to top of first 3 ch.

Round 4: sl st across each dc to next 3 ch sp, sl st in 3 ch sp, 3 ch, (2 dc, 3 ch, 3 dc) all in same 3 ch sp, 1 ch, (3 dc in next 1 ch sp, 1 ch) to next corner, *(3 dc, 3 ch, 3 dc) in corner ch sp, 1 ch, (3 dc in next 1 ch sp, 1 ch) to next corner; rep from * twice more. Join rnd with sl st to top of first 3 ch. Fasten off yarn.

CHART PATTERN

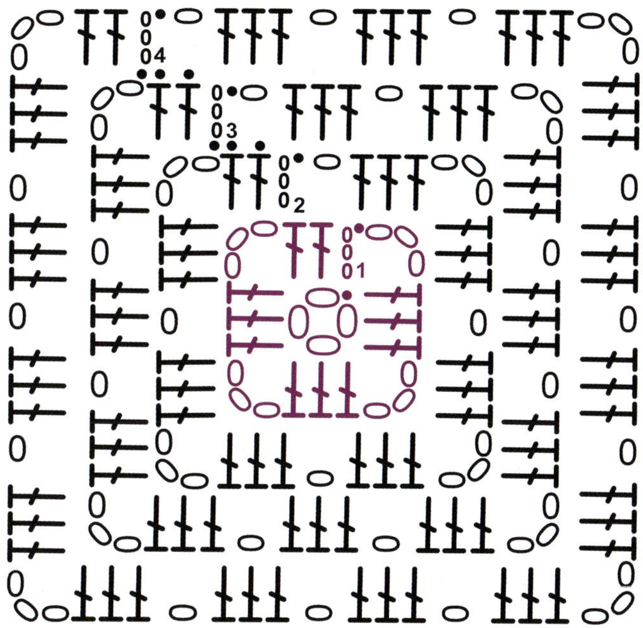

JOINING

Use the slip stitch method (see page 48) or join as you go (see pages 49–50).

6. SOLID TWO-COLOR

NOTE

To increase the size, repeat round 3 until the desired size is reached.

WRITTEN PATTERN

Using yarn A, make 4 ch, join with a sl st to form a ring.

Round 1: 3 ch (counts as first dc here and throughout), 2 dc in ring, 3 ch, (3 dc in ring, 3 ch) three times. Join rnd with sl st to top of first 3 ch. Fasten off yarn.
Attach yarn B to any corner sp of round 1.

Round 2: 3 ch, (1 dc, 3 ch, 2 dc) in same sp, 3 dc, *(2 dc, 3 ch, 2 dc) in next corner sp, 3 dc; rep from * two times more.
Join rnd with sl st to top of first 3 ch.

Round 3: 3 ch, *1 dc in each dc to next corner sp, (2 dc, 3 ch, 2 dc) into next corner sp; rep from * three times more, 1 dc in each dc to end of rnd. Join rnd with sl st to top of first 3 ch.

Round 4: as round 3. Fasten off yarn.

CHART PATTERN

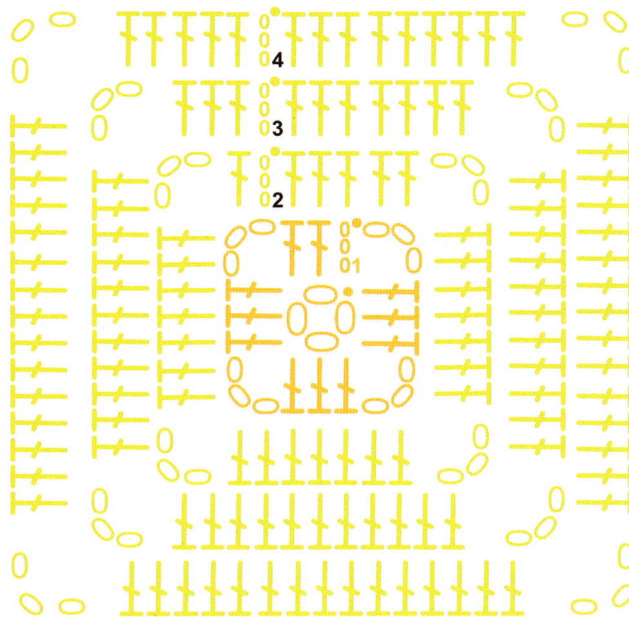

JOINING

Use the slip stitch method (see page 48).

7. HALF AND HALF

NOTE

This square is worked in joined rows – complete one row, join to the beginning of the row, then turn work and work back the other way. When changing color, leave all unused yarn where it is, to pick up later.

WRITTEN PATTERN

Using yarn A, make 4 ch, join with a sl st to form a ring.

Row 1 (RS): 3 ch (counts as first dc here and throughout), 2 dc in ring, 3 ch, 3 dc in ring, changing to yarn B in last step of last dc, continue with yarn B, leaving yarn A here, work (3 ch, 3 dc in ring) twice, 3 ch, join rnd with sl st to top of first 3 ch, turn work.

Row 2 (WS): sl st into 3 ch sp, 3 ch, 2 dc in same space, 1 ch, (3 dc, 3 ch, 3 dc) in next 3 ch sp, 1 ch, 3 dc in next 3 ch sp, changing to yarn A in last step of last st, 3 ch, 3 dc in same 3 ch sp, 1 ch, (3 dc, 3 ch, 3 dc) in next 3 ch sp, 1 ch, 3 dc in next 3 ch sp, 3 ch, join rnd with sl st to top of first 3 ch, turn work.

Row 3 (RS): sl st into 3 ch sp, 3 ch, 2 dc in same space, 1 ch, 3 dc in next 1 ch sp, 1 ch, (3 dc, 3 ch, 3 dc) in next 3 ch sp, 1 ch, 3 dc in next 1 ch sp, 1 ch, 3 dc in next 3 ch sp, changing to yarn B in last step of last st, 3 ch, 3 dc in same 3 ch sp, 1 ch, 3 dc in next 1 ch sp, 1 ch, (3 dc, 3 ch, 3 dc) in next 3 ch sp, 1 ch, 3 dc in next 1 ch sp, 1 ch, 3 dc in next 3 ch sp, 3 ch, join rnd with sl st to top of first 3 ch, turn work.

Row 4 (WS): sl st into 3 ch sp, 3 ch, 2 dc in same space, 1 ch, (3 dc in next 1 ch sp, 1 ch) to next 3 ch sp, (3 dc, 3 ch, 3 dc) in 3 ch sp, 1 ch, (3 dc in next 1 ch sp, 1 ch) to next 3 ch sp, 3 dc in 3 ch sp, changing to yarn A in last step of last st, 3 ch, 3 dc in same 3 ch sp, 1 ch, (3 dc in next 1 ch sp, 1 ch) to next 3 ch sp, (3 dc, 3 ch, 3 dc) in 3 ch sp, 1 ch, (3 dc in next 1 ch sp, 1 ch) to next 3 ch sp, 3 dc in 3 ch sp, 3 ch, join rnd with sl st to top of first 3 ch. Fasten off yarn.

CHART PATTERN

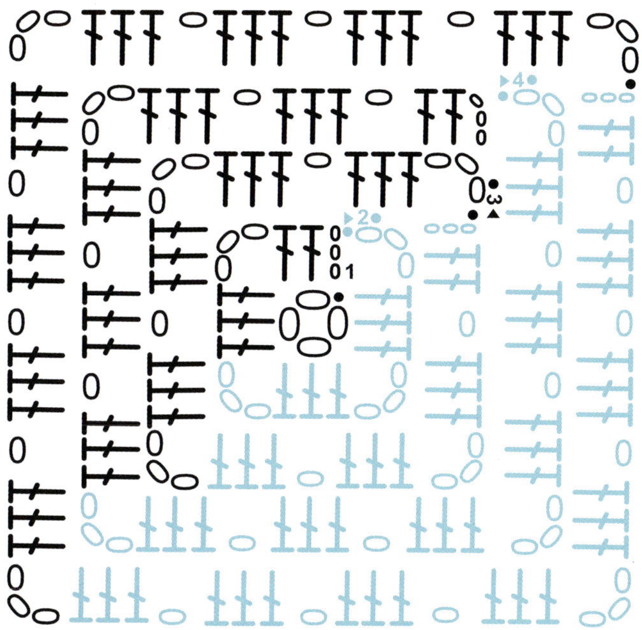

JOINING

Use the slip stitch method (see page 48) or join as you go (see pages 49–50).

8. QUARTERED

NOTE

This square is worked in joined rows – complete one row, join to the beginning of the row, then turn work and work back the other way. When changing color, leave all unused yarn where it is, to pick up later.

WRITTEN PATTERN

Using yarn A, make 4 ch, join with a sl st to form a ring.

Row 1 (RS): 3 ch (counts as first dc here and throughout), 2 dc in ring, changing to yarn B in last step of last dc, 3 ch, 3 dc in ring, changing to yarn C in last step of last dc, 3 ch, 3 dc in ring, changing to yarn D in last step of last st, 3 ch, 3 dc in ring, 3 ch, join rnd with sl st to top of first 3 ch, turn work.

Row 2 (WS): sl st into 3 ch sp, 3 ch, 2 dc in same space, 1 ch, 3 dc in next 3 ch sp, changing to yarn C in last step of last st, 3 ch, 3 dc in same ch sp, 1 ch, 3 dc in next 3 ch sp, changing to yarn B in last step of last st, 3 ch, 3 dc in same 3 ch sp, 1 ch, 3 dc in next 3 ch sp, changing to yarn A in last step of last st, 3 ch, 3 dc in same ch sp, 1 ch, 3 dc in next 3 ch sp, 3 ch, join rnd with sl st to top of first 3 ch, turn work.

Row 3 (RS): sl st into 3 ch sp, 3 ch, 2 dc in same space, 1 ch, 3 dc in next 1 ch sp, 1 ch, 3 dc in next 3 ch sp, changing to yarn B in last step of last st, 3 ch, 3 dc in same ch sp, 1 ch, 3 dc in next 1 ch sp, 1 ch, 3 dc in next 3 ch sp, changing to yarn C in last step of last st, 3 ch, 3 dc in same 3 ch sp, 1 ch, 3 dc in next 1 ch sp, 1 ch, 3 dc in next 3 ch sp, changing to yarn D in last step of last st, 3 ch, 3 dc in same ch sp, 1 ch, 3 dc in next 1 ch sp, 1 ch, 3 dc in next 3 ch sp, 3 ch, join rnd with sl st to top of first 3 ch, turn work.

Row 4 (WS): sl st into 3 ch sp, 3 ch, 2 dc in same space, 1 ch, (3 dc in next 1 ch sp, 1 ch) to next 3 ch sp, 3 dc in 3 ch sp, changing to yarn C in last step of last st, 3 ch, 3 dc in same ch sp, 1 ch, (3 dc in next 1 ch sp, 1 ch) to next 3 ch sp, 3 dc in 3 ch sp, changing to yarn B in last step of last st, 3 ch, 3 dc in same 3 ch sp, 1 ch, (3 dc in next 1 ch sp, 1 ch) to next 3 ch sp, 3 dc in 3 ch sp, changing to yarn A in last step of last st, 3 ch, 3 dc in same ch sp, 1 ch, (3 dc in next 1 ch sp, 1 ch) to next 3 ch sp, 3 dc in 3 ch sp, 3 ch, join rnd with sl st to top of first 3 ch.
Fasten off yarn.

CHART PATTERN

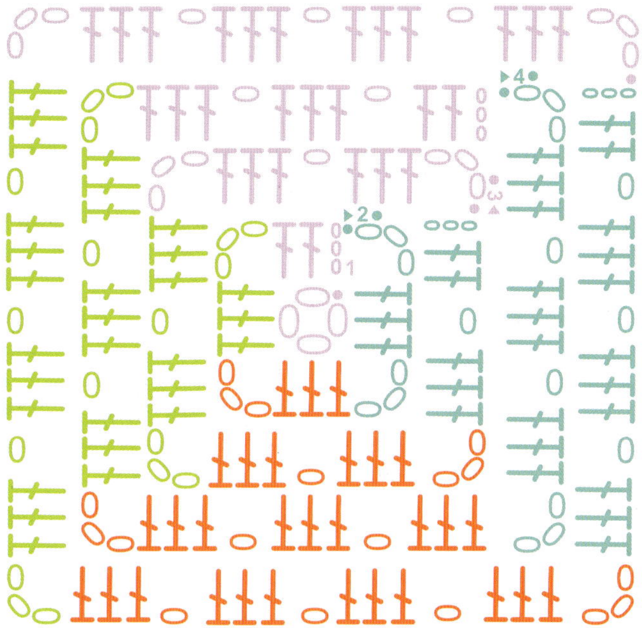

JOINING

Use the slip stitch method (see page 48) or join as you go (see pages 49–50).

9. HALF AND HALF SOLID

NOTE

When changing yarn, bring unused color with you, trapping ends inside the stitches as you go so the unused yarn is ready when you need it. To increase the size, repeat round 3, changing colors as set.

WRITTEN PATTERN

Using yarn A, make 4 ch, join with a sl st to form a ring.

Round 1: 3 ch (counts as first dc here and throughout), 2 dc in ring, 3 ch, 3 dc in ring, changing to yarn B in last step of last dc, continue with yarn B, trapping unused yarn A as you go, work 3 ch, 3 dc in ring, 3 ch, 3 dc in ring, changing back to yarn A in last step of last dc, 3 ch, join rnd with sl st to top of first 3 ch.

Round 2: 3 ch, 2 dc, (2 dc, 3 ch, 2 dc) in next 3 ch sp, 3 dc, 2 dc in next 3 ch sp, changing to yarn B in last step of last st, 3 ch, 2 dc in same 3 ch sp, 3 dc, (2 dc, 3 ch, 2 dc) in next 3 ch sp, 3 dc, 2 dc in next 3 ch sp, changing back to yarn A in last step of last st, 3 ch, 2 dc in same 3 ch sp, join rnd with sl st to top of first 3 ch.

Round 3: 3 ch, 1 dc in each dc to next 3 ch sp, (2 dc, 3 ch, 2 dc) in 3 ch sp, 1 dc in each dc to next 3 ch sp, 2 dc in 3 ch sp, changing to yarn B in last step of last st, 3 ch, 2 dc in same 3 ch sp, 1 dc in each dc across to next 3 ch sp, (2 dc, 3 ch, 2 dc) in 3 ch sp, 1 dc in each dc across to next 3 ch sp, 2 dc in next 3 ch sp, changing back to yarn A in last step of last st, 3 ch, 2 dc in same 3 ch sp, 1 dc in each dc to end, join rnd with sl st to top of first 3 ch.

Round 4: as round 3.
Fasten off yarn.

CHART PATTERN

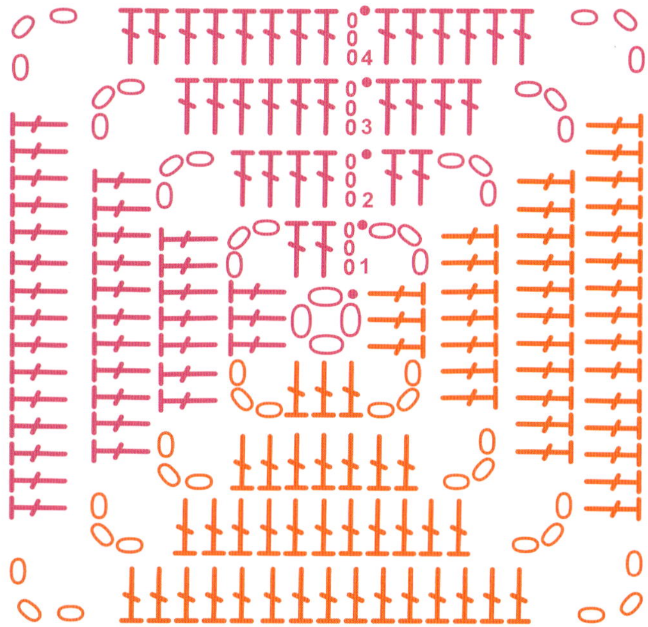

JOINING

Use the slip stitch method (see page 48).

10. QUARTERED SOLID

NOTE

This square is worked in joined rows – complete one row, join to the beginning of the row, then turn work and work back the other way. When changing color, leave all unused yarn where it is, to pick up later. To increase the size, repeat round 4, changing colors as set, until the desired size is reached.

WRITTEN PATTERN

Using yarn A, make 4 ch, join with a sl st to form a ring.

Row 1 (RS): 3 ch (counts as first dc here and throughout), 2 dc in ring, changing to yarn B in last step of last dc, 3 ch, 3 dc in ring, changing to yarn C in last step of last dc, 3 ch, 3 dc in ring, changing to yarn D in last step of last st, 3 ch, 3 dc in ring, 3 ch, join rnd with sl st to top of first 3 ch, turn work.

Row 2 (WS): sl st into 3 ch sp, 3 ch, 1 dc in same space, 3 dc, 2 dc in next 3 ch sp, changing to yarn C in last step of last st, 3 ch, 2 dc in same ch sp, 3 dc, 2 dc in next 3 ch sp, changing to yarn B in last step of last st, 3 ch, 2 dc in same 3 ch sp, 3 dc, 2 dc in next 3 ch sp, changing to yarn A in last step of last st, 3 ch, 2 dc in same ch sp, 3 dc, 2 dc in next 3 ch sp, 3 ch, join rnd with sl st to top of first 3 ch, turn work.

Row 3 (RS): sl st into 3 ch sp, 3 ch, 1 dc in same space, 1 dc in each dc to next 3 ch sp, 2 dc in 3 ch sp, changing to yarn B in last step of last st, 3 ch, 2 dc in same ch sp, 1 dc in each dc to next 3 ch sp, 2 dc in 3 ch sp, changing to yarn C in last step of last st, 3 ch, 2 dc in same 3 ch sp, 1 dc in each dc to next 3 ch sp, 2 dc in 3 ch sp, changing to yarn D in last step of last st, 3 ch, 2 dc in same ch sp, 1 dc in each dc to next 3 ch sp, 2 dc in 3 ch sp, 3 ch, join rnd with sl st to top of first 3 ch, turn work.

Row 4 (WS): sl st into 3 ch sp, 3 ch, 1 dc in same space, 1 dc in each dc to next 3 ch sp, 2 dc in 3 ch sp, changing to yarn C in last step of last st, 3 ch, 2 dc in same ch sp, 1 dc in each dc to next 3 ch sp, 2 dc in 3 ch sp, changing to yarn B in last step of last st, 3 ch, 2 dc in same 3 ch sp, 1 dc in each dc to next 3 ch sp, 2 dc in 3 ch sp, changing to yarn A in last step of last st, 3 ch, 2 dc in same ch sp, 1 dc in each dc to next 3 ch sp, 2 dc in 3 ch sp, 3 ch, join rnd with sl st to top of first 3 ch.
Fasten off yarn.

CHART PATTERN

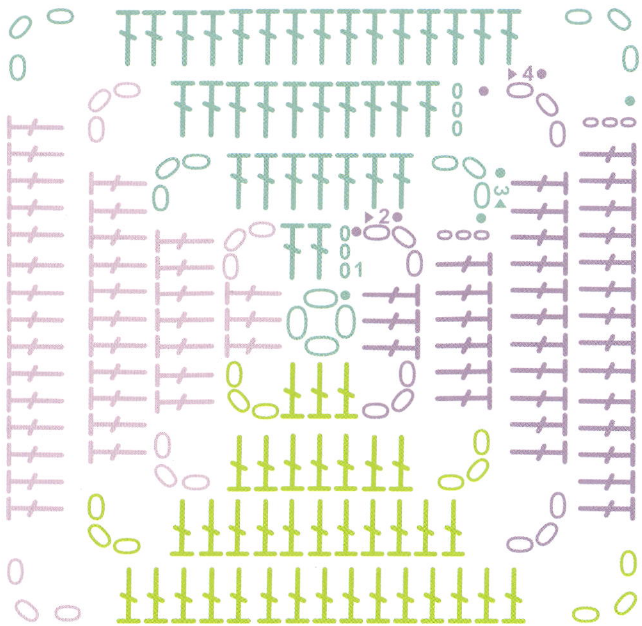

JOINING

Use the slip stitch method (see page 48).

11. MITERED

NOTE

Row 1 is joined into a round, but after that the piece is not worked in rounds but in unturned rows, with each new color added at the beginning of the last unturned row. To increase the size, repeat row 4 and row 5 alternately, changing color every row.

WRITTEN PATTERN

Using yarn A, make 4 ch, join with a sl st to form a ring.

Row 1: 3 ch (counts as first dc here and throughout), 2 dc in ring, 3 ch, (3 dc in ring, 3 ch) three times. Join rnd with sl st to top of first 3 ch. Fasten off yarn. Do not turn. Join yarn B to any corner sp of row 1.

Row 2: 3 ch (counts as first dc), 3 dc in same sp, 1 ch, (3 dc, 3 ch, 3 dc) in next 3 ch sp, 1 ch, 4 dc in next 3 ch sp. Fasten off yarn B, leaving remaining sides unworked. Do not turn. Join yarn C to top of first 3 ch of row 2.

Row 3: 4 ch (counts as 1 dc, 1 ch), miss 3 dc, 3 dc in next 1 ch sp, 1 ch, (3 dc, 3 ch, 3 dc) in next 3 ch sp, 1 ch, 3 dc in next 1 ch sp, 1 ch, miss 3 dc, 1 dc in last dc. Fasten off yarn C. Do not turn. Join yarn D to third of first 4 ch from row 3.

Row 4: 3 ch (counts as first dc), (3 dc in next 1 ch sp, 1 ch) to 3 ch corner sp, (3 dc, 3 ch, 3 dc) in 3 ch sp, (1 ch, 3 dc in next 1 ch sp) to end, 1 dc in last dc of row. Fasten off yarn D. Do not turn. Join yarn E to top of first 3 ch of row 4.

Row 5: 4 ch (counts as 1 dc, 1 ch), miss 3 dc, (3 dc in next 1 ch sp, 1 ch) to 3 ch sp, (3 dc, 3 ch, 3 dc) in next 3 ch sp, (1 ch, 3 dc in next 1 ch sp) to last 4 dc, 1 ch, miss 3 dc, 1 dc in last dc. Fasten off yarn E. Do not turn.
Join yarn F to third of first 4 ch from row 5.

Row 6: as row 4. Fasten off yarn.

CHART PATTERN

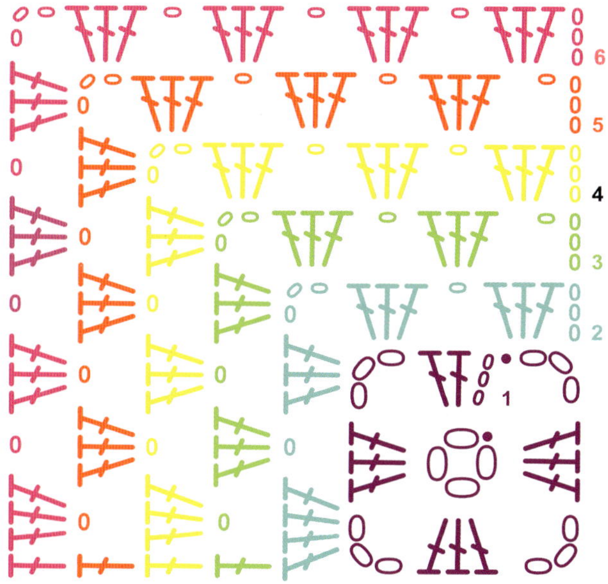

JOINING

Use the slip stitch method (see page 48).

12. MITERED SOLID

NOTE

Row 1 is joined into a round, but after that the piece is not worked in rounds but in unturned rows, with each new color added at the beginning of the last unturned row. To increase the size, repeat row 3 until the desired size is reached, changing color every round.

WRITTEN PATTERN

Using yarn A, make 4 ch, join with a sl st to form a ring.

Row 1: 3 ch (counts as first dc here and throughout), 2 dc in ring, 3 ch, (3 dc in ring, 3 ch) three times. Join rnd with sl st to top of first 3 ch. Fasten off yarn.
Attach yarn B to any corner sp of round 1.

Row 2: 3 ch, 1 dc in same sp, 3 dc, (2 dc, 3 ch, 2 dc) in next ch sp, 3 dc, 2 dc in next ch sp. Fasten off yarn B, leaving remaining sides unworked. Do not turn.
Join yarn C to top of first 3 ch of row 2.

Row 3: 3 ch, 1 dc in each dc to 3 ch sp, (2 dc, 3 ch, 2 dc) in ch sp, 1 dc in each dc to end of row. Fasten off yarn C, leaving remaining sides unworked. Do not turn.
Join yarn D to top of first 3 ch of row 3.

Rows 4–6: repeat row 3, fastening off yarn each time, working in stripes of yarns D, E and F in turn.

CHART PATTERN

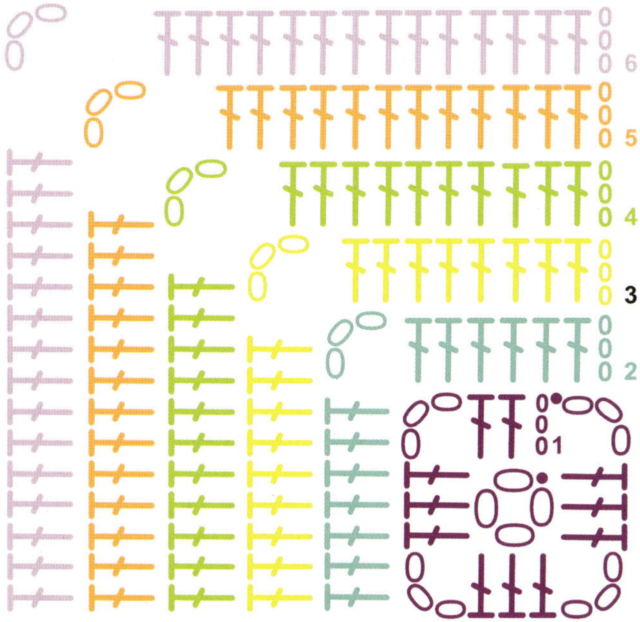

JOINING

Use the slip stitch method (see page 48).

13. STRIPE

NOTE

This square is worked in unturned rows, with each new color added at the beginning of the last unturned row. The final row is an edging working in the round.

WRITTEN PATTERN

Using yarn A, make 17 ch.

Row 1: 3 dc in fourth ch from hook (missed ch count as 1 dc), * 1 ch, miss 3 ch, 3 dc in next ch; rep from * to last ch, 1 dc in last ch. Do not turn. Fasten off yarn A.
Join yarn B into top of first stitch from row 1.

Row 2: 4 ch (counts as 1 dc, 1 ch), (3 dc in next 1 ch sp, 1 ch) to last 4 dc, miss 3 dc, 1 dc in last dc. Do not turn. Fasten off yarn B.
Join yarn C into top of first stitch from row 2.

Row 3: 3 ch (counts as 1 dc), 3 dc in next ch sp, (1 ch, 3 dc in next 1 ch sp) to last dc, 1 dc in last dc. Do not turn. Fasten off yarn C.
Join yarn D into top of first stitch from row 3.

Rows 4–7: repeat rows 2 and 3, working in stripes of yarns D, E, F and A in turn. Fasten off yarn A.
Join yarn G to top of first stitch from row 7.

Edge round: 2 ch (counts as 1 hdc), (1 hdc, 3 ch, 2 hdc) in same st, miss 2 dc, 1 hdc in next dc, 1 hdc in 1 ch sp, (3 hdc, 1 hdc in next 1 ch sp) to last 4 dc, 1 hdc in next dc, miss 2 dc, (2 hdc, 3 ch, 2 hdc) in next dc. Working down next side, 2 hdc in end of row 6 and in end of row 5, 3 hdc in end of row 4, 2 hdc in end of row 3 and in end of row 2, (2 hdc, 3 ch, 2 hdc) in unworked loop of first ch at bottom of row 1. Working along next side, work 3 hdc in next unworked ch sp, 1 hdc in bottom loop of next worked chain, 3 hdc in next unworked ch sp, 1 hdc in next worked ch, 3 hdc in next unworked ch sp, (2 hdc, 3 ch, 2 hdc) in last ch. Working along last side, work 2 hdc in beginning of row 2 and in beginning of row 3, 3 hdc in beginning of row 4, 2 hdc in beginning of row 5, and in beginning of row 6. Join rnd with sl st to top of first 2 ch.
Fasten off yarn.

CHART PATTERN

JOINING

Use the slip stitch method (see page 48).

14. DIAGONAL STRIPE

NOTE

This square is made in unturned rows, on the diagonal, with each new color added at the beginning of the last unturned row. The final row is an edging worked in the round.

WRITTEN PATTERN

Using yarn A, make 5 ch.

Row 1: (3 dc, 1 ch, 1 dc) in fifth ch from hook (missed ch counts as 1 dc, 1 ch), do not turn. Fasten off yarn A. Join yarn B with sl st to third of first ch from row 1.

Row 2: 4 ch (counts as 1 dc, 1 ch here and throughout), 3 dc in 1 ch sp, 1 ch, 3 dc in next 1 ch sp, 1 ch, 1 dc in last dc, do not turn. Fasten off yarn B.
Join yarn C with sl st to third of first ch from row 2.

Row 3: 4 ch, 3 dc in 1 ch sp, 1 ch, (3 dc in next 1 ch sp, 1 ch) to last dc, 1 dc in last dc, do not turn. Fasten off yarn C. Join yarn D with sl st to third of first ch from row 3.

Rows 4–6: repeat row 3, fastening off yarn each time, working in stripes of yarns D, E and F in turn. Fasten off yarn F. Join yarn A with sl st to third of first ch from row 6.

Row 7: 3 ch (counts as 1 dc here and throughout), (3 dc in next 1 ch sp, 1 ch) to last 4 dc, miss next 3 dc, 1 dc in last dc, do not turn. Fasten off yarn A.
Join yarn B with sl st to third of first ch from row 7.

Rows 8–11: repeat row 7, fastening off yarn each time, working in stripes of yarns B, C, D and E in turn. Fasten off yarn E.

Edge round: join yarn G with sl st in central dc of row 11, 1 ch, (2 sc, 3 ch, 2 sc) in same st, 2 sc in end of row 11 and end of row 10, 3 sc in end of row 9, 2 sc in end of row 8 and end of row 7, (2 sc, 3 ch, 2 sc) in last dc from row 6. Working down second side, 2 sc in end of row 5 and end of row 4, 3 sc in end of row 3, 2 sc in end of row 2 and end of row 1, (2 sc, 3 ch, 2 sc) in bottom chain of row 1. Working up the third side, 2 sc in end of row 1 and end of row 2, 3 sc in end of row 3, 2 sc in end of row 4 and end of row 5, (2 sc, 3 ch, 2 sc) in top of 4-ch from row 6. Working along final side of square, 2 sc in end of row 7 and end of row 8, 3 sc in end of row 9, 2 sc in end of row 10 and end of row 11. Join rnd with sl st to top of first ch (60 sc and 4 ch sps). Fasten off yarn.

CHART PATTERN

JOINING

Use the slip stitch method (see page 48).

15. MIXED

WRITTEN PATTERN

Using yarn A, make 4 ch, join with a sl st to form a ring.

Round 1: 3 ch (counts as first dc here and throughout), 2 dc in ring, 3 ch, (3 dc in ring, 3 ch) three times. Join rnd with sl st to top of first 3 ch. Fasten off yarn.
Attach yarn B to any 3 ch corner sp of round 1.

Round 2: 3 ch, (1 dc, 3 ch, 2 dc) in same sp, 3 dc, *(2 dc, 3 ch, 2 dc) in next 3 ch sp, 3 dc; rep from * twice more. Join rnd with sl st to top of first 3 ch. Fasten off yarn.
Attach yarn C to any 3 ch corner sp of round 2.

Round 3: 3 ch, (2 dc, 3 ch, 3 dc) in same sp, 1 ch, miss 3 dc, 3 dc in next dc, 1 ch, *(3 dc, 3 ch, 3 dc) in next 3 ch sp, 1 ch, miss 3 dc, 3 dc in next dc, 1 ch; rep from * twice more. Join rnd with sl st to top of first 3 ch.
Fasten off yarn.
Attach yarn D to any 3 ch corner sp of round 3.

Round 4: 3 ch, (1 dc, 3 ch, 2 dc) in same sp, 1 dc in each dc and 1 ch sp to next 3 ch sp, *(2 dc, 3 ch, 2 dc) in 3 ch sp, 1 dc in each dc and 1 ch sp to next 3 ch sp; rep from * twice more. Join rnd with sl st to top of first 3 ch.
Fasten off yarn.

CHART PATTERN

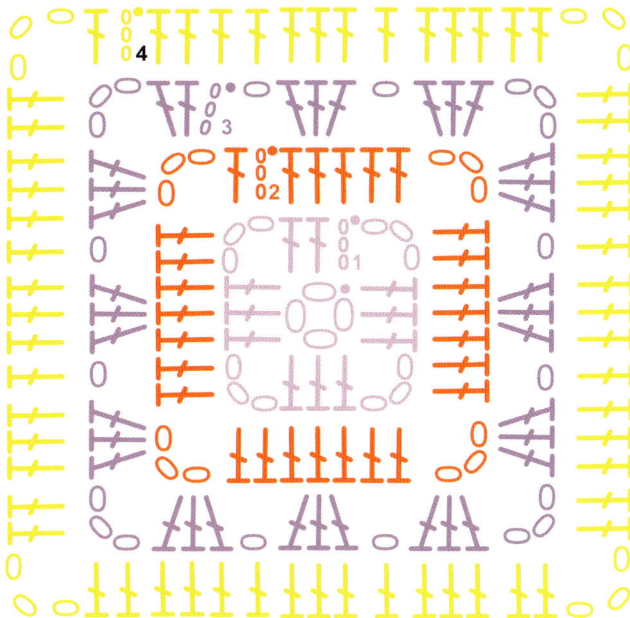

JOINING

Use the slip stitch method (see page 48).

16. BLOCK STITCH

WRITTEN PATTERN

Using yarn A, make 4 ch, join with a sl st to form a ring.

Round 1: 3 ch (counts as first dc here and throughout), 2 dc in ring, 3 ch, (3 dc in ring, 3 ch) three times. Join rnd with sl st to top of first 3 ch. Fasten off yarn.
Attach yarn B to any 3 ch corner sp of round 1.

Round 2: 1 ch (does not count as st), * (1 sc, 3 ch, 1 sc) in 3 ch sp, 3 ch, miss 3 dc; rep from * three times more. Join rnd with sl st to top of first ch. Fasten off yarn.
Attach yarn C to any 3 ch corner sp of round 2.

Round 3: 3 ch, (2 dc, 3 ch, 3 dc) in same sp, 1 ch, 3 dc in next ch sp, 1 ch, * (3 dc, 3 ch, 3 dc) in next ch sp, 1 ch, 3 dc in next ch sp, 1 ch; rep from * twice more. Join rnd with sl st to top of first 3 ch. Fasten off yarn.
Attach yarn D to any 3 ch corner sp of round 3.

Round 4: 1 ch, * (1 sc, 3 ch, 1 sc) in 3 ch sp, (3 ch, miss 3 dc, 1 sc in next 1 ch sp) twice, 3 ch; rep from * three times more. Join rnd with sl st to top of first ch. Fasten off yarn.
Attach yarn E to any 3 ch corner sp of round 4.

Round 5: 3 ch, (2 dc, 3 ch, 3 dc) in same sp, (3 dc) in each ch sp to next corner sp, * (3 dc, 3 ch, 3 dc) in corner ch sp, (3 dc) in each ch sp to next corner sp; rep from * twice more. Join rnd with sl st to top of first 3 ch.
Fasten off yarn.

CHART PATTERN

JOINING

Use the slip stitch method (see page 48).

17. LACE HOLES

WRITTEN PATTERN

Using yarn A, make 4 ch, join with a sl st to form a ring.

Round 1: 3 ch (counts as first dc here and throughout), 2 dc in ring, 3 ch, (3 dc in ring, 3 ch) three times. Join rnd with sl st to top of first 3 ch.

Round 2: sl st across to next ch sp, 3 ch, (1 dc, 3 ch, 2 dc) in 3 ch sp, 1 dc, miss next dc, 1 ch, 1 dc in next st, * (2 dc, 3 ch, 2 dc) in corner sp, 1 dc, miss next dc, 1 ch, 1 dc in next st; rep from * twice more. Join rnd with sl st to top of first 3 ch.

Round 3: sl st across to next ch sp, 3 ch, (1 dc, 3 ch, 2 dc) in 3 ch sp, 2 dc, 1 ch, miss next dc, 1 dc in next ch sp, 1 ch, miss next dc, 2 dc, * (2 dc, 3 ch, 2 dc) in 3 ch sp, 2 dc, 1 ch, miss next dc, 1 dc in next ch sp, 1 ch, miss next dc, 2 dc; rep from * twice more. Join rnd with sl st to top of first 3 ch.

Round 4: sl st across to next ch sp, 3 ch, (1 dc, 3 ch, 2 dc) in 3 ch sp, 3 dc, (1 ch, miss next dc, 1 dc in next st) three times, 2 dc, * (2 dc, 3 ch, 2 dc) in 3 ch sp, 3 dc, (1 ch, miss next dc, 1 dc in next st) three times, 2 dc; rep from * twice more. Join rnd with sl st to top of first 3 ch.
Fasten off yarn.

CHART PATTERN

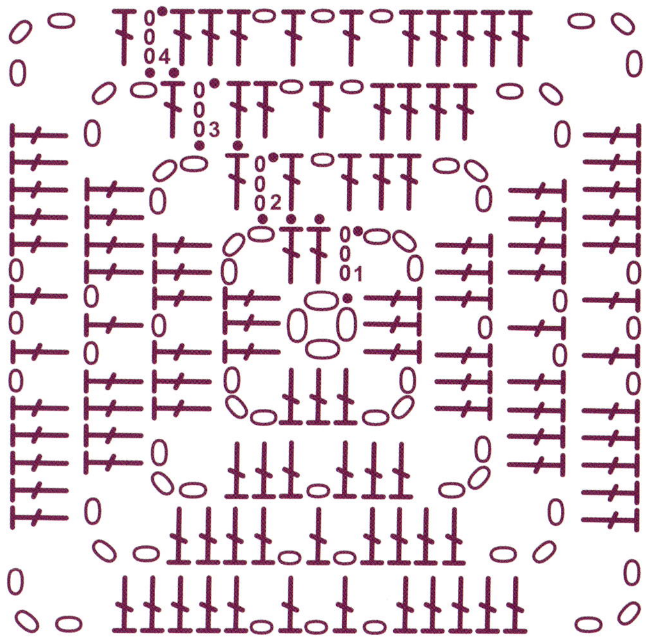

JOINING

Use the slip stitch method (see page 48).

18. CIRCLE TO SQUARE

WRITTEN PATTERN

Using yarn A, make 4 ch.

Round 1: work 11 dc in fourth ch from hook (missed 3 ch counts as 1 dc). Join rnd with sl st to top of first 3 ch (12 dc). Fasten off yarn. Attach yarn B to any stitch from round 1.

Round 2: 3 ch (counts as 1 dc here and throughout), 1 dc in same st, 2 dc in each st around. Join rnd with sl st to top of first 3 ch (24 dc). Fasten off yarn. Attach yarn C to any stitch from round 2.

Round 3: 3 ch, 2 dc in next st, (1 dc in next st, 2 dc in next st) around. Join rnd with sl st to top of first 3 ch (36 dc). Fasten off yarn. Attach yarn D to any stitch from round 3.

Round 4: 1 ch (does not count as st), 1 sc in same st, 4 sc, 1 hdc, 2 dc in next st, 3 ch, 2 dc in next st, 1 hdc, * 5 sc, 1 hdc, 2 dc in next st, 3 ch, 2 dc in next st, 1 hdc; rep from * twice more. Join rnd with sl st to top of first ch (44 sts and 4 ch sps). Fasten off yarn. Attach yarn E to any 3 ch corner sp from round 4.

Round 5: 3 ch, * (1 dc, 3 ch, 2 dc) in same sp, 1 dc in each st to next 3 ch sp, * (2 dc, 3 ch, 2 dc) in 3 ch sp, 1 dc in each st to next 3 ch sp; rep from * twice more. Join rnd with sl st to top of first 3 ch (60 dc and 4 ch sps).
Fasten off yarn.

CHART PATTERN

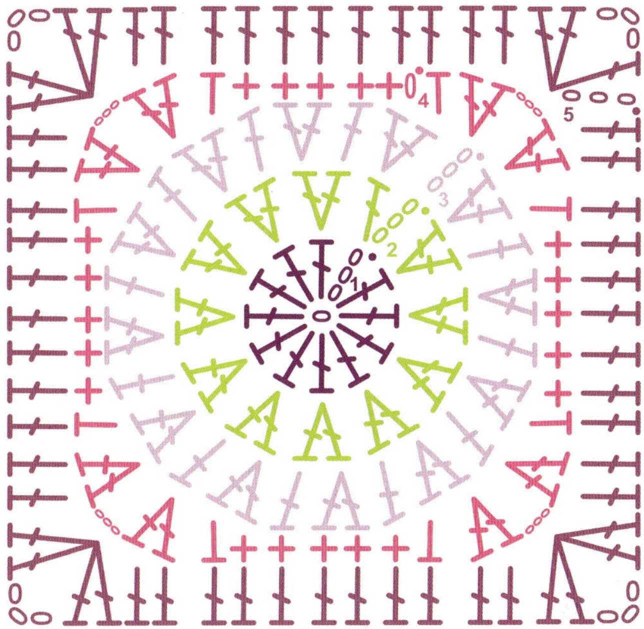

JOINING

Use the slip stitch method (see page 48).

19. GRANNY CIRCLE TO SQUARE

SPECIAL STITCH

2 dc cluster (cl2) (see page 32).

WRITTEN PATTERN

Using yarn A, make 5 ch.

Round 1: work (1 dc, 1 ch) eleven times into fifth ch from hook (missed 4 ch counts as 1 dc, 1 ch). Join rnd with sl st to top of first 3 ch (12 dc and 12 ch sps). Fasten off yarn. Attach yarn B to any 1 ch sp from round 1.

Round 2: 3 ch (counts as 1 dc here and throughout), 1 dc in same sp, 2 ch, (cl2, 2 ch) in each 1 ch sp around. Join rnd with sl st to top of first 3 ch (12 clusters and 12 ch sps). Fasten off yarn.
Attach yarn C to any ch sp from round 2.

Round 3: 3 ch, 2 dc in same sp, 1 ch, (3 dc in next sp, 1 ch) around. Join rnd with sl st to top of first 3 ch (36 dc and 12 ch sps). Fasten off yarn.
Attach yarn D to any ch sp from round 3.

Round 4: 3 ch, 2 dc in same ch sp, 1 ch, 3 dc in next ch sp, 1 ch, (3 tr, 3 ch, 3 tr) in next ch sp, 1 ch, * (3 dc in next ch sp, 1 ch) twice, (3 tr, 3 ch, 3 tr) in next ch sp, 1 ch; rep from * twice more. Join rnd with sl st to top of first 3 ch (48 sts and 16 ch sps).
Fasten off yarn.

CHART PATTERN

JOINING

Use the slip stitch method (see page 48) or join as you go (see pages 49–50).

20. STARBURST

SPECIAL STITCHES

2 dc cluster (cl2) and and 3 dc cluster (cl3) (see page 32).

WRITTEN PATTERN

Using yarn A, make 4 ch.

Round 1: work 15 dc in fourth ch from hook (missed 3 ch counts as 1 dc). Join rnd with sl st to top of first 3 ch (16 dc). Fasten off yarn. Attach yarn B to any st from round 1.

Round 2: 3 ch (counts as 1 dc here and throughout), 1 dc in same sp, 1 ch, (cl2, 1 ch) in each st around. Join rnd with sl st to top of first 3 ch (16 clusters and 16 ch sps). Fasten off yarn.
Attach yarn C to any ch sp from round 2.

Round 3: 3 ch, cl2 in same sp, 3 ch, (cl3 in next ch sp, 3 ch) around. Join rnd with sl st to top of first 3 ch (16 clusters and 16 ch sps). Fasten off yarn.
Attach yarn D to any ch sp from round 3.

Round 4: 3 ch, (2 dc, 3 ch, 3 dc) in same sp, 3 hdc in next ch sp, 3 sc in next ch sp, 3 hdc in next ch sp, * (3 dc, 3 ch, 3 dc) in next ch sp, 3 hdc in next ch sp, 3 sc in next ch sp, 3 hdc in next ch sp; rep from * twice more. Join rnd with sl st to top of first 3 ch (60 sts and 4 ch sps).
Fasten off yarn.

CHART PATTERN

JOINING

Use the slip stitch method (see page 48).

21. PUFF CIRCLE TO SQUARE

SPECIAL STITCH

Puff stitch (see page 32).

WRITTEN PATTERN

Using yarn A, make 4 ch.

Round 1: work 11 dc in fourth ch from hook (missed 3 ch count as 1 dc). Join rnd with sl st to top of first 3 ch (12 dc). Fasten off yarn. Attach yarn B to any stitch from round 1.

Round 2: 3 ch (does not count as st here and throughout), 1 puff in same st, 2 ch, (1 puff, 2 ch) in each st around. Join rnd with sl st to top of first 3 ch (12 puffs and 12 ch sps). Fasten off yarn.
Attach yarn C to any ch sp from round 2.

Round 3: 3 ch, (1 puff, 2 ch, 1 puff) in each ch sp around. Join rnd with sl st to top of first 3 ch (24 puffs and 12 ch sps). Fasten off yarn.
Attach yarn D to any ch sp from round 3.

Round 4: 3 ch (counts as 1 dc here), 2 dc in same ch sp, 1 ch, 3 dc in next ch sp, 1 ch, (3 tr, 3 ch, 3 tr) in next ch sp, 1 ch, * (3 dc in next ch sp, 1 ch) twice, (3 tr, 3 ch, 3 tr) in next ch sp, 1 ch; rep from * twice more. Join rnd with sl st to top of first ch (48 sts and 16 ch sps).
Fasten off yarn.

CHART PATTERN

JOINING

Use the slip stitch method (see page 48) or join as you go (see pages 49–50).

22. STAR PUFF

SPECIAL STITCH

Puff stitch (see page 32).

WRITTEN PATTERN

Using yarn A, make 4 ch, join with a sl st to form a ring.

Round 1: 3 ch (does not count as st here), (1 puff, 2 ch) six times into ring. Join rnd with sl st to top of first 3 ch (6 puffs and 6 ch sps). Fasten off yarn.
Attach yarn B to any ch sp from round 1.

Round 2: 3 ch (counts as 1 dc here), 4 dc in same sp, 1 ch, (5 dc, 1 ch) in each rem ch sp around. Join rnd with sl st to top of first 3 ch (30 dc and 6 ch sps). Fasten off yarn.
Attach yarn C to any ch sp from round 2.

Round 3: 3 ch (does not count as st here), *1 puff in ch sp, 3 ch, 1 puff in central dc of next 5 dc group, 3 ch; rep from * five more times. Join rnd with sl st to top of first 3 ch (12 puffs and 12 ch sps). Fasten off yarn.
Attach yarn D to any ch sp from round 3.

Round 4: 3 ch (counts as 1 dc here), 2 dc in same ch sp, 1 ch, 3 dc in next ch sp, 1 ch, (3 tr, 3 ch, 3 tr) in next ch sp, 1 ch, * (3 dc in next ch sp, 1 ch) twice, (3 tr, 3 ch, 3 tr) in next ch sp, 1 ch; rep from * twice more. Join rnd with sl st to top of first 3 ch (48 sts and 16 ch sps).
Fasten off yarn.

CHART PATTERN

JOINING

Use the slip stitch method (see page 48) or join as you go (see pages 49–50).

23. POPCORN CORNERS

SPECIAL STITCH

Popcorn stitch (pop) (see page 32).

NOTE

The first pop in each round will be made up of the first 3 ch and 4 more dc.

WRITTEN PATTERN

Note that the first pop in each round will be made up of the first 3 ch and 4 more dc.

Using yarn A, make 4 ch, join with a sl st to form a ring.

Round 1: 3 ch (counts as 1 dc here and throughout), (pop, 3 ch) four times into the ring. Join rnd with sl st to top of first ch (4 popcorns and 4 ch sps). Fasten off yarn.
Attach yarn B to any ch sp from round 1.

Round 2: 3 ch, *(pop, 3 ch, pop) in 3 ch sp, 3 dc in pop; rep from * around. Join rnd with sl st to top of first 3 ch (20 sts and 4 ch sps). Fasten off yarn.
Attach yarn C to any ch sp from round 2.

Round 3: 3 ch, *(pop, 3 ch, pop) in 3 ch sp, 2 dc in pop, 3 dc, 2 dc in next pop; rep from * three more times.
Join rnd with sl st to top of first 3 ch (36 sts and 4 ch sps).
Fasten off yarn.
Attach yarn D to any ch sp from round 3.

Round 4: 3 ch, *(pop, 3 ch, pop) in 3 ch sp, 2 dc in pop, 1 dc in each st to next pop, 2 dc in pop; rep from * three more times. Join rnd with sl st to top of first 3 ch (52 sts and 4 ch sps).
Fasten off yarn.

CHART PATTERN

JOINING

Use the slip stitch method (see page 48).

24. POPCORN CENTER

SPECIAL STITCH

Popcorn stitch (pop) (see page 32).

NOTE

The first pop in each round will be made up of the first 3 ch and 4 more dc.

WRITTEN PATTERN

Note that the first pop in round 1 will be made up of the first 3 ch and 4 more dc.

Using yarn A, make 4 ch, join with a sl st to form a ring.

Round 1: 3 ch (counts as 1 dc here and throughout), (pop, 3 ch) six times into the ring. Join rnd with sl st to top of first 3 ch (6 popcorns and 6 ch sps). Fasten off yarn.
Attach yarn B to any ch sp from round 1.

Round 2: 3 ch, 4 dc in same 3 ch sp, 1 ch, * 5 dc in next 3 ch sp, 1 ch; rep from * four more times. Join rnd with sl st to top of first 3 ch (30 dc). Fasten off yarn.
Attach yarn C to the third dc in any 5 dc group from round 2.

Round 3: 3 ch (counts as 1 dc here and throughout), 2 dc in same st, 1 ch, 3 dc in next ch sp, 1 ch, * 3 dc in third dc of next 5 dc group, 1 ch, 3 dc in next ch sp, 1 ch; rep from * four more times. Join rnd with sl st to top of first 3 ch (36 sts and 12 ch sps). Fasten off yarn. Attach yarn D to any ch sp from round 3.

Round 4: 3 ch, 2 dc in same ch sp, 1 ch, 3 dc in next ch sp, 1 ch, (3 tr, 3 ch, 3 tr) in next ch sp, 1 ch, * (3 dc in next ch sp, 1 ch) twice, (3 tr, 3 ch, 3 tr) in next ch sp, 1 ch; rep from * twice more. Join rnd with sl st to top of first 3 ch (48 sts and 16 ch sps).
Fasten off yarn.

CHART PATTERN

JOINING

Use the slip stitch method (see page 48) or join as you go (see pages 49–50).

25. POPCORN DAISY

SPECIAL STITCH

Popcorn stitch (pop) (see page 32).

NOTE

The first pop in round 2 will be made up of the first 3 ch and 4 more dc.

WRITTEN PATTERN

Note that the first pop in round 2 will be made up of the first 3 ch and 4 more dc.

Using yarn A, make 4 ch.

Round 1: work 7 hdc in fourth ch from hook (missed 3 ch counts as 1 hdc). Join rnd with sl st to top of first 3 ch (8 hdc). Fasten off yarn. Attach yarn B to any stitch from round 1.

Round 2: 3 ch (counts as 1 dc here and throughout), (pop, 2 ch) in each st around. Join rnd with sl st to top of first 3 ch (8 popcorns and 8 ch sps). Fasten off yarn. Attach yarn C to any ch sp from round 2.

Round 3: 3 ch, 2 dc in same ch sp, 1 ch, (3 tr, 3 ch, 3 tr) in next ch sp, 1 ch, * 3 dc in next ch sp, 1 ch, (3 tr, 3 ch, 3 tr) in next ch sp, 1 ch; rep from * twice more. Join rnd with sl st to top of first 3 ch (36 sts and 12 ch sps). Fasten off yarn. Attach yarn D to any 3 ch sp from round 3.

Round 4: 3 ch, (2 dc, 3 ch, 3 dc) all in same 3 ch sp, 1 ch, (3 dc in next 1 ch sp, 1 ch) twice, *(3 dc, 3 ch, 3 dc) in corner ch sp, 1 ch, (3 dc in next 1 ch sp, 1 ch) twice; rep from * twice more. Join rnd with sl st to top of first 3 ch (48 dc and 16 ch sps).
Fasten off yarn.

CHART PATTERN

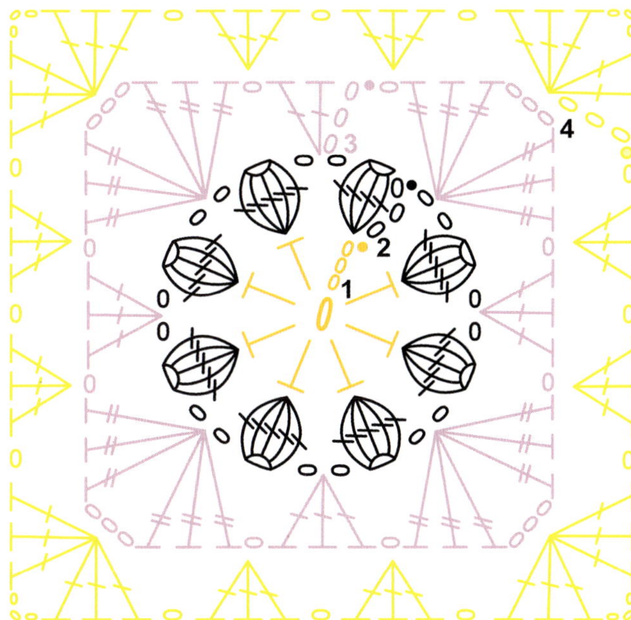

JOINING

Use the slip stitch method (see page 48) or join as you go (see pages 49–50).

26. POPCORN FLOWER

SPECIAL STITCHES

Popcorn stitch (pop), puff stitch, 2 dc cluster (cl2) (see page 32).

NOTE

The first pop in round 3 will be made up of the first 3 ch and 4 more dc.

WRITTEN PATTERN

Note that the first pop in round 3 will be made up of the first 3 ch and 4 more dc.

Using yarn A, make 4 ch, join with a sl st to form a ring.

Round 1: 3 ch (counts as first part of cl2 here), 1 dc in ring, 2 ch, (cl2, 2 ch) five times into the ring. Join rnd with sl st to top of first 3 ch (6 cl2 and 6 ch sps). Fasten off yarn. Attach yarn B to any ch sp from round 1.

Round 2: 3 ch (does not count as a stitch here), (puff, 2 ch, puff, 1 ch) in each ch sp around. Join rnd with sl st to top of first 3 ch (12 puffs and 12 ch sps). Fasten off yarn. Attach yarn C to any ch sp from round 2.

Round 3: 3 ch (counts as first st in pop), (1 pop, 3 ch) in each ch sp around. Join rnd with sl st to top of first 3 ch (12 pops and 12 ch sps). Fasten off yarn.
Attach yarn D to any ch sp from round 3.

Round 4: 3 ch, 2 dc in same ch sp, 1 ch, 3 dc in next ch sp, 1 ch, (3 tr, 3 ch, 3 tr) in next ch sp, 1 ch, * (3 dc in next ch sp, 1 ch) twice, (3 tr, 3 ch, 3 tr) in next ch sp, 1 ch; rep from * twice more. Join rnd with sl st to top of first 3 ch (48 sts and 16 ch sps).
Fasten off yarn.

CHART PATTERN

JOINING

Use the slip stitch method (see page 48) or join as you go (see pages 49–50).

27. GRANNY STAR CIRCLE

WRITTEN PATTERN

Using yarn A, make 4 ch, join with a sl st to form a ring.

Round 1: 3 ch (counts as 1 dc here and throughout), (1 dc, 2 ch) in ring, (2 dc, 2 ch) five times into ring. Join rnd with sl st to top of first 3 ch (12 dc and 6 ch sps).
Fasten off yarn.
Attach yarn B to any ch sp from round 1.

Round 2: 3 ch, (1 dc, 1 ch, 2 dc) in same sp, 1 ch, work (2 dc, 1 ch) twice in each rem ch sp around. Join rnd with sl st to top of first 3 ch (24 dc and 12 ch sps).
Fasten off yarn.
Attach yarn C to any ch sp from round 2.

Round 3: 3 ch, 2 dc in same sp, 1 ch, (3 dc in next ch sp, 1 ch) around. Join rnd with sl st to top of first 3 ch (36 dc and 12 ch sps). Fasten off yarn.
Attach yarn D to any ch sp from round 3.

Round 4: 3 ch, 2 dc in same ch sp, 1 ch, 3 dc in next ch sp, 1 ch, (3 tr, 3 ch, 3 tr) in next st, 1 ch, * (3 dc in next ch sp, 1 ch) twice, (3 tr, 3 ch, 3 tr) in next ch sp, 1 ch; rep from * twice more.
Join rnd with sl st to top of first 3 ch (48 sts and 16 ch sps).
Fasten off yarn.

CHART PATTERN

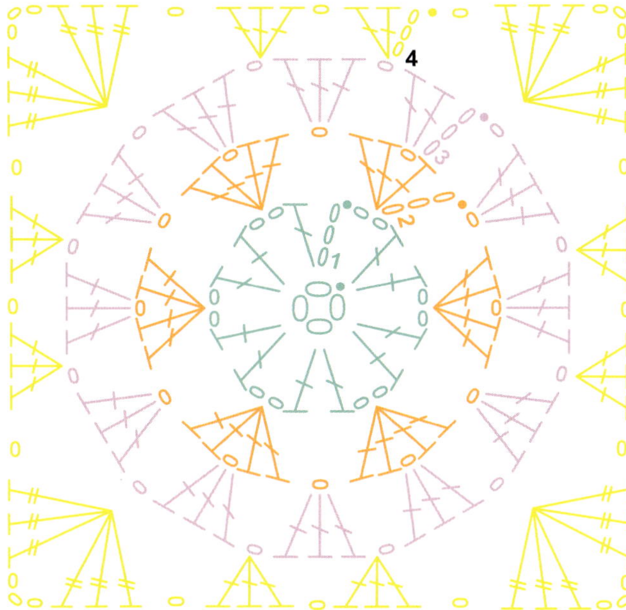

JOINING

Use the slip stitch method (see page 48) or join as you go (pages 49–50).

28. PETALS

SPECIAL STITCH

2 dc cluster (cl2) (see page 32).

WRITTEN PATTERN

Using yarn A, make 4 ch, join with a sl st to form a ring.

Round 1: 1 ch (does not count as st here and throughout), 8 sc in ring. Join rnd with sl st to top of first ch (8 sc).
Fasten off yarn.
Attach yarn B to any st from round 1.

Round 2: 3 ch (counts as 1 dc here and throughout), 1 dc in same st, 3 ch, (cl2, 3 ch) in each st around. Join rnd with sl st to top of first 3 ch (8 clusters and 8 ch sps).
Fasten off yarn.
Attach yarn C to any ch sp from round 2.

Round 3: 3 ch, 2 dc in same sp, (3 dc, 3 ch, 3 dc) in next sp, * 3 dc in next ch sp, (3 dc, 3 ch, 3 dc) in next ch sp; rep from * twice more. Join rnd with sl st to top of first 3 ch (36 dc and 4 ch sps). Fasten off yarn.
Attach yarn D to any ch sp from round 3.

Round 4: 1 ch, * (2 sc, 3 ch, 2 sc) in same sp, 1 sc in each st to next ch sp; rep from * three more times. Join rnd with sl st to top of first ch (52 sc and 4 ch sps). Fasten off yarn.
Attach yarn E to any ch sp from round 4.

Round 5: 3 ch, (2 dc, 3 ch, 3 dc) all in same 3 ch sp, 1 ch, miss 4 sts, 3 dc in next st, 1 ch, miss 3 sts, 3 dc in next st, 1 ch, *(3 dc, 3 ch, 3 dc) in corner ch sp, 1 ch, miss 4 sts, 3 dc in next st, 1 ch, miss 3 sts, 3 dc in next st, 1 ch; rep from * twice more. Join rnd with sl st to top of first 3 ch (48 sts and 16 ch sps).
Fasten off yarn.

CHART PATTERN

JOINING

Use the slip stitch method (see page 48) or join as you go (see pages 49–50).

29. CLUSTER FLOWER

SPECIAL STITCHES

2 dc cluster (cl2), 3 dc cluster (cl3) (see page 32).

WRITTEN PATTERN

Using yarn A, make 4 ch, join with a sl st to form a ring.

Round 1: 2 ch (counts as hdc here), 7 hdc in ring. Join rnd with sl st to top of first ch (8 hdc). Fasten off yarn.
Attach yarn B to any st from round 1.

Round 2: 3 ch (counts as 1 dc here and throughout), cl2 in same st, 3 ch, (cl3, 3 ch) in each st around. Join rnd with sl st to top of first 3 ch (8 clusters and 8 ch sps). Fasten off yarn.
Attach yarn C to any ch sp from round 2.

Round 3: 3 ch, 2 dc in same sp, 1 ch, (3 dc, 3 ch, 3 dc) in next sp, 1 ch, * 3 dc in next sp, 1 ch, (3 dc, 3 ch, 3 dc) in next sp, 1 ch; rep from * twice more. Join rnd with sl st to top of first 3 ch (36 dc and 12 ch sps). Fasten off yarn.
Attach yarn D to any 3 ch sp from round 3.

Round 4: 1 ch, * (1 sc, 3 ch, 1 sc) in 3 ch sp, 3 ch, (1 sc in next ch sp, 3 ch) twice; rep from * three more times. Join rnd with sl st to top of first ch (16 sc and 16 ch sps). Fasten off yarn. Attach yarn E to any corner 3 ch sp from round 4.

Round 5: 3 ch, (2 dc, 3 ch, 3 dc) all in same corner sp, 3 dc in each ch sp to corner 3 ch sp, *(3 dc, 3 ch, 3 dc) in corner ch sp, 3 dc in each ch sp to corner 3 ch sp; rep from * twice more. Join rnd with sl st to top of first 3 ch (60 dc and 4 ch sps).
Fasten off yarn.

CHART PATTERN

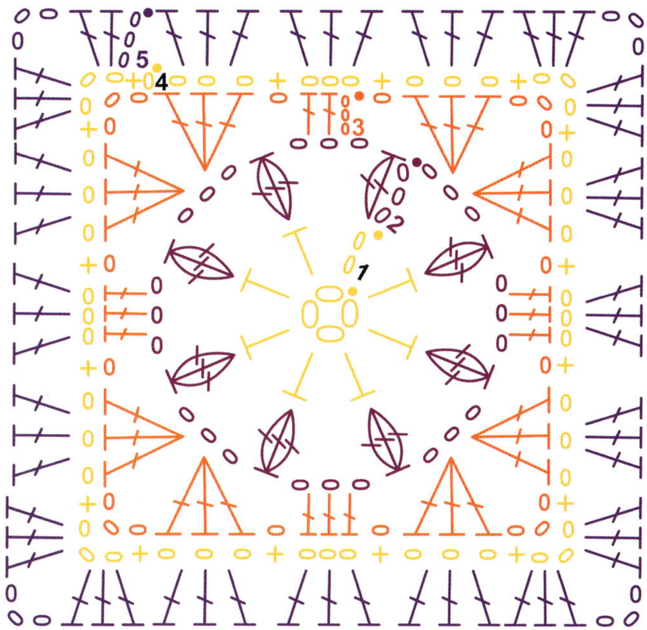

JOINING

Use the slip stitch method (see page 48).

30. BLOOM

SPECIAL STITCHES

2 dc cluster (cl2), 3 dc cluster (cl3), 3 tr cluster (trcl3) (see page 32).

WRITTEN PATTERN

Using yarn A, make 4 ch, join with a sl st to form a ring.

Round 1: 1 ch (does not count as st here and throughout), 12 sc in ring. Join rnd with sl st to top of first ch (12 sc). Fasten off yarn.
Attach yarn B to any st from round 1.

Round 2: 1 ch, (1 sc, 1 ch) in each st around. Join rnd with sl st to top of first ch (12 sc and 12 ch sps). Fasten off yarn. Attach yarn C to any ch sp from round 2.

Round 3: 3 ch (counts as 1 dc here and throughout), cl2 in same ch sp, 2 ch, (cl3, 2 ch) in each ch sp around. Join rnd with sl st to top of first 3 ch (12 clusters and 12 ch sps). Fasten off yarn. Attach yarn D to any ch sp from round 3.

Round 4: 1 ch, 1 sc in ch sp, 5 ch, 1 sc in next ch sp, 5 ch, * (trcl3, 3 ch, trcl3) in next ch sp, 5 ch, ** (1 sc in next ch sp, 5 ch) twice; rep from * around, ending last rep at **. Join rnd with sl st to top of first ch (16 sts and 16 ch sps). Fasten off yarn. Attach yarn E to any 3 ch sp from round 4.

Round 5: 3 ch, (2 dc, 3 ch, 3 dc) all in same 3 ch sp, * 3 dc in next ch sp, 1 ch, 1 dc in next ch sp, 1 ch, 3 dc in next ch sp, **(3 dc, 3 ch, 3 dc) in corner ch sp; rep from * around, ending last rep at **. Join rnd with sl st to top of first ch (52 dc and 12 ch sps).
Fasten off yarn.

CHART PATTERN

JOINING

Use the slip stitch method (see page 48).

31. IN A MUDDLE

NOTE

To increase the size of this square, repeat round 4 until the desired size is reached, changing color every round.

WRITTEN PATTERN

Using yarn A, make 4 ch, join with a sl st to form a ring.

Round 1: 3 ch (counts as first dc here and throughout), 2 dc in ring, 3 ch, (3 dc in ring, 3 ch) three times. Join rnd with sl st to top of first 3 ch. Fasten off yarn.
Attach yarn B to any 3 ch sp of round 1.

Round 2: 3 ch, (2 dc, 3 ch, 3 dc) in same sp, 1 ch, *(3 dc, 3 ch, 2 dc) in next 3 ch sp, 3 dc, (2 dc, 3 ch, 2 dc) in next 3 ch sp, 3 dc, (2 dc, 3 ch, 3 dc) in last 3 ch sp, 1 ch. Join rnd with sl st to top of first 3 ch. Fasten off yarn.
Attach yarn C to first 3 ch sp of round 2.

Round 3: 3 ch, (2 dc, 3 ch, 3 dc) in same sp, 1 ch, 3 dc in next 1 ch sp, 1 ch, (3 dc, 3 ch, 2 dc) in next 3 ch sp, 1 dc in each dc to next 3 ch sp, (2 dc, 3 ch, 2 dc) in 3 ch sp, 1 dc in each dc to next 3 ch sp, (2 dc, 3 ch, 3 dc) in next 3 ch sp, 1 ch, 3 dc in next 1 ch sp, 1 ch.
Join rnd with sl st to top of first 3 ch. Fasten off yarn.
Attach yarn D to first 3 ch sp of round 3.

Round 4: 3 ch, (2 dc, 3 ch, 3 dc) all in same 3 ch sp, 1 ch, (3 dc in next 1 ch sp, 1 ch) to next 3 ch sp, (3 dc, 3 ch, 2 dc) in 3 ch sp, 1 dc in each dc to next 3 ch sp, (2 dc, 3 ch, 2 dc) in 3 ch sp, 1 dc in each dc to next 3 ch sp, (2 dc, 3 ch, 3 dc) in 3 ch sp, 1 ch, (3 dc in next 1 ch sp, 1 ch) to end of round. Join rnd with sl st to top of first 3 ch.
Fasten off yarn.

CHART PATTERN

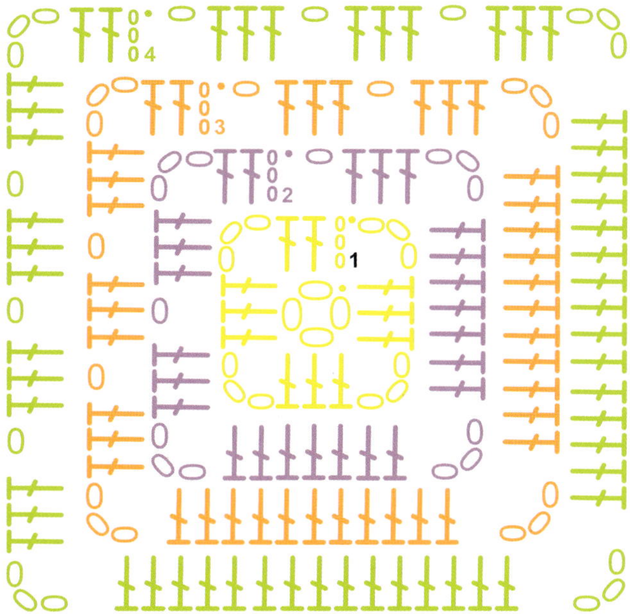

JOINING

Use the slip stitch method (see page 48).

32. LITTLE LINES

SPECIAL STITCH

Back loop only (blo) (see page 27).

NOTE

To increase the size of this square, alternate the last two rounds until the desired size has been reached, changing color every round.

WRITTEN PATTERN

Using yarn A, make 4 ch, join with a sl st to form a ring.

Round 1: 3 ch (counts as first dc here and throughout), 2 dc in ring, 3 ch, (3 dc in ring, 3 ch) three times. Join rnd with sl st to top of first ch. Fasten off yarn. Attach yarn B to any 3 ch sp of round 1.

Round 2: 1 ch (does not count as st here and throughout), * (1 sc, 3 ch, 1 sc) in 3 ch sp, 3 sc blo; rep from * three times. Join rnd with sl st to top of first ch (20 sts and 4 ch sps). Fasten off yarn. Attach yarn C to any 3 ch sp of round 2.

Round 3: 3 ch, (1 dc, 3 ch, 2 dc) in same sp, 1 dc blo in each st to next ch sp, *(2 dc, 3 ch, 2 dc) in next corner sp, 1 dc blo in each st to next ch sp; rep from * twice more. Join rnd with sl st to top of first 3 ch (36 dc and 4 ch sps). Fasten off yarn.
Attach yarn D to any 3 ch sp of round 3.

Round 4: 1 ch (does not count as st here and throughout), * (1 sc, 3 ch, 1 sc) in 3 ch sp, 1 sc blo in each st to next 3 ch sp; rep from * three more times. Join rnd with sl st to top of first ch (44 sts and 4 ch sps). Fasten off yarn.
Attach yarn E to any 3 ch sp of round 4.

Round 5: 3 ch, (1 dc, 3 ch, 2 dc) in same sp, 1 dc blo in each st to next ch sp, *(2 dc, 3 ch, 2 dc) in next corner sp, 1 dc blo in each st to next ch sp; rep from * twice more. Join rnd with sl st to top of first 3 ch (60 dc and 4 ch sps). Fasten off yarn.

CHART PATTERN

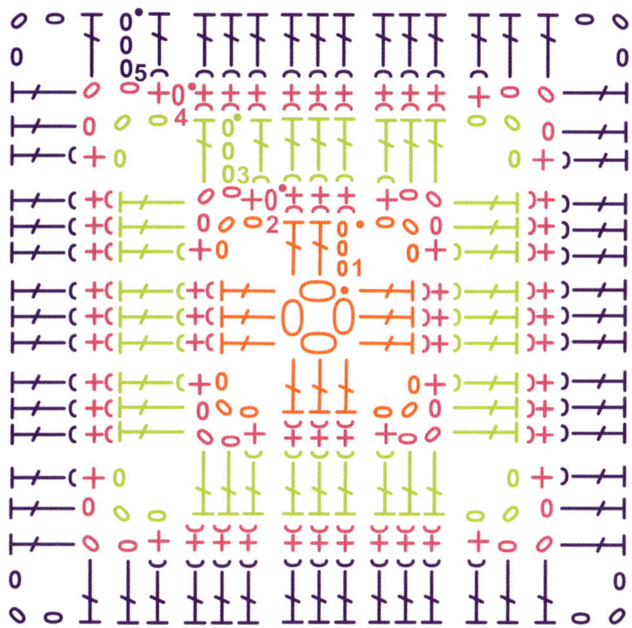

JOINING

Use the slip stitch method (see page 48).

33. MINI SQUARES

NOTE

This square is worked in joined rows – complete one row, join to the beginning of the row, then turn work and work back the other way. When changing color, leave all unused yarn where it is, to pick up later.

WRITTEN PATTERN

Using yarn A, make 4 ch, join with a sl st to form a ring.

Row 1: 3 ch (counts as first dc here and throughout), (1 dc, 3 ch, 2 dc) in ring, changing to yarn B in last step of last dc, (2 dc, 3 ch, 2 dc) in ring, changing to yarn C in last step of last dc, (2 dc, 3 ch, 2 dc) in ring, changing to yarn D in last step of last dc, (2 dc, 3 ch, 2 dc) in ring. Join rnd with sl st to top of first 3 ch, turn work (16 dc).

Row 2: 3 ch, 1 dc, (2 dc, 3 ch, 2 dc) in next 3 ch sp, 2 dc, changing to yarn C in last step of last st, 2 dc, (2 dc, 3 ch, 2 dc) in next 3 ch sp, 2 dc, changing to yarn B in last step of last st, 2 dc, (2 dc, 3 ch, 2 dc) in next 3 ch sp, 2 dc, changing to yarn A in last step of last st, 2 dc, (2 dc, 3 ch, 2 dc) in next 3 ch sp, 2 dc.
Join rnd with sl st to top of first ch, turn work (32 dc).

Row 3: 3 ch, 1 dc in each dc to next 3 ch sp, (2 dc, 3 ch, 2 dc) in next 3 ch sp, 4 dc, changing to yarn B in last step of last st, 4 dc, (2 dc, 3 ch, 2 dc) in next 3 ch sp, 4 dc, changing to yarn C in last step of last st, 4 dc, (2 dc, 3 ch, 2 dc) in next 3 ch sp, 4 dc, changing to yarn D in last step of last st, 4 dc, (2 dc, 3 ch, 2 dc) in next 3 ch sp, 4 dc.
Join rnd with sl st to top of first ch, turn work (48 dc).

Row 4: 3 ch, 1 dc in each dc to next 3 ch sp, (2 dc, 3 ch, 2 dc) in next 3 ch sp, 6 dc, changing to yarn C in last step of last st, 6 dc, (2 dc, 3 ch, 2 dc) in next 3 ch sp, 6 dc, changing to yarn B in last step of last st, 6 dc, (2 dc, 3 ch, 2 dc) in next 3 ch sp, 6 dc, changing to yarn A in last step of last st, 6 dc, (2 dc, 3 ch, 2 dc) in next 3 ch sp, 6 dc.
Join rnd with sl st to top of first ch (64 dc).
Fasten off yarn.

CHART PATTERN

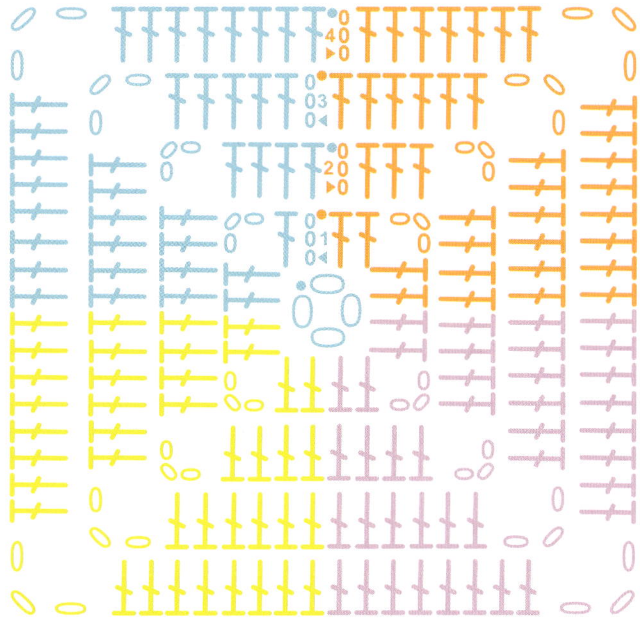

JOINING

Use the slip stitch method (see page 48).

34. SUN

SPECIAL STITCHES

Dc 2 sts together (dc2tog), dc 3 sts together (dc3tog) (see page 32).

WRITTEN PATTERN

Using yarn A, make 4 ch, join with a sl st to form a ring.

Round 1: 1 ch (does not count as st), 8 sc in ring.
Join rnd with sl st to top of first ch (8 sc).
Fasten off yarn.
Attach yarn B to any st from round 1.

Round 2: 3 ch (counts as 1 dc here and throughout), 2 dc in same st, 3 dc in each st around. Join rnd with sl st to top of first 3 ch (24 dc).

Round 3: 3 ch, dc2tog, 4 ch, (dc3tog, 4 ch) around. Join rnd with sl st to top of first 3 ch (8 sts and 8 ch sps). Fasten off yarn.
Attach yarn C to any ch sp from round 3.

Round 4: 3 ch, (2 dc, 3 ch, 3 dc) in same sp, 1 ch, 3 dc in next 4 ch sp, 1 ch, *(3 dc, 3 ch, 3 dc) in next 4 ch sp, 1 ch, 3 dc in next 4 ch sp, 1 ch; rep from * twice more. Join rnd with sl st to top of first 3 ch. Fasten off yarn.
Attach yarn D to any 3 ch corner sp of round 4.

Round 5: 3 ch, (2 dc, 3 ch, 3 dc) all in same 3 ch sp, 1 ch, (3 dc in next 1 ch sp, 1 ch) to next corner, *(3 dc, 3 ch, 3 dc) in corner ch sp, 1 ch, (3 dc in next 1 ch sp, 1 ch) to next corner; repeat from * twice more. Join rnd with sl st to top of first 3 ch.
Fasten off yarn.

CHART PATTERN

JOINING

Use the slip stitch method (see page 48) or join as you go (see pages 49–50).

35. PETALS & LEAVES

SPECIAL STITCHES

Popcorn stitch (pop), tr cluster (trcl2 and trcl3) (see page 32).

NOTE

The first pop in each round will be made up of the first 3 ch and 4 more dc.

WRITTEN PATTERN

Note that the first pop in round 3 will be made up of the first 3 ch and 4 more dc.

Using yarn A, make 4 ch.

Round 1: work 15 dc in fourth ch from hook (missed 3 ch counts as 1 dc). Join rnd with sl st to top of first 3 ch (16 dc). Fasten off yarn. Attach yarn B to any stitch from round 1.

Round 2: 4 ch (counts as 1 dc, 1 ch), (1 dc, 1 ch) in each st around. Join rnd with sl st to top of first 3 ch (16 dc and 16 ch sps). Fasten off yarn.
Attach yarn C to any ch sp from round 2.

Round 3: 3 ch, (1 pop, 2 ch) in each ch sp around. Join rnd with sl st to top of first 3 ch (16 popcorns and 16 ch sps). Fasten off yarn.
Attach yarn D to any ch sp from round 3.

Round 4: 3 ch, 2 dc in same ch sp, 1 ch, 1 dc in next ch sp, 2 ch, (trcl2, 3 ch, trcl3, 3 ch, trcl2) in next ch sp, 2 ch, 1 dc in next ch sp, 1 ch, * 3 dc in next ch sp, 1 ch, 1 dc in next ch sp, 2 ch, (trcl2, 3 ch, trcl3, 3 ch, trcl2) in next ch sp, 2 ch, 1 dc in next ch sp, 1 ch; rep from * twice more. Join rnd with sl st to top of first 3 ch (32 sts and 24 ch sps). Fasten off yarn.

CHART PATTERN

JOINING

Use the slip stitch method (see page 48).

36. ROSETTE

SPECIAL STITCH

Popcorn stitch (pop) (see page 32).

NOTE

The first pop in each round will be made up of the first 3 ch and 4 more dc.

WRITTEN PATTERN

Note that the first pop in rounds 2 and 3 will be made up of the first 3 ch and 4 more dc.

Using yarn A, make 4 ch, join with a sl st to form a ring.

Round 1: 1 ch (does not count as st here and throughout), 8 sc in ring. Join rnd with sl st to top of first ch (8 sc).

Round 2: 3 ch (counts as 1 dc here and throughout), (pop, 2 ch) in each st around. Join rnd with sl st to top of first 3 ch (8 popcorns and 8 ch sp). Fasten off yarn. Attach yarn B to any ch sp from round 2.

Round 3: 3 ch, (pop, 2 ch) twice in each ch sp around. Join rnd with sl st to top of first 3 ch (16 popcorns and 16 ch sps). Fasten off yarn. Attach yarn C to any ch sp from round 3.

Round 4: 2 ch (counts as 1 hdc), 2 hdc in same sp, 1 ch, (3 hdc, 1 ch) in each ch sp around. Join rnd with a sl st to top of first 2 ch (48 hdc and 16 ch sps). Fasten off yarn. Attach yarn D to any ch sp from round 4.

Round 5: 3 ch, (2 dc, 3 ch, 3 dc) all in same 3 ch sp, * 1 hdc in next 1 ch sp, 3 sc, 1 sc in 1 ch sp, 3 sc, 1 hdc in next ch sp, ** (3 dc, 3 ch, 3 dc) in next ch sp; rep from * around, ending last rep at **. Join rnd with sl st to top of first 3 ch (60 sts and 4 ch sps).
Fasten off yarn.

CHART PATTERN

JOINING

Use the slip stitch method (see page 48).

37. FLOWER POWER

SPECIAL STITCHES

Puff stitch (puff) and spiked single crochet (spsc) (see pages 32 and 33).

NOTE

Stitches made in round 3 are worked into unworked stitches from round 1, as shown by the spiked single crochet symbols.

WRITTEN PATTERN

Using yarn A, make 4 ch.

Round 1: work 15 dc in fourth ch from hook (missed 3 ch counts as 1 dc). Join rnd with sl st to top of first 3 ch (16 dc). Fasten off yarn. Attach yarn B to any stitch from round 1.

Round 2: 3 ch (counts as 1 dc here and throughout), 2 dc in same st, miss next st, 1 ch, *3 dc in next st, miss next st, 1 ch; rep from * around. Join rnd with sl st to top of first 3 ch (24 dc and 8 ch sps). Fasten off yarn. Attach yarn C to any ch sp from round 2.

Round 3: 1 ch (does not count as st), *work 1 spsc down into the next unworked st from round 1, working around ch sp from round 2, 5 ch; rep from * around. Join rnd with sl st to top of first ch (8 long sc and 8 ch sps).

Round 4: sl st to next ch sp, 3 ch, (2 dc, 3 ch, 3 dc) in same ch sp, 1 ch, (1 hdc, 1 puff, 1 hdc) in next ch sp, 1 ch, * (3 dc, 3 ch, 3 dc) in next ch sp, 1 ch, (1 hdc, 1 puff, 1 hdc) in next ch sp, 1 ch; rep from * twice more. Join rnd with sl st to top of first 3 ch (36 sts and 12 ch sps). Fasten off yarn. Attach yarn D to any 3 ch corner sp of round 4.

Round 5: 3 ch, (2 dc, 3 ch, 3 dc) all in same 3 ch sp, 1 ch, (3 dc in next 1 ch sp, 1 ch) to next corner, *(3 dc, 3 ch, 3 dc) in corner ch sp, 1 ch, (3 dc in next 1 ch sp, 1 ch) to next corner; rep from * twice more. Join rnd with sl st to top of first 3 ch (48 sts and 16 ch sps).
Fasten off yarn.

CHART PATTERN

JOINING

Use the slip stitch method (see page 48) or join as you go (see pages 49–50).

38. SCALLOP CENTER

WRITTEN PATTERN

Using yarn A, make 4 ch, join with a sl st to form a ring.

Round 1: 3 ch (counts as first dc here and throughout), 2 dc in ring, 3 ch, (3 dc in ring, 3 ch) three times. Join rnd with sl st to top of first 3 ch (12 dc). Fasten off yarn. Attach yarn B to any 3 ch sp of round 1.

Round 2: 1 ch (does not count as st), *(1 sc, 3 ch , 1 sc) in 3 ch sp, 3 ch; rep from * three more times. Join rnd with sl st to top of first ch (8 sc and 8 ch sps).

Round 3: sl st into next ch sp, 3 ch, 8 dc in same sp, 1 sc in next ch sp, * 9 dc in next ch sp, 1 sc in next ch sp; rep from * twice more. Join rnd with sl st to top of first 3 ch (40 sts). Fasten off yarn. Attach yarn C to central dc of any 9 dc group from round 3.

Round 4: 6 ch (counts as 1 dc, 3 ch), 1 dc in same st, * 1 hdc in each of next 3 dc, 1 tr in next dc, 1 tr in next sc, 1 tr in next dc, 1 hdc in each of next 3 dc, ** (1 dc, 3 ch, 1 dc) in next dc; rep from *, ending last rep at **. Join rnd with sl st to third ch of first 6 ch (44 sts and 4 ch sps). Fasten off yarn.
Attach yarn D to any 3 ch sp from round 4.

Round 5: 3 ch, (1 dc, 3 ch, 2 dc) in same sp, 1 dc in each st to next corner sp, *(2 dc, 3 ch, 2 dc) into next corner sp, 1 dc in each st to next corner sp; rep from * twice more. Join rnd with sl st to top of first 3 ch (60 dc and 4 ch sps). Fasten off yarn.

CHART PATTERN

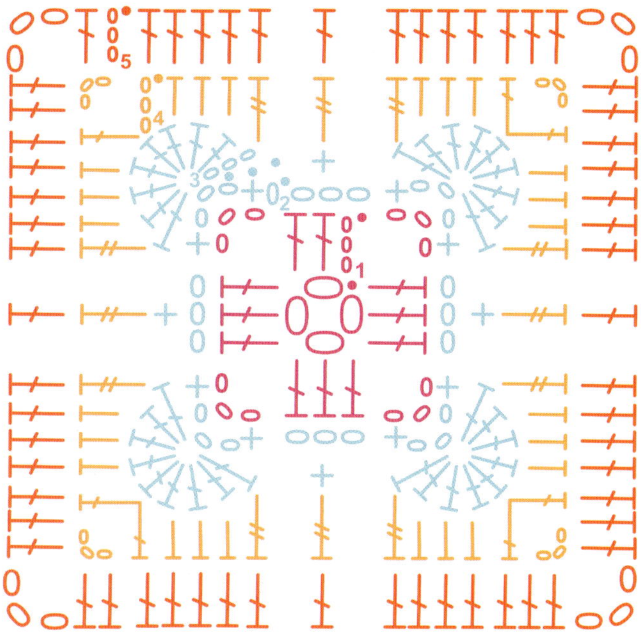

JOINING

Use the slip stitch method (see page 48).

39. PETALS & LACE

WRITTEN PATTERN

Using yarn A, make 4 ch, join with a sl st to form a ring.

Round 1: 1 ch (does not count as st), (1 sc, 3 ch), four times into ring. Join rnd with sl st to top of first ch (4 sc and 4 ch sps). Fasten off yarn. Attach yarn B to any 3 ch sp of round 1.

Round 2: 3 ch (counts as 1 dc here and throughout), (2 dc, 3 ch, 3 dc) in 3 ch sp, 1 ch, * (3 dc, 3 ch, 3 dc) in next 3 ch sp, 1 ch; rep from * twice more. Join rnd with sl st to top of first 3 ch (24 dc and 8 ch sps). Fasten off yarn. Attach yarn C to any 3 ch sp of round 2.

Round 3: 6 ch (counts as 1 dc, 3 ch), 1 dc in same sp, 1 ch, (1 dc, 2 ch, 1 dc) in 1 ch sp, 1 ch, * (1 dc, 3 ch, 1 dc) in next 3 ch sp, 1 ch, (1 dc, 2 ch, 1 dc) in 1 ch sp, 1 ch; rep from * twice more. Join rnd with sl st to third ch of first 6 ch (16 dc and 16 ch sps). Fasten off yarn. Attach yarn D to any 3 ch sp from round 3.

Round 4: 3 ch, (2 dc, 3 ch, 3 dc) in same sp, * 1 sc in next 1 ch sp, 3 sc in next 2 ch sp, 1 sc in next 1 ch sp, ** (3 dc, 3 ch, 3 dc) in next 3 ch sp; rep from * around, ending last rep at **. Join rnd with sl st to top of first 3 ch (44 sts and 4 ch sps). Fasten off yarn. Attach yarn E to any 3 ch sp from round 4.

Round 5: 3 ch, (2 dc, 3 ch, 3 dc) all in same 3 ch sp, * 1 ch, 3 dc in next sc, 1 ch, miss next 3 sc, 3 dc in next sc, 1 ch, ** (3 dc, 3 ch, 3 dc) in corner ch sp; rep from * around, ending last rep at **. Join rnd with sl st to top of first 3 ch. Fasten off yarn.

CHART PATTERN

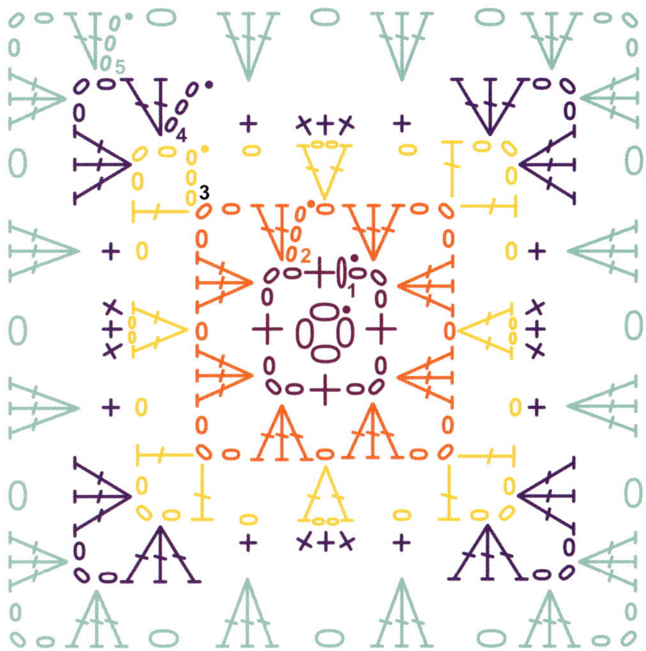

JOINING

Use the slip stitch method (see page 48) or join as you go (see pages 49–50).

40. DIAMOND

SPECIAL STITCH

Back loop only (blo) (see page 27).

WRITTEN PATTERN

Using yarn A, make 4 ch, join with a sl st to form a ring.

Round 1: 3 ch (counts as first dc here and throughout), 3 dc in ring, 3 ch, (4 dc in ring, 3 ch) three times. Join rnd with sl st to top of first 3 ch (16 dc). Fasten off yarn.
Attach yarn B to any 3 ch sp of round 1.

Round 2: 1 ch (does not count as st here and throughout), 1 sc in same sp, 3 ch, 1 dc in each of next 4 dc, 3 ch, * 1 sc in next 3 ch sp, 3 ch, 1 dc in each of next 4 dc, 3 ch; rep from * twice more. Join rnd with sl st to top of first ch (20 sts and 8 ch sps). Fasten off yarn.
Attach yarn C to first 3 ch sp of any corner from round 2.

Round 3: 1 ch, 1 sc in same sp, 3 ch, 1 sc in next 3 ch sp, 3 ch, 1 dc in each of next 4 dc, * (3 ch, 1 sc in next 3 ch sp) twice, 3 ch, 1 dc in each of next 4 dc; rep from * twice more, 3 ch. Join rnd with sl st to top of first ch (24 sts and 12 ch sps). Fasten off yarn.
Attach yarn D to first 3 ch sp of any corner from round 3.

Round 4: 3 ch, 1 dc in same sp, 3 dc in next ch sp, 2 dc in next ch sp, *miss 1 dc, 3 dc in next st, 3 ch, 3 dc in next st, ** 2 dc in next ch sp, 3 dc in next ch sp, 2 dc in next ch sp; rep from * around, ending last rep at **. Join rnd with sl st to top of first 3 ch (52 dc and 4 ch sps). Fasten off yarn.
Attach yarn E to any 3 ch sp from round 4.

Round 5: 1 ch (does not count as st), (1 sc, 3 ch, 1 sc) in same sp, 1 sc blo in each st to next 3 ch sp, * (1 sc, 3 ch, 1 sc) in next ch sp, 1 sc blo in each st to next ch sp; rep from * twice more. Join rnd with sl st to top of first ch (60 sts and 4 ch sps).
Fasten off yarn.

CHART PATTERN

JOINING

Use the slip stitch method (see page 48).

41. LEAVES

SPECIAL STITCHES

Dc two stitches together (dc2tog), dc three stitches together (dc3tog), 3 dc cluster (cl3) (see page 32).

WRITTEN PATTERN

Using yarn A, make 4 ch, join with a sl st to form a ring.

Round 1: 3 ch (counts as first dc here and throughout), 2 dc in ring, 3 ch, (3 dc in ring, 3 ch) three times. Join rnd with sl st to top of first 3 ch (12 dc and 4 ch sps).
Fasten off yarn.
Attach yarn B to any 3 ch sp from round 1.

Round 2: 3 ch, (2 dc, 3 ch, 3 dc) in same sp, 1 ch, *(3 dc, 3 ch, 3 dc) in next 3 ch sp, 1 ch; rep from * twice more. Join rnd with sl st to top of first 3 ch (24 dc and 4 ch sps).

Round 3: 3 ch, 1 dc in each of next 2 dc, * 2 ch, (1 dc, 3 ch, 1 dc) in 3 ch sp, 2 ch, 1 dc in each of next 3 dc, 1 ch, ** 1 dc in each of next 3 dc; rep from * around, ending last rep at **. Join rnd with sl st to top of first 3 ch (32 dc and 16 ch sps).

Round 4: 2 ch (counts as first dc of dc3tog group), dc2tog, 4 ch, * (cl3, 3 ch, cl3) in next 3 ch sp, 4 ch, (dc3tog across next 3 dc, 4 ch) twice; rep from * twice more, (cl3, 3 ch, cl3) in next 3 ch sp, 4 ch, dc3tog across next 3 dc, 4 ch. Join rnd with sl st to top of first 2 ch (16 sts and 16 ch sps). Fasten off yarn.

CHART PATTERN

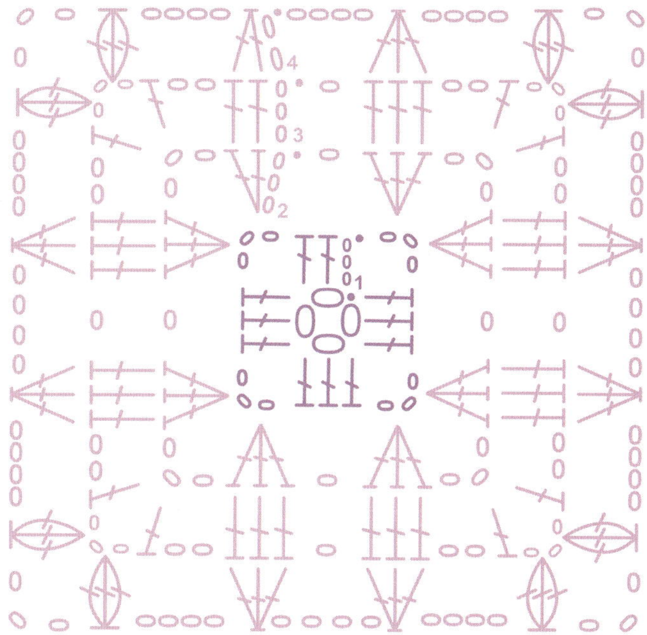

JOINING

Use the slip stitch method (see page 48).

42. AFRICAN FLOWER

SPECIAL STITCHES

Back loop only (blo) and spiked single crochet (spsc) (see pages 27 and 33).

NOTE

Spiked single crochet stitches in round 4 are worked down into unworked chain spaces from round 2, working over the single crochet from round 3.

WRITTEN PATTERN

Using yarn A, make 4 ch, join with a sl st to form a ring.

Round 1: 3 ch (counts as 1 dc here and throughout) 1 dc in ring, 1 ch (2 dc, 1 ch) seven times in ring. Join rnd with sl st to top of first 3 ch (16 dc and 8 ch sps). Fasten off yarn. Attach yarn B to any 1 ch sp from round 1.

Round 2: 3 ch, (1 dc, 2 ch, 2 dc) all in the same sp, 1 ch, * (2 dc, 2 ch, 2 dc, 1 ch) in each ch sp around. Join round with sl st to top of first 3 ch (32 dc and 16 ch sps).

Round 3: 1 ch (does not count as st here or throughout), * 5 dc in next 2 ch sp, 1 sc in next 1 ch sp; rep from * seven more times. Join round with sl st to top of first ch. Fasten off yarn. Attach yarn C to first dc of any 5 dc group from round 3 in blo.

Round 4: 1 ch, * 1 sc blo in each of the next 5 dc, work 1 spsc, by inserting hook down under the next 1 ch sp from round 2, working the sc around the 1 sc from round 3; rep from * seven more times. Join round with sl st to top of first ch. Fasten off yarn.
Attach yarn D to any spsc from round 4.

Round 5: 3 ch, (3 dc, 3 ch, 4 dc) in same st, * miss 2 sc, 1 sc blo in each of next 3 sts, 1 hdc in next spsc, 1 sc blo in each of next 3 sts, ** (4 dc, 3 ch, 4 dc) in next spsc; rep from * around, ending last rep at **. Join round with sl st to top of first 3 ch.
Fasten off yarn.

CHART PATTERN

JOINING

Use the slip stitch method (see page 48).

43. POPCORN

SPECIAL STITCH

Popcorn (pop) (see page 32).

WRITTEN PATTERN

Using yarn A, make 4 ch, join with a sl st to form a ring.

Round 1: 3 ch (counts as first dc here and throughout), 2 dc in ring, 3 ch, (3 dc in ring, 3 ch) three times. Join rnd with sl st to top of first 3 ch (12 dc and 4 ch sps).
Fasten off yarn.
Attach yarn B to any 3 ch sp from round 1.

Round 2: 3 ch, (1 dc, 3 ch, 2 dc) in 3 ch sp, miss next dc, 1 pop in next st, * (2 dc, 3 ch, 2 dc) in corner sp, miss next dc, 1 pop in next st; rep from * around. Join rnd with sl st to top of first 3 ch (20 sts and 4 ch sps). Fasten off yarn.
Attach yarn C to any 3 ch sp from round 2.

Round 3: 3 ch, (1 dc, 3 ch, 2 dc) in 3 ch sp, * 1 dc, 1 pop in next st, 1 dc in pop, 1 pop in next st, 1 dc, ** (2 dc, 3 ch, 2 dc) in 3 ch sp; rep from * around, ending last rep at **. Join rnd with sl st to top of first 3 ch (36 sts and 4 ch sps).
Fasten off yarn.
Attach yarn D to any 3 ch sp from round 3.

Round 4: 3 ch, (1 dc, 3 ch, 2 dc) in 3 ch sp, * 1 dc, 1 pop in next st, 1 dc in each of next 2 sts, 1 pop in next st, 1 dc in each of next 2 sts, 1 pop in next st, 1 dc, ** (2 dc, 3 ch, 2 dc) in 3 ch sp; rep from * around, ending last rep at **. Join rnd with sl st to top of first 3 ch (52 sts and 4 ch sps).
Fasten off yarn.

CHART PATTERN

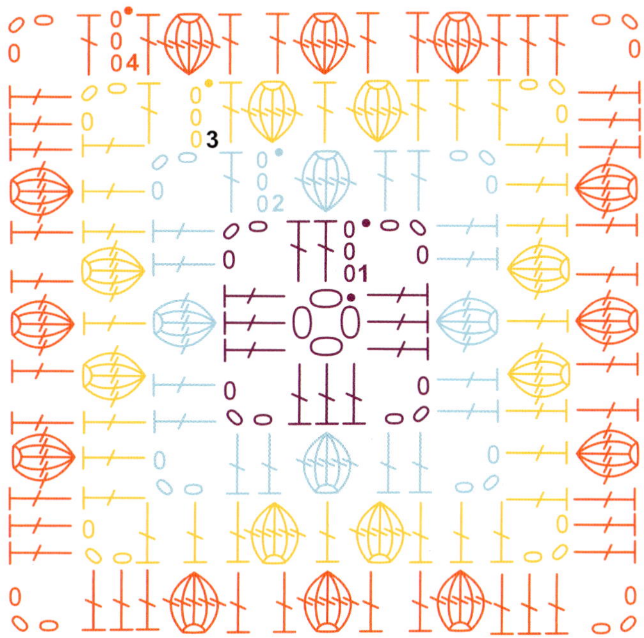

JOINING

Use the slip stitch method (see page 48).

44. DIAMOND SCALLOPS

WRITTEN PATTERN

Using yarn A, make 4 ch, join with a sl st to form a ring.

Round 1: 6 ch (counts as 1 dc and 3 ch), (1 dc, 3 ch) three times in ring. Join rnd with sl st to third ch of first 6 ch (4 dc and 4 ch sps). Fasten off yarn. Attach yarn B to any dc from round 1.

Round 2: 1 ch (does not count as st here or throughout), 1 sc in same st, (3 dc, 1 ch, 3 dc) in next ch sp, * 1 sc in next dc, (3 dc, 1 ch, 3 dc) in next ch sp; rep from * twice more. Join round with sl st to top of first ch (28 sts and 4 ch sps). Fasten off yarn.
Attach yarn C to any 1 ch sp from round 2.

Round 3: 1 ch, 1 sc in same sp, * 1 ch, (1 dc, 2 ch, 1 dc, 1 ch) twice all in next sc, ** 1 sc in next 1 ch sp; rep from * around, ending last rep at **. Join round with sl st to top of first ch.

Round 4: 1 ch, 1 sc in same st, * (3 dc, 1 ch, 3 dc) in next 2 ch sp, 1 sc in next 1 ch sp, (3 dc, 1 ch, 3 dc) in next 2 ch sp, ** 1 sc in next sc; rep from * around, ending last rep at **. Join round with sl st to top of first ch. Fasten off yarn. Attach yarn D to any sc that was worked into a ch sp in round 4.

Round 5: 3 ch, (2 dc, 3 ch, 3 dc) in same st, * 1 ch, 1 sc in next 1 ch sp, 1 ch, (1 dc, 2 ch, 1 hdc, 2 ch, 1 dc) all worked into next sc, 1 ch, 1 sc in next 1 ch sp, 1 ch, ** (3 dc, 3 ch, 3 dc) all in next sc; rep from * around, ending last rep at **. Join round with sl st to top of first 3 ch.
Fasten off yarn.

CHART PATTERN

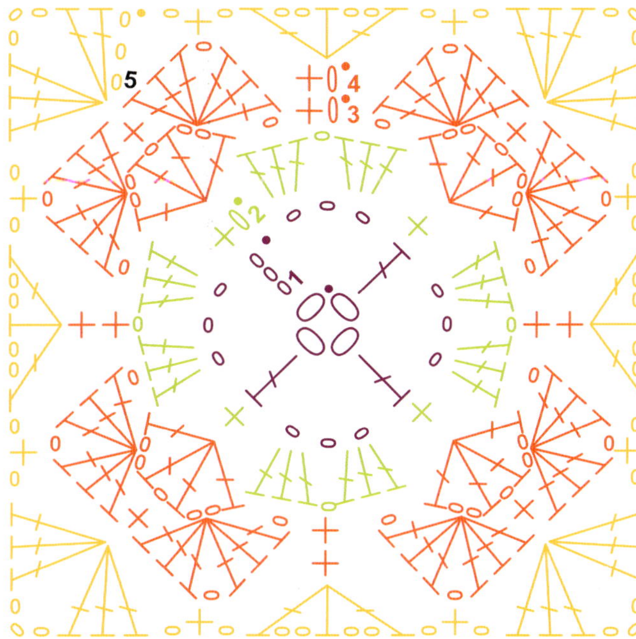

JOINING

Use the slip stitch method (see page 48).

45. MEDALLION

SPECIAL STITCH

Raised treble front (RtrF) (see page 33).

WRITTEN PATTERN

Using yarn A, make 4 ch, join with a sl st to form a ring.

Round 1: 2 ch (counts as 1 hdc), 7 hdc in ring. Join rnd with sl st to top of first 2 ch (8 hdc). Fasten off yarn.
Attach yarn B to any stitch from round 1.

Round 2: 1 ch (does not count as st here or throughout), (1 sc, 1 ch) in each st around. Join rnd with sl st to top of first ch (8 sc and 8 ch sps). Fasten off yarn.
Attach yarn C to any ch sp from round 2.

Round 3: 3 ch (counts as 1 dc here and throughout), 2 dc in same sp, 1 ch, (3 dc, 1 ch) in each ch sp around. Join rnd with sl st to top of first 3 ch (24 sts and 8 ch sps).
Fasten off yarn.
Reattach yarn B to first dc of any 3 dc group from round 3.

Round 4: 2 ch (counts as 1 hdc), 3 dc in next dc, 1 hdc in next dc, 1 RtrF around next sc from round 2, 1 hdc in next dc, * 3 dc in next dc, 1 hdc in next dc, 1 RtrF around next sc from round 2, ** 1 hdc in next dc; rep from * around, ending last rep at **. Join rnd with sl st to top of first 2 ch (48 sts).
Fasten off yarn.
Attach yarn D to any RtrF from round 4.

Round 5: 1 ch, 1 sc in same st, 3 ch, (3 dc, 3 ch, 3 dc) in next RtrF, 3 ch, * 1 sc in next RtrF, 3 ch, (3 dc, 3 ch, 3 dc) in next RtrF, 3 ch; rep from * twice more. Join rnd with sl st to top of first ch (28 sts and 12 ch sps). Fasten off yarn.
Attach yarn E to any corner 3 ch sp from round 5.

Round 6: 3 ch, (2 dc, 3 ch, 3 dc) all in same 3 ch sp, 1 ch, (3 dc in next 3 ch sp, 1 ch) to next corner, * (3 dc, 3 ch, 3 dc) in corner ch sp, 1 ch, (3 dc in next 3 ch sp, 1 ch) to next corner; rep from * twice more. Join rnd with sl st to top of first 3 ch (48 dc and 16 ch sps).
Fasten off yarn.

CHART PATTERN

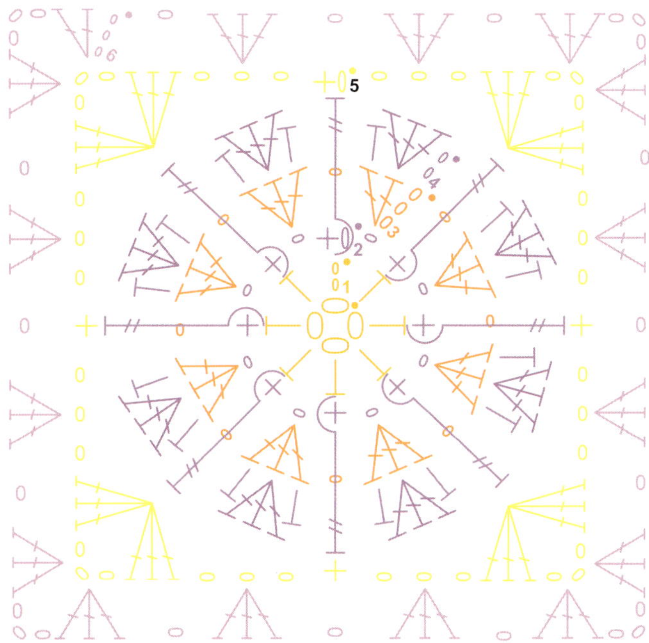

JOINING

Use the slip stitch method (see page 48) or join as you go (see pages 49–50).

46. 3D FLOWER

NOTE

Round 5 is worked behind the petals made on rounds 3 and 4 – the stitches are made into unworked spaces of round 2, as denoted by the arrows.

WRITTEN PATTERN

Using yarn A, make 4 ch, join with a sl st to form a ring.

Round 1: 1 ch (does not count as st here or throughout), 8 sc in ring. Join rnd with sl st to top of first ch (8 sc). Fasten off yarn.
Attach yarn B to any stitch from round 1.

Round 2: 1 ch, 1 sc in first st, 1 ch, (1 sc in next st, 1 ch) around. Join rnd with sl st to top of first ch (8 sc and 8 ch sps).

Round 3: 1 ch, (1 sc in next sc, 3 ch) around. Join rnd with sl st to top of first ch (8 sc and 8 ch sps).

Round 4: 1 ch, * (1 sc, 1 hdc, 5 dc, 1 hdc, 1 sc) all into next 3 ch sp, 1 sl st in next sc; rep from * around (8 petals made). Fasten off yarn.
Attach yarn C to any unworked 1 ch sp of round 2: you will have to work behind the petals of the flower already made in rounds 3 and 4.

Round 5: 1 ch, (2 sc, 2 ch) in each unworked ch sp from round 2. Join rnd with sl st to top of first ch (16 sc and 8 ch sps).

Round 6: 3 ch (counts as 1 dc here and throughout), 1 dc in same st, 1 dc in next st, (2 dc in next st or sp, 1 dc in next st or sp) around. Join rnd with sl st to top of first 3 ch (36 sts). Fasten off yarn.
Attach yarn D to first stitch of round 6.

Round 7: 3 ch, 1 dc in same st, 3 ch, 2 dc in next st, 1 hdc, 5 sc, 1 hdc, * 2 dc in next st, 3 ch, 2 dc in next st, 1 hdc, 5 sc, 1 hdc; rep from * twice more. Join rnd with sl st to top of first 3 ch (44 sts and 4 ch sps).

Round 8: 3 ch, 1 dc in next st, * (2 dc, 3 ch, 2 dc) in next ch sp, 1 dc in each st to next 3 ch sp; rep from * twice more, (2 dc, 3 ch, 2 dc) in next ch sp, 1 dc in each st to end. Join rnd with sl st to top of first 3 ch (60 dc and 4 ch sps). Fasten off yarn.

CHART PATTERN

JOINING

Use the slip stitch method (see page 48).

47. V-STITCH

SPECIAL STITCH

V stitch (V st) (see page 32).

WRITTEN PATTERN

Using yarn A, make 4 ch, join with a sl st to form a ring.

Round 1: 3 ch (counts as first dc here and throughout), 2 dc in ring, 3 ch, (3 dc in ring, 3 ch) three times. Join rnd with sl st to top of first 3 ch (12 dc and 4 ch sps).
Fasten off yarn.
Attach yarn B to any 3 ch sp of round 1.

Round 2: 5 ch (counts as 1 dc, 2 ch here and throughout), (1 dc, 3 ch, V st) all in same sp, 1 ch, *(V st, 3 ch, V st) all in next 3 ch sp, 1 ch; rep from * twice more. Join rnd with sl st to third ch of first 5 ch (16 dc and 16 ch sps).
Fasten off yarn.
Attach yarn C to any 3 ch corner sp of round 2.

Round 3: 3 ch, (2 dc, 3 ch, 3 dc) in same sp, 1 ch, 3 dc in next 1 ch sp, 1 ch, *(3 dc, 3 ch, 3 dc) in next 3 ch sp, 1 ch, 3 dc in next 1 ch sp, 1 ch; rep from * twice more. Join rnd with sl st to top of first 3 ch (36 dc and 12 ch sps). Fasten off yarn.
Attach yarn D to any 3 ch corner sp of round 3.

Round 4: 5 ch, (1 dc, 3 ch, V st) all in same sp, 1 ch, (V st in next 1 ch sp, 1 ch) twice, *(V st, 3 ch, V st) all in next 3 ch sp, 1 ch, (V st in next 1 ch sp, 1 ch) twice; rep from * twice more. Join rnd with sl st to third ch of first 5 ch (32 dc and 32 ch sps).
Fasten off yarn.

CHART PATTERN

JOINING

Use the slip stitch method (see page 48) or join as you go (see pages 49–50).

48. WHEEL SPOKE

WRITTEN PATTERN

Using yarn A, make 4 ch.

Round 1: work 11 dc in fourth ch from hook (missed ch count as 1 dc). Join rnd with sl st to top of first 3 ch (12 dc). Fasten off yarn. Attach yarn B to any dc from round 1.

Round 2: 5 ch (counts as 1 dc, 2 ch), (1 dc, 2 ch) in each dc around. Join rnd with sl st to third ch of first 5 ch (12 dc and 12 ch sps). Fasten off yarn.
Attach yarn C to any dc from round 2.

Round 3: 1 ch (does not count as st here or throughout), * 1 sc in dc, (1 hdc, 1 dc, 1 ch, 1 dc, 1 hdc) in 2 ch sp; rep from * around. Join rnd with sl st to top of first ch (60 sts and 12 ch sps). Fasten off yarn.
Attach yarn D to any ch sp from round 3.

Round 4: 1 ch, 1 sc in ch sp, 5 ch, 1 sc in next ch sp, 5 ch, (2 dc, 3 ch, 2 dc) in next ch sp, 5 ch, * (1 sc in next ch sp, 5 ch) twice, (2 dc, 3 ch, 2 dc) in next ch sp, 5 ch; rep from * twice more. Join rnd with sl st to top of first ch (24 sts and 16 ch sps).
Fasten off yarn.

CHART PATTERN

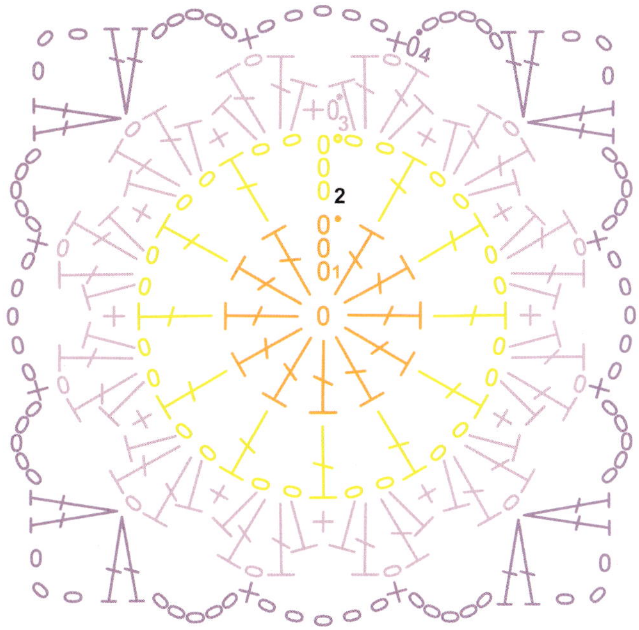

JOINING

Use the slip stitch method (see page 48).

49. FLORAL CROWN

SPECIAL STITCHES

2dc cluster (cl2), 3dc cluster (cl3), picot, spiked double crochet (spdc) and spiked half double crochet (sphdc) (see pages 32 and 33).

NOTE

Some stitches in round 5 are worked into unworked chain spaces from round 3, as shown by the sphdc and spdc symbols.

WRITTEN PATTERN

Using yarn A, make 4 ch, join with a sl st to form a ring.

Round 1: 1 ch (does not count as st here or throughout), 8 sc in ring. Join rnd with sl st to top of first ch (8 sc). Fasten off yarn.
Attach yarn B to any st from round 1.

Round 2: 3 ch (counts as 1 dc here and throughout), cl2 in same st, 3 ch, (cl3, 3 ch) in each st around. Join rnd with sl st to top of first 3 ch (8 clusters and 8 ch sps). Fasten off yarn.
Attach yarn C to any ch sp from round 2.

Round 3: 1 ch (does not count as st here or throughout), (1 sc, 4 ch) in each ch sp around. Join rnd with sl st to top of first ch (8 sc and 8 ch sps).

Round 4: * 2 ch, 1 sc in next ch sp, 2 ch, sl st in next sc, (1 hdc, 3 dc, 3 ch, 3 dc, 1 hdc) all in next ch sp, sl st in next sc; rep from * three more times (36 sts and 12 ch sps). Fasten off yarn.
Attach yarn D to any 3 ch corner sp from round 4.

Round 5: 3 ch, (cl2, 3 ch, cl3) in same sp, * 5 ch, (1 hdc, 2 dc, picot, 1 dc, 1 hdc) all in next ch sp from round 3, working over sc and ch sp from round 4, 5 ch, ** (cl3, 3 ch, cl3) in next 3 ch sp; rep from * around, ending last rep at **. Join rnd with sl st to top of first 3 ch (28 sts and 12 ch sps). Fasten off yarn.

CHART PATTERN

JOINING

Slip stitch (see page 48) or, if joining to other floral crowns, join as you go (see pages 49–50) on the last round, joining with a slip stitch at the center of every chain space and picot.

50. CHECKERBOARD

SPECIAL STITCH

Spiked double crochet (spdc) (see page 33).

NOTE

Some stitches made in rounds 3 and 5 are worked into unworked stitches from two rounds below, as shown by spdc symbols. Work over the chains from the round below when hooking these.

WRITTEN PATTERN

Using yarn A, make 4 ch, join with a sl st to form a ring.

Round 1: 3 ch (counts as first dc here and throughout), 2 dc in ring, 3 ch, (3 dc in ring, 3 ch) three times. Join rnd with sl st to top of first 3 ch (12 dc and 4 ch sps). Fasten off yarn. Attach yarn B to any 3 ch sp of round 1.

Round 2: 3 ch, (2 dc, 3 ch, 3 dc) in same sp, 1 ch, *(3 dc, 3 ch, 3 dc) in next 3 ch sp, 1 ch; rep from * twice more. Join rnd with sl st to top of first 3 ch (24 dc and 8 ch sps). Fasten off yarn.
Attach yarn C to any 3 ch corner sp of round 2.

Round 3: 1 ch (does not count as st here and throughout), * 3 sc in 3 ch sp, 1 sc in each of next 3 dc, 1 spdc in each of the next 3 dc from round 1, working over ch sp from round 2, 1 sc in each of next 3 dc; rep from * three more times. Join rnd with sl st to top of first ch (48 sts). Fasten off yarn.
Attach yarn D to first sc of any 3 sc corner from round 3.

Round 4: 3 ch, * (1 dc, 3 ch, 1 dc) in next sc, 1 dc in next sc, miss next 3 sc, 3 ch, 1 dc in each of next 3 spdc, miss 3 sc, 3 ch, ** 1 dc in next sc; rep from * around, ending last rep at **. Join rnd with sl st to top of first 3 ch (28 dc and 12 ch sps). Fasten off yarn.
Reattach yarn C to any 3 ch corner sp from round 4.

Round 5: 1 ch, * (2 sc, 1 ch, 2 sc) in corner sp, 1 sc in each of next 2 dc, 1 spdc in each of the next unworked 3 sc from round 3, working over ch sp from round 4, 1 sc in each of next 3 dc, 1 spdc in each of next 3 unworked sc from round 3 as before, 1 sc in each of last 2 dc; rep from * three more times. Join rnd with sl st to top of first ch (68 sts and 4 ch sps). Fasten off yarn.

CHART PATTERN

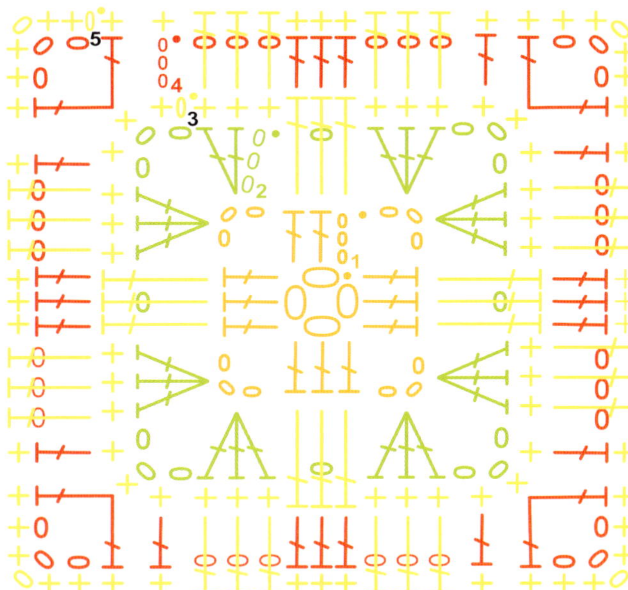

JOINING

Use the slip stitch method (see page 48).

51. CALENDULA

SPECIAL STITCHES

3 tr cluster (trcl3), 2 tr cluster (trcl2) (see page 32).

WRITTEN PATTERN

Using yarn A, make 4 ch, join with a sl st to form a ring.

Round 1: 4 ch (counts as 1 dc, 1 ch), (1 dc, 1 ch) 11 times in ring. Join rnd with sl st to third ch of first 4 ch (12 dc and 12 ch sp). Fasten off yarn.
Attach yarn B to any ch sp from round 1.

Round 2: 4 ch (counts as 1 tr), trcl2 in same sp, 3 ch, (trcl3, 3 ch) in each ch sp around. Join rnd with sl st to top of first 4 ch (12 clusters and 12 ch sps).Fasten off yarn.
Attach yarn C to any ch sp from round 2.

Round 3: 3 ch (counts as 1 dc), 2 dc in same ch sp, 1 ch, 3 dc in next ch sp, 1 ch, * (3 tr, 3 ch, 3 tr) in next ch sp, 1 ch, ** (3 dc in next ch sp, 1 ch) twice; rep from * around, ending last rep at **. Join rnd with sl st to top of first 3 ch (48 sts and 16 ch sps).
Fasten off yarn.

CHART PATTERN

JOINING

Use the slip stitch method (see page 48) or join as you go (see pages 49–50).

52. MARIGOLD

SPECIAL STITCHES

Puff stitch (puff), popcorn (pop) (see page 32).

WRITTEN PATTERN

Using yarn A, make 4 ch.

Round 1: work 11 dc in fourth ch from hook (missed 3 ch count as 1 dc). Join rnd with sl st to top of first 3 ch (12 dc). Fasten off yarn.
Attach yarn B to any st from round 1.

Round 2: 2 ch (does not count as a st), (puff, 2 ch) in each st around. Join rnd with sl st to top of first 2 ch (12 puffs and 12 ch sps). Fasten off yarn.
Attach yarn C to any ch sp from round 2.
Note 3 ch at beg of next round counts as first dc of pop, so only make 4 more dc in this st.

Round 3: 3 ch (counts as 1 dc here and throughout), (1 pop, 3 ch) in each ch sp around. Join rnd with sl st to top of first ch (12 pops and 12 ch sps). Fasten off yarn.
Attach yarn D to any ch sp from round 3.

Round 4: 3 ch, 2 dc in same ch sp, 1 ch, 3 dc in next ch sp, 1 ch, (3 tr, 3 ch, 3 tr) in next ch sp, 1 ch, * (3 dc in next ch sp, 1 ch) twice, (3 tr, 3 ch, 3 tr) in next 3 ch sp, 1 ch; rep from * around. Join rnd with sl st to top of first 3 ch (48 sts and 16 ch sps).
Fasten off yarn.

CHART PATTERN

JOINING

Use the slip stitch method (see page 48) or join as you go (see pages 49–50).

53. GEUM

SPECIAL STITCHES

Popcorn (pop), 3 dc cluster (cl3) (see page 32).

WRITTEN PATTERN

Using yarn A, make 4 ch, join with a sl st to form a ring.

Round 1: 1 ch, 8 sc in ring. Join rnd with sl st to top of first ch (8 sc). Fasten off yarn.
Attach yarn B to any st from round 1.
Note 3 ch at beg of next round counts as first dc of pop, so only make four more dc in this st.

Round 2: 3 ch (counts as 1 dc here and throughout), (pop, 2 ch) in each st around. Join rnd with sl st to top of first 3 ch (8 popcorns and 8 ch sps). Fasten off yarn.
Attach yarn C to any ch sp from round 2.

Round 3: 3 ch, 2 dc in same ch sp, 1 ch, (3 dc, 1 ch) in each ch sp around. Join rnd with sl st to top of first 3 ch (24 sts and 8 ch sps). Fasten off yarn.
Attach yarn D to any ch sp from round 3.

Round 4: 1 ch, 1 sc in same sp, * 3 ch, (cl3, 3 ch, cl3) in next ch sp, 3 ch, ** 1 sc in next ch sp; rep from * in each ch sp around, ending last rep at **. Join rnd with sl st to top of first ch (12 sts and 12 ch sps). Fasten off yarn.
Attach yarn E to any corner 3 ch sp from round 4.

Round 5: 3 ch, (2 dc, 3 ch, 3 dc) in same ch sp, * (1 ch, 3 dc in next ch sp) twice, 1 ch, ** (3 dc, 3 ch, 3 dc) in next 3 ch sp; rep from * around, ending last rep at **. Join rnd with sl st to top of first 3 ch (48 sts and 16 ch sps).
Fasten off yarn.

CHART PATTERN

JOINING

Use the slip stitch method (see page 48) or join as you go (see pages 49–50).

54. RUDBECKIA

SPECIAL STITCH

2 dc cluster (cl2) (see page 32).

WRITTEN PATTERN

Using yarn A, make 4 ch, join with a sl st to form a ring.

Round 1: 1 ch (does not count as st here or throughout), 12 sc in ring. Join rnd with sl st to top of first ch (12 sc). Attach yarn B to any st from round 1.

Round 2: 3 ch (counts as first dc here and throughout), 1 dc in same st, 2 ch, (cl2 in next st, 2 ch) around. Join rnd with sl st to top of first 3 ch (12 cl). Fasten off yarn. Attach yarn C to any ch sp from round 2.

Round 3: 3 ch, 2 dc in same ch sp, 2 ch, (3 dc, 2 ch) in each ch sp around. Join rnd with sl st to top of first 3 ch (36 dc and 12 ch sps).

Round 4: sl st to next ch sp, 3 ch, 2 dc in same ch sp, 1 ch, 3 dc in next ch sp, 1 ch, * (3 tr, 3 ch, 3 tr) in next ch sp, 1 ch, ** (3 dc in next ch sp, 1 ch) twice; rep from * around, ending last rep at **. Join rnd with sl st to top of first 3 ch (48 sts and 16 ch sps).
Fasten off yarn.

CHART PATTERN

JOINING

Use the slip stitch method (see page 48) or join as you go (see pages 49–50).

55. MALLOW

SPECIAL STITCHES

2 dc cluster (cl2), 3 dc cluster (cl3) (see page 32).

WRITTEN PATTERN

Using yarn A, make 4 ch, join with a sl st to form a ring.

Round 1: 2 ch (counts as 1 hdc), 7 hdc in ring. Join rnd with sl st to top of first 2 ch (8 hdc). Fasten off yarn.
Attach yarn B to any st from round 1.

Round 2: 3 ch (counts as 1 dc here and throughout), cl2 in same st, 2 ch, (cl3, 2 ch) in each st around. Join rnd with sl st to top of first 3 ch (8 clusters and 8 ch sps). Fasten off yarn.
Attach yarn C to any ch sp from round 2.

Round 3: 1 ch, * (1 sc, 1 hdc, 1 dc, 1 hdc, 1 sc) in ch sp, 1 ch; rep from * in each ch sp around. Join rnd with sl st to top of first ch (8 petals). Fasten off yarn.
Attach yarn D to any ch sp from round 3.

Round 4: 1 ch, 1 sc in same sp, * 3 ch, (cl2, 3 ch, cl2) in next ch sp, 3 ch, ** 1 sc in next ch sp; rep from * in each ch sp around, ending last rep at **. Join rnd with sl st to top of first ch (12 sts and 12 ch sps). Fasten off yarn.
Attach yarn E to any corner 3 ch sp from round 4.

Round 5: 3 ch, (2 dc, 3 ch, 3 dc) in same ch sp, * 1 dc in next cl, 3 dc in next ch sp, 1 dc in next sc, 3 dc in next ch sp, 1 dc in next cl, ** (3 dc, 3 ch, 3 dc) in next 3 ch sp; rep from * around, ending last rep at **. Join rnd with sl st to top of first 3 ch (60 sts and 4 ch sps).
Fasten off yarn.

CHART PATTERN

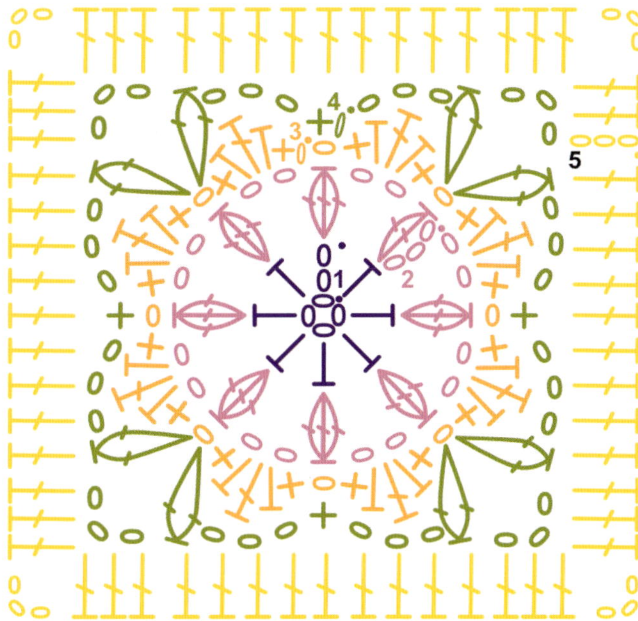

JOINING

Use the slip stitch method (see page 48).

56. GERBERA

SPECIAL STITCHES

2 dc cluster (cl2), 3 dc cluster (cl3), 4 dc cluster (cl4) (see page 32).

WRITTEN PATTERN

Using yarn A, make 4 ch, join with a sl st to form a ring.

Round 1: 2 ch (counts as 1 hdc), 15 hdc in ring. Join rnd with sl st to top of first 2 ch (16 hdc).
Fasten off yarn.
Attach yarn B to any st from round 1.

Round 2: 3 ch (counts as 1 dc here and throughout), 1 dc in same st, 1 ch, (cl2, 1 ch) in each st around. Join rnd with sl st to top of first 3 ch (16 clusters and 16 ch sps).
Fasten off yarn.
Attach yarn C to any ch sp from round 2.

Round 3: 3 ch, cl2 in same sp, 2 ch, (cl3, 2 ch) in each sp around. Join rnd with sl st to top of first 3 ch (16 clusters and 16 ch sps). Fasten off yarn.
Attach yarn D to any cluster from round 3.

Round 4: 2 ch (counts as 1 hdc), 2 hdc in same st, 1 ch, 3 hdc in next cluster, 1 ch, * miss next cluster, (cl4, 5 ch, cl4) in next ch sp, 1 ch, miss next cluster, ** (3 hdc in next cluster, 1 ch) twice; rep from * around, ending last rep at **. Join rnd with sl st to top of first 2 ch (32 sts and 16 ch sps).
Fasten off yarn.

CHART PATTERN

JOINING

Use the slip stitch method (see page 48) or join as you go (see pages 49–50).

57. CHAMOMILE
(3D MOTIF)

NOTE

The four black sc stitches indicate where the flower should be attached to the background granny square (see page 45).

WRITTEN PATTERN

Using yarn A, make 4 ch, join with a sl st to form a ring.

Round 1: 1 ch (does not count as st here or throughout), 8 sc in ring. Join rnd with sl st to top of first ch (8 sc).

Round 2: 1 ch, (1 scflo, 2 scflo in next st) around.
Join rnd with sl st to top of first ch (12 scflo).
Fasten off yarn.
Attach yarn B to any st from round 2.

Round 3: * 2 ch, 3 dc in next st, 2 ch, sl st in next st; rep from * around (6 petals made).
Fasten off yarn.

Background

Attach yarn C to unworked blo of any indicated (black) st on round 1 of chart and work as for Solid Background Granny Square (page 47).

When working the first round of background, insert hook into marked (black) stitches from round 1 of the Chamomile chart.

CHART PATTERN

JOINING

Use the slip stitch method (see page 48).

58. FLEABANE

SPECIAL STITCH

3 dc cluster (cl3) (see page 32).

WRITTEN PATTERN

Using yarn A, make 4 ch, join with a sl st to form a ring.

Round 1: 1 ch (does not count as st here or throughout), 8 sc in ring. Join rnd with sl st to top of first ch (8 sc). Fasten off yarn. Attach yarn B to any st from round 1.

Round 2: 1 ch, (1 sc, cl3 in same st) (1 sc, cl3) in each st around. Join rnd with sl st to top of first ch (8 clusters and 8 sc). Fasten off yarn. Attach yarn C to any sc from round 2.

Round 3: 3 ch, 2 dc in same sc, 2 ch, (3 dc, 2 ch) in each sc around. Join rnd with sl st to top of first 3 ch (24 dc and 8 ch sps).

Round 4: sl st across each dc to next 2 ch sp, 2 ch (counts as 1 hdc), 2 hdc in same ch sp, 1 ch * (3 dc, 3 ch, 3 dc) in next ch sp, 1 ch, ** 3 hdc in next ch sp, 1 ch; rep from * around, ending last rep at **. Join rnd with sl st to top of 2 ch (36 sts and 12 ch sps).

Round 5: sl st to next ch sp, 3 ch, (counts as 1 dc), 2 dc in same sp, 1 ch, (3 dc, 3 ch, 3 dc) in next ch sp, 1 ch, * (3 dc in next ch sp, 1 ch) twice, (3 dc, 3 ch, 3 dc) in next ch sp, 1 ch; rep from * around, finishing with 3 dc in next ch sp, 1 ch. Join rnd with sl st to top of first 3 ch (48 sts and 16 ch sps).
Fasten off yarn.

CHART PATTERN

JOINING

Use the slip stitch method (see page 48) or join as you go (see pages 49–50).

59. DIANTHUS

SPECIAL STITCH

Spiked single crochet (spsc) (see page 33).

NOTE

Work the spsc in round 4 over the ch sp from round 3 and down into the next unworked sc from round 2.

WRITTEN PATTERN

Using yarn A, make 4 ch.

Round 1: work 15 dc in fourth ch from hook (missed 3 ch counts as 1 dc). Join rnd with sl st to top of first 3 ch (16 dc). Fasten off yarn.
Attach yarn B to any st from round 1.

Round 2: 1 ch (does not count as a st here or throughout), 2 sc in each st around. Join rnd with sl st to top of first ch (32 sc). Fasten off yarn.
Attach yarn C to any sc from round 2.

Round 3: 1 ch, * 1 hdc in same st, 2 dc in next st, 1 hdc in next st, 1 ch, miss next st; rep from * around. Join rnd with sl st to top of first ch (32 sts and 8 ch sps). Fasten off yarn.
Attach yarn D to first st of round 3.

Round 4: 1 ch, 1 sc in same st, *(2 sc in next st) twice, 1 sc in next st, 1 spsc down into next missed sc from round 2, working over ch sp from round 3, ** 1 sc in next st; rep from * around, ending last rep at **. Join rnd with sl st to top of first ch (56 sts). Fasten off yarn.
Attach yarn E to any spsc from round 4.

Round 5: 1 ch, 1 sc in same st, 5 ch, (1 sc in next spsc, 5 ch) around. Join rnd with sl st to top of first ch (8 sc and 8 ch sps).

Round 6: 3 ch (counts as 1 dc), * 4 dc in next 5 ch sp, (3 tr, 3 ch, 3 tr) in next sc, 4 dc in next 5 ch sp, ** 1 dc in next sc; rep from * around, ending last rep at **. Join rnd with sl st to top of first 3 ch (60 sts and 4 ch sps).
Fasten off yarn.

CHART PATTERN

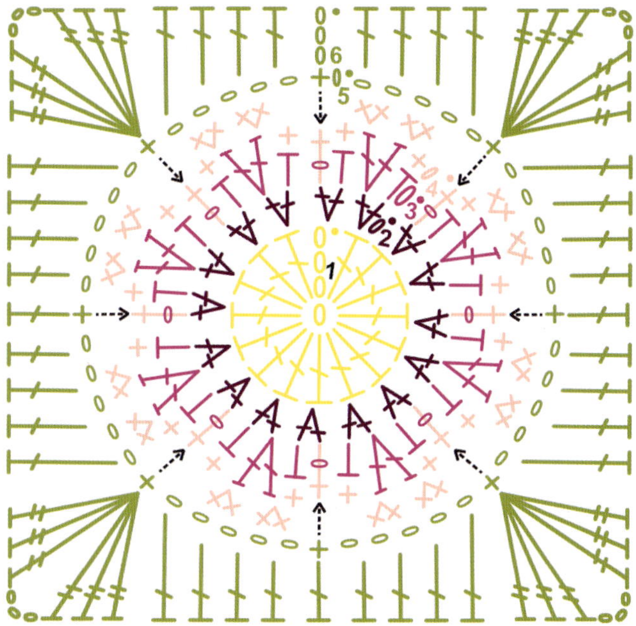

JOINING

Use the slip stitch method (see page 48).

60. LILY
(3D MOTIF)

SPECIAL STITCH

Picot (see page 33).

NOTE

The four black sc stitches indicate where the flower should be attached to the background granny square (see page 45).

WRITTEN PATTERN

Using yarn A, make 4 ch, join with a sl st to form a ring.

Round 1: 1 ch (does not count as st here or throughout), (2 sc, 3 ch) six times in ring. Join rnd with sl st to top of first ch (12 sc and 6 ch sps). Fasten off yarn.
Attach yarn B with a sl st to any ch sp from round 1.

Round 2: 1 ch, (1 sc, 1 hdc, 1 dc, 1 tr, 1 ch, 1 tr, 1 dc, 1 hdc, 1 sc, 1 ch) in each ch sp around. Join rnd with sl st to top of first ch (6 petals). Fasten off yarn.
Attach yarn C with a sl st to a ch sp at the base of any petal from round 2.

Round 3: * 1 sc in each of next 2 sts, 1 hdc in next st, 2 dc in next st, (1 tr, picot, 1 tr) in 1 ch sp at the peak of petal, 2 dc in next st, 1 hdc in next st, 1 sc in each of next 2 sts, sl st in ch sp; rep from * around (6 petals). Fasten off yarn.

Background

Attach yarn D to unworked blo of any indicated stitch on round 1 of chart and work as for the Background Granny Square (page 46).

When working the first round of background, insert hook into marked (black) stitches from round 1 of the Lily chart.

CHART PATTERN

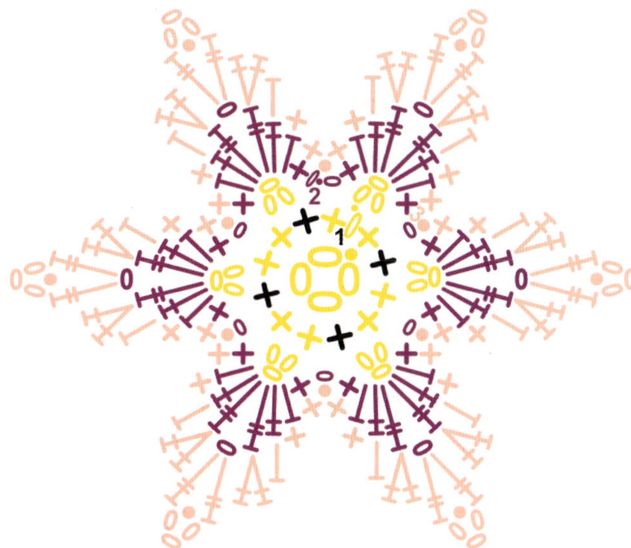

JOINING

Use the slip stitch method (see page 48) or join as you go (see pages 49–50).

61. CAMELLIA

WRITTEN PATTERN

Using yarn A, make 4 ch, join with a sl st to form a ring.

Round 1: 1 ch (does not count as st here or throughout), 8 sc in ring. Join rnd with sl st to top of first ch (8 sc). Fasten off yarn. Attach yarn B to any st from round 1.

Round 2: 1 ch, (1 sc, 1 ch) in each st around. Join rnd with sl st to top of first ch (8 sc and 8 ch sps). Fasten off yarn. Attach yarn C to any ch sp from round 2.

Round 3: 3 ch (counts as 1 dc here), 2 dc in same ch sp, 1 ch, (3 dc in ch sp, 1 ch) around. Join rnd with sl st to top of first 3 ch (24 dc and 8 ch sps). Fasten off yarn.
Attach yarn B to any ch sp from round 3.

Round 4: 1 ch, (1 sc, 3 ch) in each ch sp around.
Join rnd with sl st to top of first ch (8 sc and 8 ch sps).
Fasten off yarn.
Attach yarn D to any ch sp from round 4.

Round 5: 1 ch, * (1 sc, 1 hdc, 3 dc, 1 hdc, 1 sc) in ch sp, 1 ch; rep from * around. Join rnd with sl st to top of first ch (8 petals). Fasten off yarn.
Attach yarn E to any ch sp from round 5.

Round 6: (1 ch, 1 sc in same ch sp, 4 ch) in each ch sp around. Join rnd with sl st to top of first ch (8 sc and 8 ch sps).

Round 7: 2 ch (counts as 1 hdc), 2 hdc in first sc, 1 ch, 3 hdc in next sc, 1 ch, * (3 dc, 3 ch, 3 dc) in next ch sp, 1 ch, ** (3 hdc in next sc, 1 ch) twice; rep from *, ending last rep at **. Join rnd with sl st to top of first 2 ch (48 sts and 16 ch sps).
Fasten off yarn.

CHART PATTERN

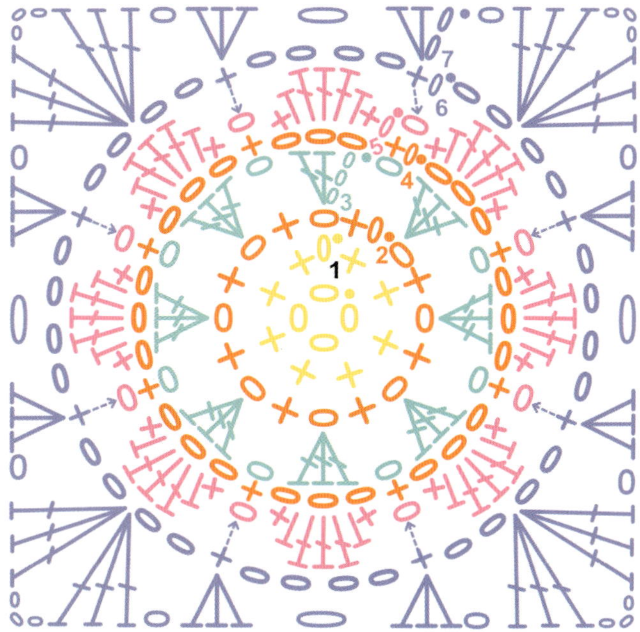

JOINING

Use the slip stitch method (see page 48) or join as you go (see pages 49–50).

62. CALIFORNIA SUNLIGHT

SPECIAL STITCH

3 tr cluster (trcl3) (see page 32).

WRITTEN PATTERN

Using yarn A, make 4 ch.

Round 1: work 15 dc in fourth ch from hook (missed 3 ch counts as 1 dc). Join rnd with sl st to top of first 3 ch (16 dc). Fasten off yarn.
Attach yarn B to any st from round 1.

Round 2: 1 ch (does not count as st), 1 sc in same st, * 3 ch, trcl3 flo in next st, 3 ch, ** 1 sc in next st; rep from *, ending last rep at **. Join rnd with sl st to top of first ch (8 petals). Fasten off yarn.
All the sts of the next round are worked into blo of clusters from round 2.
Attach yarn C to blo of any trcl3 from round 2.

Round 3: 1 ch, 1 scblo in same st, 4 ch, (1 scblo in next trcl3, 4 ch) around. Join rnd with sl st to top of first ch (8 sc and 8 ch sps).

Round 4: 3 ch (counts as 1 dc), 2 dc in first sc, 1 ch, 3 dc in next sc, 1 ch, * (3 tr, 3 ch, 3 tr) in next 4 ch sp, 1 ch, ** (3 dc in next sc, 1 ch) twice; rep from *, ending last rep at **. Join rnd with sl st to top of first 3 ch (48 sts and 16 ch sps).
Fasten off yarn.

CHART PATTERN

JOINING

Use the slip stitch method (see page 48) or join as you go (see pages 49–50).

63. COREOPSIS

SPECIAL STITCHES

2 dc cluster (cl2), 3 dc cluster (cl3), 3 tr cluster (trcl3), popcorn (pop) (see page 32).

WRITTEN PATTERN

Using yarn A, make 4 ch, join with a sl st to form a ring.

Round 1: 1 ch (does not count as st here or throughout), 12 sc in ring. Join rnd with sl st to top of first ch (12 sc). Fasten off yarn.
Attach yarn B to any st from round 1.

Round 2: 1 ch, 1 sc in same st, 1 ch, (1 sc, 1 ch) in each st around. Join rnd with sl st to top of first ch (12 sc and 12 ch sps). Fasten off yarn.
Attach yarn C to any ch sp from round 2.
Note that the 3 ch at the start of the next rnd counts as the first dc of pop, so you only need to make four more dc in this st.

Round 3: 3 ch (counts as 1 dc here and throughout), pop in same ch sp, 2 ch, (pop, 2 ch) in each ch sp around. Join rnd with sl st to top of first ch (12 pop and 12 ch sps). Fasten off yarn.
Attach yarn D to any 2 ch sp from round 3.

Round 4: 3 ch, cl2 in same 2 ch sp, 3 ch, * trcl3 in next pop, 3 ch, cl3 in next 2 ch sp, 2 ch, 1 dc in next 2 ch sp, 2 ch, ** cl3 in next 2 ch sp, 3 ch; rep from * around, ending last rep at **. Join rnd with sl st to top of first 3 ch (16 sts and 16 ch sps). Fasten off yarn.
Attach yarn E to any trcl3 from round 4.

Round 5: 2 ch (counts as 1 hdc), (1 hdc, 2 ch, 2 hdc) in same st, * 2 hdc in next 3 ch sp, 1 hdc in next cl, 2 hdc in next 2 ch sp, 1 hdc in next dc, 2 hdc in next 2 ch sp, 1 hdc in next cl, 2 hdc in next 3 ch sp, ** (2 hdc, 2 ch, 2 hdc) in next trcl3; rep from * around, ending last rep at **. Join rnd with sl st to top of first 2 ch (60 sts and 4 ch sps).
Fasten off yarn.

CHART PATTERN

JOINING

Use the slip stitch method (see page 48).

64. GERANIUM

SPECIAL STITCH

Spiked double crochet (spdc) (see page 33).

NOTE

Work the spdc in round 4 over the ch sps from rounds 2 and 3 and down into the next unworked sc from round 1.

WRITTEN PATTERN

Using yarn A, make 4 ch, join with a sl st to form a ring.

Round 1: 1 ch (does not count as st), 8 sc in ring. Join rnd with sl st to top of first ch (8 sc). Fasten off yarn. Attach yarn B to any st from round 1.

Round 2: 2 ch (counts as 1 hdc), (1 hdc, 3 ch, 2 hdc) in same st, 1 ch, miss next st, * (2 hdc, 3 ch, 2 hdc) in next st, 1 ch, miss next st; rep from * around. Join rnd with sl st to top of first 2 ch (16 hdc and 8 ch sps).

Round 3: sl st to next 3 ch sp, 3 ch (counts as 1 dc here and throughout), (2 dc, 3 ch, 3 dc) in same sp, 1 ch, * (3 dc, 3 ch, 3 dc) in next 3 ch sp, 1 ch; rep from * twice more. Join rnd with sl st to top of first 3 ch (24 dc and 8 ch sps). Fasten off yarn.
Attach yarn C to any 3 ch sp from round 3.

Round 4: 3 ch, (2 dc, 3 ch, 3 dc) in same sp, 1 ch, * 1 dc in next 1 ch sp, 1 spdc down into next missed st from round 1, 1 dc back into same 1 ch sp in round 3 as before, 1 ch, ** (3 dc, 3 ch, 3 dc) in next 3 ch sp, 1 ch; rep from *, ending last rep at **. Join rnd with sl st to top of first 3 ch (36 sts and 12 ch sps). Fasten off yarn.
Attach yarn D to any 3 ch corner sp from round 4.

Round 5: 3 ch, (2 dc, 3 ch, 3 dc) in 3 ch sp, 1 ch, (3 dc in next 1 ch sp, 1 ch) to next corner, * (3 dc, 3 ch, 3 dc) in corner ch sp, 1 ch, (3 dc in next 1 ch sp, 1 ch) to next corner; rep from * around. Join rnd with sl st to top of first 3 ch (48 sts and 16 ch sps).
Fasten off yarn.

CHART PATTERN

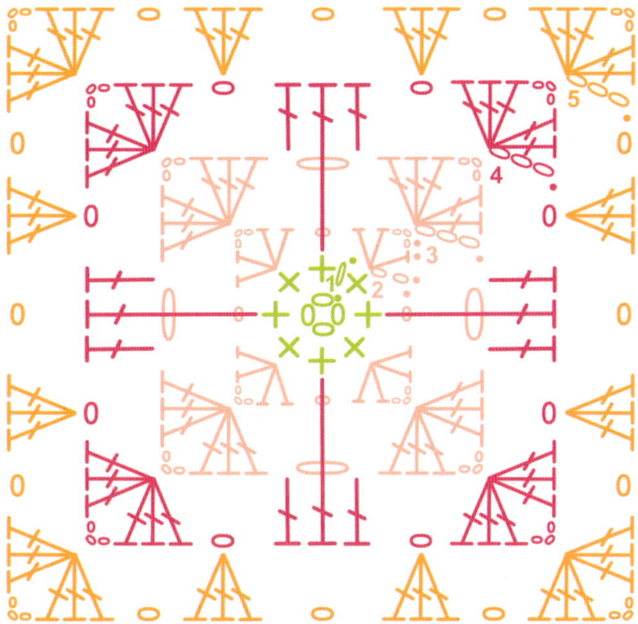

JOINING

Use the slip stitch method (see page 48) or join as you go (see pages 49–50).

65. DAHLIA

SPECIAL STITCHES

Picot, popcorn (pop) (see pages 32 and 33).

WRITTEN PATTERN

Using yarn A, make 4 ch, join with a sl st to form a ring.

Round 1: 1 ch, (1 sc, picot) eight times in ring. Join rnd with sl st to top of first ch (8 sc and 8 picots).
Fasten off yarn.
Attach yarn B to any sc from round 1.
Note 3 ch at beg of rounds 2 and 3 counts as first dc of pop, so only make four more dc in this st.

Round 2: 3 ch (counts as 1 dc here and throughout), (pop, 2 ch) in each sc around. Join rnd with sl st to top of first 3 ch (8 popcorns and 8 ch sp).
Fasten off yarn.
Attach yarn C to any 2 ch sp from round 2.

Round 3: 3 ch, (pop, 2 ch) twice in each 2 ch sp around. Join rnd with sl st to top of first 3 ch (16 popcorns and 16 ch sps). Fasten off yarn.
Attach yarn D to any 2 ch sp from round 3.

Round 4: 3 ch, 2 dc in same 2 ch sp, 1 ch, 3 dc in next 2 ch sp, 1 ch, * (3 tr, 3 ch) in next 2 ch sp, (3 tr, 1 ch) in next 2 ch sp, ** (3 dc in next 2 ch sp, 1 ch) twice; rep from * around, ending last rep at **. Join rnd with sl st to top of first 3 ch (48 sts and 16 ch sps).
Fasten off yarn.

CHART PATTERN

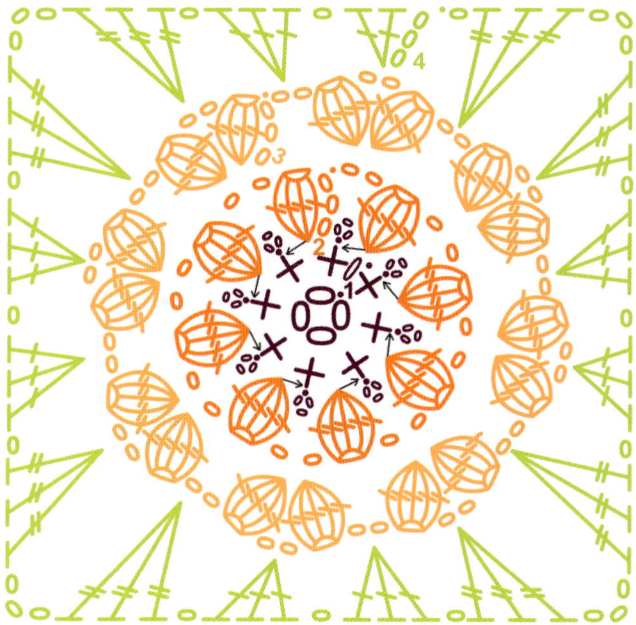

JOINING

Use the slip stitch method (see page 48) or join as you go (see pages 49–50).

66. PEONY

NOTES

In the chart opposite, the lower seven petals are faded slightly to show clearly where stitches from round 4 should be inserted.

Crochet round 4 by working behind the petals from round 3, inserting the hook into the unworked blo of indicated stitches from round 2 (see page 43).

WRITTEN PATTERN

Using yarn A, make 4 ch.

Round 1: work 15 dc in fourth ch from hook (missed 3 ch counts as 1 dc). Join rnd with sl st to top of first 3 ch (16 dc).
Fasten off yarn.
Attach yarn B to any st from round 1.

Round 2: 3 ch (counts as 1 dc here and throughout), 1 dc in same st, 2 dc in each st around. Join rnd with sl st to top of first 3 ch (32 dc).
Fasten off yarn.
Attach yarn C to any st from round 2.

Round 3: 1 ch, 1 sc in same st, miss next st, 9 dc in flo of next st, miss next st, * 1 sc in next st, miss next st, 9 dc in flo of next st, miss next st; rep from * around. Join rnd with sl st to top of first ch (8 petals).
Fasten off yarn.
All the sts of the next round are worked into unworked blo of sts at center base of petals from round 3.
Attach yarn D to unworked blo of any st from round 3 that has a petal worked into it.

Round 4: 2 ch (counts as 1 hdc), 2 hdcblo in same st, 1 ch, * (3 dc, 3 ch, 3 dc) in unworked blo of next petal stitch, 1 ch, ** 3 hdc in unworked blo of next petal st, 1 ch; rep from *, ending last rep at **. Join rnd with sl st to top of first 2 ch (36 sts and 12 ch sps).

Round 5: sl st across each hdc to next 1 ch sp, sl st in 1 ch sp, 3 ch, 2 dc in same sp, 1 ch, * (3 dc, 3 ch, 3 dc) in corner ch sp, 1 ch, (3 dc in next 1 ch sp, 1 ch) ** twice; rep from * around, ending rep at **. Join rnd with sl st to top of first 3 ch (48 sts and 16 ch sps).
Fasten off yarn.

CHART PATTERN

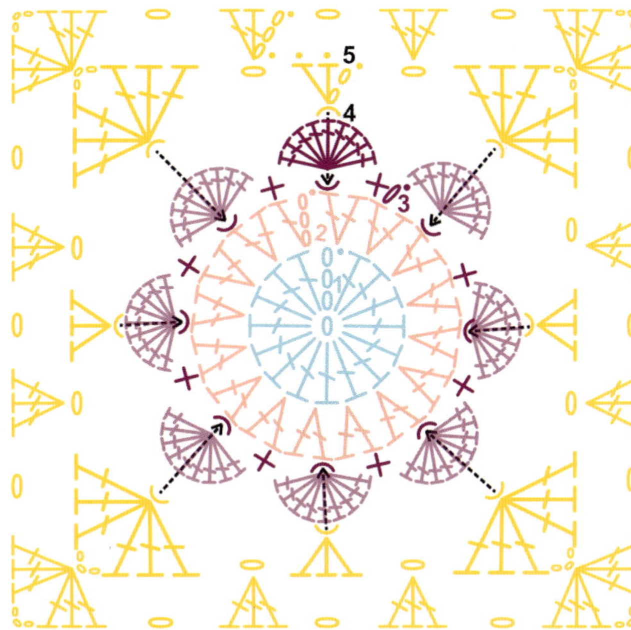

JOINING

Use the slip stitch method (see page 48) or join as you go (see pages 49–50).

67. PRIMROSE

SPECIAL STITCH

5 tr cluster (trcl5) (see page 32).

WRITTEN PATTERN

Using yarn A, make 4 ch.

Round 1: work 15 dc in fourth ch from hook (missed 3 ch counts as 1 dc). Join rnd with sl st to top of first 3 ch (16 dc).
Fasten off yarn.
Attach yarn B to any st from round 1.

Round 2: 2 ch (counts as 1 hdc), 1 trcl5 in next st, (1 hdc in next st, 1 trcl5 in next st) around. Join rnd with sl st to top of first 2 ch (8 cl and 8 hdc).
Fasten off yarn.
Attach yarn C to any hdc from round 2.

Round 3: 1 ch, 1 sc in same st, 1 ch, (3 dc, 3 ch, 3 dc) in next hdc, 1 ch, * 1 sc in next hdc, 1 ch, (3 dc, 3 ch, 3 dc) in next hdc, 1 ch; rep from * around. Join rnd with sl st to top of first ch (28 sts and 12 ch sps).
Fasten off yarn.
Attach yarn D to any 3 ch corner sp from round 3.

Round 4: 3 ch (counts as 1 dc), (2 dc, 3 ch, 3 dc) all in same 3 ch sp, * 1 ch, (3 dc in next 1 ch sp, 1 ch) twice, ** (3 dc, 3 ch, 3 dc) in corner ch sp; rep from * around, ending last rep at **. Join rnd with sl st to top of first 3 ch.
Fasten off yarn.

CHART PATTERN

JOINING

Use the slip stitch method (see page 48) or join as you go (see pages 49–50).

68. ROSE CAMPION

SPECIAL STITCHES

4 dc cluster (cl4), 5 dc cluster (cl5), spiked double crochet (spdc) (see pages 32 and 33).

NOTE

Work the spdc in round 4 down into the ch sp from round 2, working over the sc from round 3.

WRITTEN PATTERN

Using yarn A, make 4 ch, join with a sl st to form a ring.

Round 1: 4 ch (counts as 1 dc, 1 ch), (1 dc, 1 ch) seven times in ring. Join rnd with sl st to third of first 4 ch (8 sts and 8 ch sps).
Fasten off yarn.
Attach yarn B to any ch sp from round 1.

Round 2: 3 ch (counts as 1 dc here and throughout), cl4 in same ch sp, 3 ch, (cl5, 3 ch) in each ch sp around. Join rnd with sl st to top of first 3 ch (8 clusters and 8 ch sps).
Fasten off yarn.
Attach yarn C to any ch sp from round 2.

Round 3: 1 ch, 1 sc in same ch sp, 1 ch, * (3 dc, 3 ch, 3 dc) in next ch sp, 1 ch, ** 1 sc in next ch sp, 1 ch; rep from * around, ending last rep at **. Join rnd with sl st to top of first ch (28 sts and 12 ch sps).
Fasten off yarn.
Attach yarn D to any 3 ch corner sp from round 3.

Round 4: 3 ch, (2 dc, 3 ch, 3 dc) in same ch sp, * 1 dc in each of next 3 dc, 1 dc in 1 ch sp, 1 spdc back down into next ch sp from round 2, working over the sc from round 3, 1 dc in 1 ch sp, 1 dc in each of next 3 dc, ** (3 dc, 3 ch, 3 dc) in next 3 ch sp; rep from * around, ending last rep at **.
Join rnd with sl st to top of first 3 ch.
Fasten off yarn.

CHART PATTERN

JOINING

Use the slip stitch method (see page 48).

69. WATERLILY

NOTE

The arrows show where to insert the hook when working behind previously made petals. Make a note of which loop each stitch should be worked into when working behind (see page 43).

WRITTEN PATTERN

Using yarn A, make 4 ch, join with a sl st to form a ring.

Round 1: 3 ch (counts as 1 dc here and throughout), 2 dc in ring, 3 ch, (3 dc in ring, 3 ch) three times.
Join rnd with sl st to top of first 3 ch (12 dc).
Fasten off yarn.
Attach yarn B to any corner sp of round 1.

Round 2: 1 ch (does not count as a st here or throughout), 1 sc in same ch sp, * miss next dc, 7 dc in flo of next dc, miss next dc, ** 1 sc in next ch sp; rep from * around, ending last rep at **. Join rnd with sl st to top of first ch (4 petals and 4 sc).
Fasten off yarn.
Attach yarn C to unworked blo of central dc from any 3 dc group from round 1.

Round 3: 3 ch (counts as 1 dc), 2 dcblo in next unworked dc from round 1, * (2 dc, 3 ch, 2 dc) in next sc from round 2, 2 dcblo in unworked dc from round 1, ** 1 dc in unworked blo of next dc from round 1, 2 dcblo in next unworked dc from round 1; rep from * around, ending last rep at **.
Join rnd with sl st to top of first 3 ch (36 dc and 4 ch sps).

Round 4: 1 ch, 1 sc in same st, * miss 2 dc, 7 dc in flo of next dc, miss next dc, 1 sc in next 3 ch sp, miss next dc, 7 dc in flo of next dc, miss 2 dc, ** 1 sc in next dc; rep from * around, ending last rep at **. Join rnd with sl st to top of first ch (8 petals and 8 sc).
Fasten off yarn.
Attach yarn D to sc at any corner from round 4.

Round 5: 3 ch, *(2 dc, 3 ch, 3 dc) in same sc, * 1 ch, working behind petals from round 4, (3 dc in unworked blo of next dc from round 3 that has a petal worked into it, 1 ch) twice, ** (3 dc, 3 ch, 3 dc) in next corner sc from round 4; rep from * around, ending last rep at **. Join rnd with sl st to top of first 3 ch (48 dc and 16 ch sps).
Fasten off yarn.

CHART PATTERN

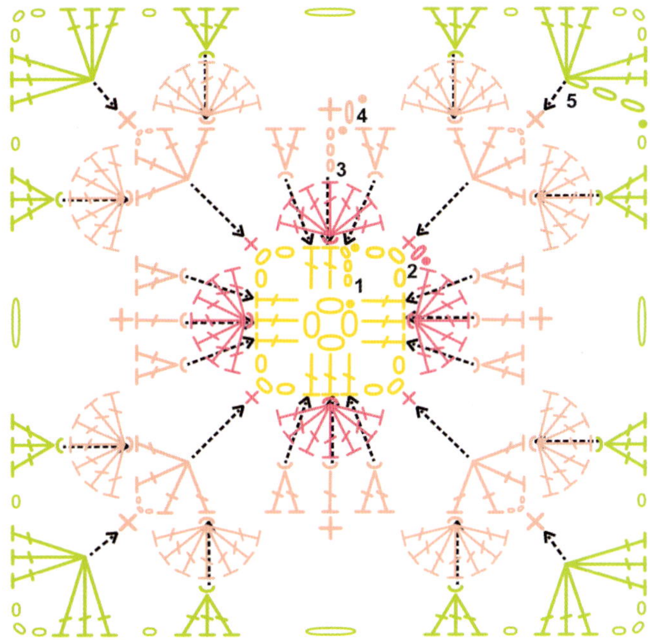

JOINING

Use the slip stitch method (see page 48) or join as you go (see pages 49–50).

70. ASTER
(3D MOTIF)

NOTE

The four black sc stitches indicate where the flower should be attached to the background granny square (see page 45).

WRITTEN PATTERN

Using yarn A, make 4 ch, join with a sl st to form a ring.

Round 1: 1 ch (does not count as st here or throughout), 12 sc in ring. Join rnd with sl st to top of first ch (12 sc).
Fasten off yarn.
Attach yarn B to flo of any st from round 1.

Round 2: (3 ch, 2 dcflo in same st, 3 ch, sl st flo in next st) around (12 petals).
Fasten off yarn.

Background

Attach yarn C to unworked blo of any indicated stitch on round 1 of chart and work as for Background Granny Square (page 46).

When working the first round of background, insert hook into marked (black) stitches from round 1 of the Aster chart.

CHART PATTERN

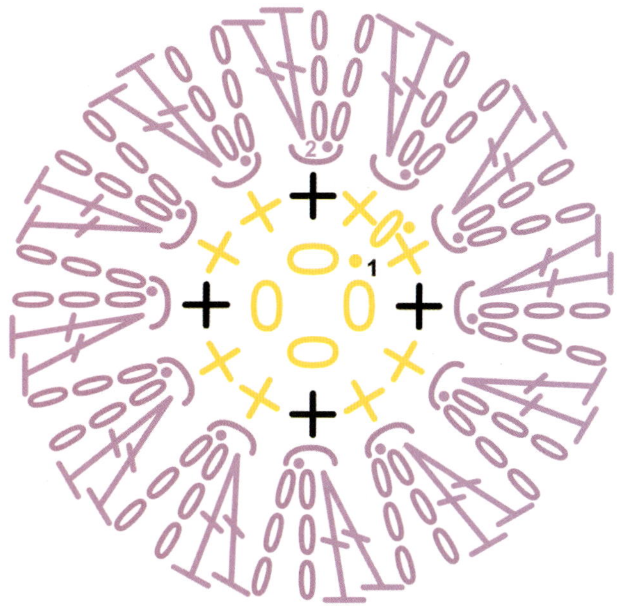

JOINING

Use the slip stitch method (see page 48) or join as you go (see pages 49–50).

71. POPPY

SPECIAL STITCH

Spiked treble crochet (sptr) (see page 33).

NOTE

Work the sptr in round 5 in front of the next sc from round 4 and down into the unworked flo of the sc from round 3.

WRITTEN PATTERN

Using yarn A, make 4 ch, join with a sl st to form a ring.

Round 1: 1 ch (does not count as st here or throughout), 8 sc in ring. Join rnd with sl st to top of first ch (8 sc).

Round 2: 1 ch, 2 sc in each st around. Join rnd with sl st to top of first ch (16 sc).
Fasten off yarn.
Attach yarn B to any st from round 2.

Round 3: 1 ch, * 1 sc in next st, (1 hdc, 1 dc) in next st, 3 dc in next st, (1 dc, 1 hdc) in next st; rep from * around. Join rnd with sl st to top of first ch (32 sts).

Round 4: 1 ch, 1 scblo in first st, * 1 hdc in next st, (1 hdc, 1 dc) in next st, 2 dc in next st, 3 dc in next st, 2 dc in next st, (1 dc, 1 hdc) in next st, 1 hdc in next st, ** 1 scblo in next st; rep from * around, ending last rep at **. Join rnd with sl st to top of first ch (56 sts).
Fasten off yarn.
Attach yarn C to central dc of any 3 dc group from round 4.

Round 5: 1 ch, (1 sc, 1 ch, 1 sc) in same st, * 2 sc, hdc2tog, dc2tog, 1 sptr down into the flo of the next sc from round 3, dc2tog, hdc2tog, 2 sc, ** (1 sc, 1 ch, 1 sc) in next st; rep from * around, ending last rep at **. Join rnd with sl st to top of first ch (44 sts and 4 ch sps).

Round 6: 3 ch (counts as 1 dc), (2 dc, 3 ch, 2 dc) in ch sp, * 1 dc in each st to next ch sp, (2 dc, 3 ch, 2 dc) in ch sp; rep from * to last ch sp, 1 dc in each st to end. Join rnd with sl st to top of first ch (60 sts and 4 ch sps).
Fasten off yarn.

CHART PATTERN

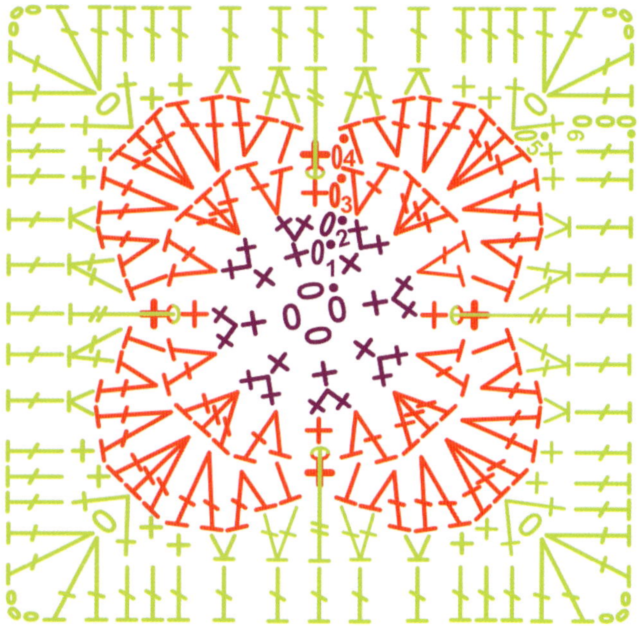

JOINING

Use the slip stitch method (see page 48).

72. BLANKET FLOWER
(3D MOTIF)

NOTE

The four black sc stitches indicate where the flower should be attached to the background granny square (see page 45).

WRITTEN PATTERN

Using yarn A, make 4 ch, join with a sl st to form a ring.

Round 1: 1 ch (does not count as st), 8 sc in ring. Join rnd with sl st to top of first ch (8 sc).

Round 2: 2 ch (counts as 1 hdc here and throughout), 1 hdcflo in same st, 2 hdcflo in each rem st around. Join rnd with sl st to top of first 2 ch (16 hdcflo).

Round 3: 2 ch, 1 hdc in same st, 1 hdc in next st, (2 hdc in next st, 1 hdc in next st) around. Join rnd with sl st to top of first 2 ch (24 htr). Fasten off yarn.
Attach yarn B to any st from round 3.

Round 4: * 3 ch, 3 dc in next st, 3 ch, sl st in next st; rep from * around. Join rnd with sl st to bottom of first 3 ch (12 petals). Fasten off yarn.

Background

Attach yarn C to unworked blo of any indicated stitch on round 1 of chart and work as for Background Granny Square (page 46).

When working the first round of background, insert hook into marked (black) stitches from round 1 of the Blanket Flower chart.

CHART PATTERN

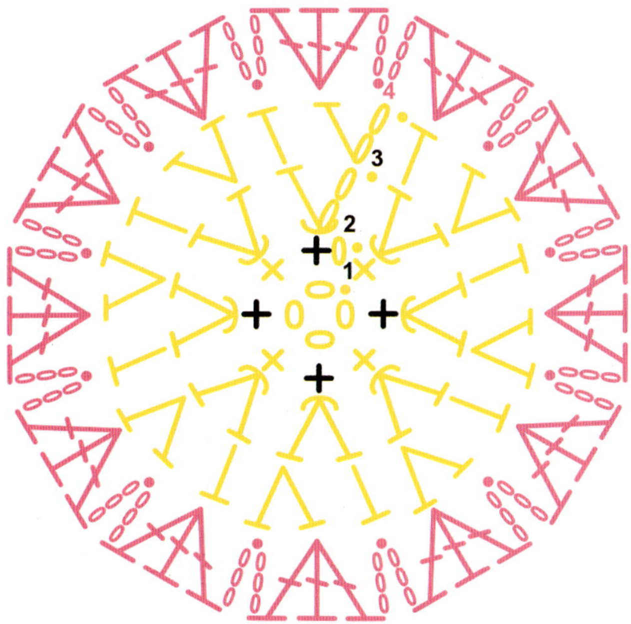

JOINING

Use the slip stitch method (see page 48) or join as you go (see pages 49–50).

73. PANSY
(3D MOTIF)

NOTE

The four black stitches indicate where the flower is attached to the background (see page 45).

Work four identical petals, as shown in the chart opposite (two are faded to show how they overlap). Each begins with a new yarn on round 4: labelled 4a, b, c, or d.

WRITTEN PATTERN

Using yarn A, make 4 ch, join with a sl st to form a ring.

Round 1: 1 ch (does not count as st here or throughout), 8 sc in ring. Join rnd with sl st to top of first ch (8 sc). Fasten off yarn. Attach yarn B to any st from round 1.

Round 2: 1 ch, 1 sc in same st, (3 ch, miss next st, 1 sc in next st) three times, 3 ch, miss next st. Join rnd with sl st to top of first ch (4 ch sps and 4 sc).

Round 3: sl st in first sc, * (1 sc, 1 hdc, 3 dc, 1 hdc, 1 sc) in next 3 ch sp, sl st in next sc; rep from * around (4 petals). Do not fasten off yarn.

Round 4: sl st into first sc of next petal, * 3 ch, 1 dc in same st, 2 dc in each of next 2 sts, 3 dc in next st, 2 dc in each of next 2 sts, 1 dc in next st, 3 ch, sl st in same st. Fasten off yarn.
With right side facing, attach yarn C to first sc of next petal; rep from * three times more in yarn C (4 petals made). Fasten off yarn.

Background

Attach yarn D to any indicated (black) stitch on round 1 of chart and work as for Background Granny Square (page 46).

When working the first round of background, insert hook into marked stitches from round 1 of the Pansy chart – note you can work into the whole of the stitch when beginning the background.

CHART PATTERN

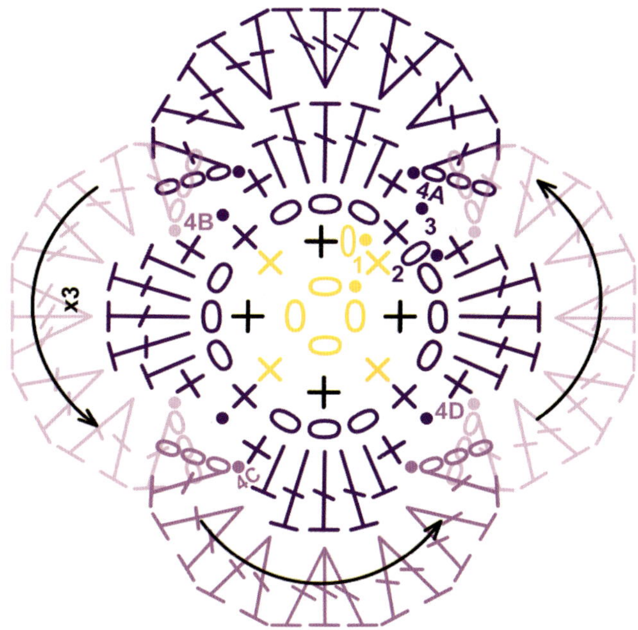

JOINING

Use the slip stitch method (see page 48) or join as you go (see pages 49–50).

74. FORGET-ME-NOT
(3D MOTIF)

SPECIAL STITCH

Picot (see page 33).

NOTES

In the chart opposite, arrows show where to insert round 3 sts: work behind round 2 petals into the unworked blo of sts from round 2. The four black sc stitches indicate where the flower is attached to the background (see page 45).

WRITTEN PATTERN

Using yarn A, make 4 ch, join with a sl st to form a ring.

Round 1: 1 ch (does not count as st here or throughout), 10 sc in ring. Join rnd with sl st to top of first ch (10 sc). Fasten off yarn.

Attach yarn B to flo of any st from round 1.

Round 2: (2 ch, 3 dcflo in next st, 2 ch, sl st flo in next st) around (5 petals). Fasten off yarn.

Attach yarn C to unworked blo of a st between petal in round 2.

Round 3: 1 ch, 1 scblo in same st, 3 ch, miss next st from round 2, (1 scblo in next st from round 2, 3 ch, miss next st from round 2) around. Join rnd with sl st to top of first ch (5 ch sps and 5 scblo).

Round 4: sl st in first sc, * (1 sc, 1 hdc, 2 dc, 1 picot, 1 dc, 1 hdc, 1 sc) in next ch sp, sl st in next sc; rep from * around (5 leaves). Fasten off yarn.

Background

Attach yarn D to unworked blo of any indicated (black) stitch on round 1 of chart and work as for Solid Background Granny Square (page 47).

When working the first round of background, insert hook into marked stitches from round 1 of the Forget-Me-Not chart.

CHART PATTERN

JOINING

Use the slip stitch method (see page 48).

75. SUNFLOWER

NOTE

In the chart opposite, arrows show where to insert the round 5 sts: work behind the round 4 petals into the unworked blo of the sts from round 3.

WRITTEN PATTERN

Using yarn A, make 4 ch.

Round 1: work 11 dc in fourth ch from hook (missed 3 ch counts as 1 dc). Join rnd with sl st to top of first 3 ch (12 dc).

Round 2: 3 ch (counts as 1 dc here and throughout), 1 dc in same st, 2 dc in each st around. Join rnd with sl st to top of first 3 ch (24 dc).

Round 3: 3 ch, 2 dc in next st, (1 dc in next st, 2 dc in next st) around. Join rnd with sl st to top of first 3 ch (36 dc).
Fasten off yarn.
Attach yarn B to flo of any st from round 3.

Note: all the stitches of the next round are worked into flo of sts from round 3.

Round 4: 1 ch (does not count as st), (1 sc, 1 hdc, 1 dc) in flo of same st, 1 ch, (1 dc, 1 hdc) in flo of next st, * (1 sc, 1 hdc, 1 dc) in flo of next st, 1 ch, (1 dc, 1 hdc) in flo of next st; rep from * around. Join rnd with sl st to top of first ch (18 petals).
Fasten off yarn.
Attach yarn C to unworked blo of any st from round 3.

Note: all the stitches of the next round are worked into unworked blo of sts from round 3.

Round 5: 4 ch (counts as 1 tr), (2 tr, 3 ch, 3 tr) in blo of same st, 1 ch, (miss next 2 sts from round 3, 3 dcblo in next st, 1 ch) twice, miss next 2 sts from round 3, * (3 tr, 3 ch, 3 tr) in blo of next st, 1 ch, (miss next 2 sts, 3 dcblo in next st, 1 ch) twice, miss next 2 sts; rep from * around. Join rnd with sl st to top of first 4 ch (48 sts and 16 ch sps).
Fasten off yarn.

CHART PATTERN

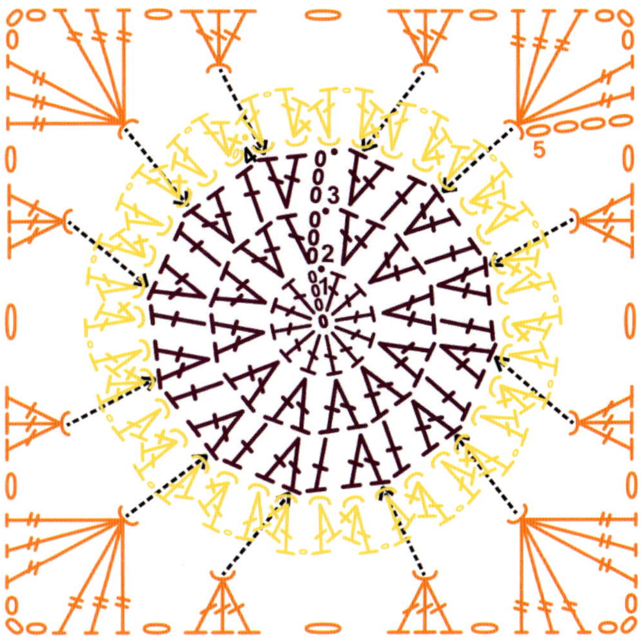

JOINING

Use the slip stitch method (see page 48) or join as you go (see pages 49–50).

76. ANEMONE
(3D MOTIF)

SPECIAL STITCHES

Split cluster (splcl), spiked single crochet (spsc) (see page 33).

NOTE

The four black sc stitches show where the flower attaches to the background (see page 45). Work the spsc in round 5 around the sc from round 4 and down into the ch sp from round 3.

WRITTEN PATTERN

Using yarn A, make 4 ch, join with a sl st to form a ring.

Round 1: 1 ch (does not count as st here or throughout), 12 sc in ring. Join rnd with sl st to top of first ch (12 sc). Fasten off yarn.
Attach yarn B to flo of any st from round 1 – the next round will be worked into flo of each st.

Round 2: 2 ch (does not count as st), working through only front loops around, * splcl, 3 ch; rep from * five more times. Join rnd with sl st to top of first 2 ch (6 petals). Fasten off yarn.
Attach yarn C to any ch sp from round 2.

Round 3: 3 ch, (1 dc, 2 ch, 2 dc) in the same ch sp, 1 ch * (2 dc, 2 ch, 2 dc, 1 ch) in each ch sp around. Join rnd with sl st to top of first 3 ch (24 dc and 12 ch sps).

Round 4: 1 ch, * 7 dc in next 2 ch sp, 1 sc in next 1 ch sp; rep from * around. Join rnd with sl st to top of first ch (6 petals). Fasten off yarn.
Attach yarn D to blo of first dc of any 7 dc group from round 4.

Round 5: 1 ch, * 1 scblo in each of the next 7 dc, work 1 spsc by inserting hook down under the next 1 ch sp from round 3, working the sc over the 1 sc from round 4; rep from * around. Join rnd with sl st to top of first ch.
Fasten off yarn.

Background

Attach yarn E to unworked blo of any indicated (black) stitch on round 1 of chart and work as for Background Granny Square (page 46).

When working the first round of background, insert hook into marked (black) stitches from round 1 of the Anemone chart.

CHART PATTERN

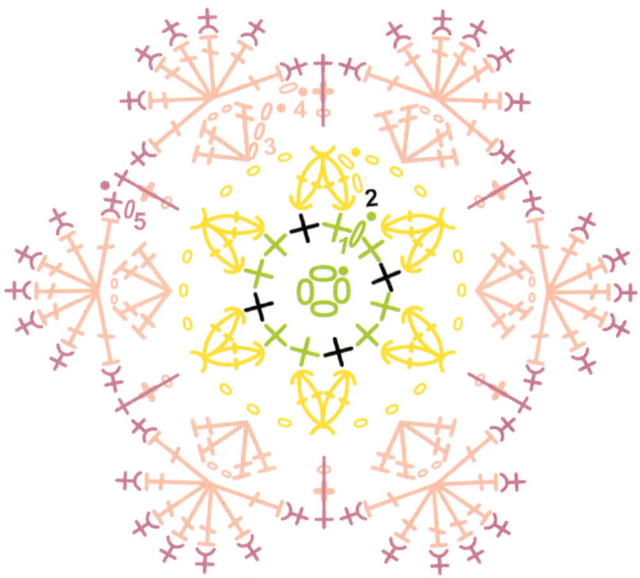

JOINING

Use the slip stitch method (see page 48) or join as you go (see pages 49–50).

77. AURICULA

SPECIAL STITCH

Spiked single crochet (spsc) (see page 33).

NOTE

Work the spsc in round 5 over the ch sp from round 4 and down into the unworked sc from round 3.

WRITTEN PATTERN

Using yarn A, make 2 ch.

Round 1: work 6 sc in second chain from hook. Join rnd with sl st to top of first ch (6 sc). Fasten off yarn.
Attach yarn B to any st from round 1.

Round 2: 1 ch (does not count as a st here or throughout), 2 sc in each st around. Join rnd with sl st to top of first ch (12 sc). Fasten off yarn.
Attach yarn C to any st from round 2.

Round 3: 1 ch, (1 sc in each of next 2 sts, 2 sc in next st) around. Join rnd with sl st to top of first ch (16 sc).
Fasten off yarn.
Attach yarn D to any st from round 3.

Round 4: 2 ch (counts as 1 hdc), (2 dc, 1 hdc) in same st, 1 ch, miss next st, * (1 hdc, 2 dc, 1 hdc) in next st, 1 ch, miss next st; rep from * around. Join rnd with sl st to top of first ch (8 petals). Fasten off yarn.
Attach yarn E to any unworked st from round 3.

Round 5: 1 ch, 1 spsc in same stitch, working around 1 ch from round 4 and down into the unworked sc from round 3, 4 ch, * 1 spsc into next unworked st from round 3, working around 1 ch from round 4, 4 ch; rep from * around. Join rnd with sl st to top of first ch.

Round 6: sl st to next ch sp, 3 ch (counts as 1 dc here and throughout), 2 dc in same ch sp, 1 ch, (3 dc, 3 ch, 3 dc) in next ch sp, 1 ch*, 3 dc in next ch sp, 1 ch, (3 dc, 3 ch, 3 dc) in next ch sp, 1 ch; rep from * around. Join rnd with sl st to top of first 3 ch (36 dc and 12 ch sps).
Fasten off yarn.
Attach yarn F to any corner 3 ch sp from round 6.

Round 7: 3 ch, (2 dc, 3 ch, 3 dc) in same ch sp, 1 ch, (3 dc in next 1 ch sp, 1 ch) twice, * (3 dc, 3 ch, 3 dc) in next ch sp, 1 ch, (3 dc in next ch sp, 1 ch) twice; rep from * around.
Join rnd with sl st to top of first 3 ch (48 dc and 16 ch sps).
Fasten off yarn.

CHART PATTERN

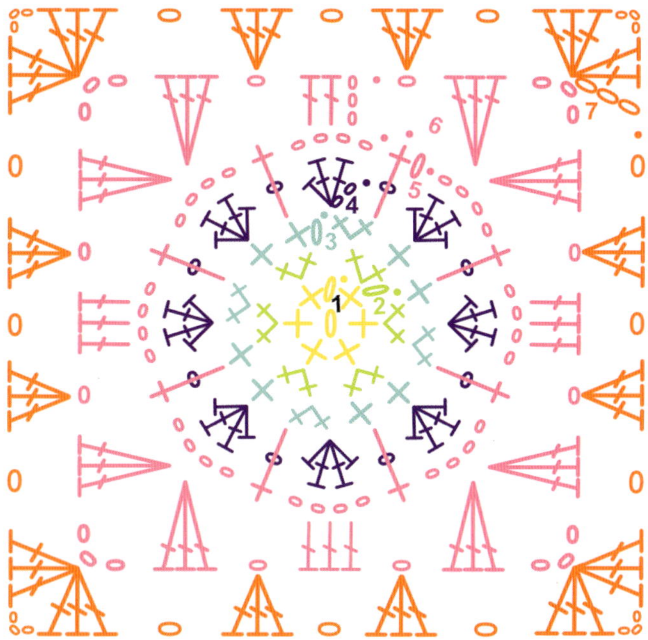

JOINING

Use the slip stitch method (see page 48) or join as you go (see pages 49–50).

78. CLEMATIS
(3D MOTIF)

SPECIAL STITCHES

Picot, spiked single crochet (spsc) (see page 33).

NOTE

The four black sc stitches show where the flower attaches to the background (see page 45).

Work the spsc in round 3 over the ch sp from round 2 and down into the flo of the next unworked sc in round 1.

WRITTEN PATTERN

Using yarn A, make 4 ch, join with a sl st to form a ring.

Round 1: 1 ch (does not count as st here or throughout), 12 sc in ring. Join rnd with sl st to top of first ch (12 sc).
Fasten off yarn.
Attach yarn B to flo of any stitch from round 1.

Round 2: 1 ch, * (1 scflo, picot) in next st, 1 ch, miss next st; rep from * around (6 scflo, 6 picot and 6 ch sps).
Fasten off yarn.
Attach yarn C to any ch sp from round 2.

Round 3: 1 ch, 1 spsc down into the flo of next unworked sc from round 1, working over the chain space from round 2, 5 ch, miss next picot, * 1 spscflo in next unworked st from round 1, 5 ch, miss next picot; rep from * around. Join rnd with sl st to top of first ch (6 spscflo and 6 ch sps).

Round 4: * (2 sc, 1 hdc, 1 dc, 1 hdc, 2 sc) in next ch sp, sl st in next spscflo; rep from * around (6 petals).
Fasten off yarn.
Attach yarn D to blo of any dc from round 4.

Round 5: 1 ch, * (1 scblo, 1 ch, 1 scblo) in dc, 1 scblo in each st to next sl st, sl st in next sl st, 1 scblo in each st to next dc; rep from * around (6 petals).
Fasten off yarn.

Background

Attach yarn E to unworked blo of any indicated (black) stitch on round 1 of chart and work as for Solid Background Granny Square (page 47).

When working the first round of background, insert hook into marked stitches from round 1 of the Clematis chart.

CHART PATTERN

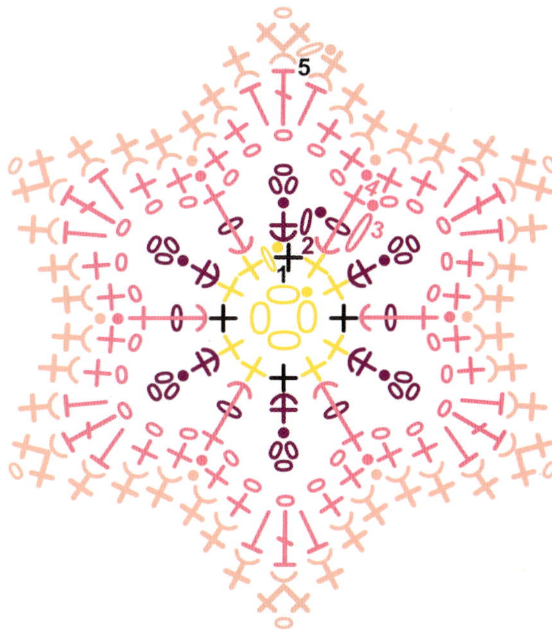

JOINING

Use the slip stitch method (see page 48).

79. PINCUSHION

NOTE

In the chart opposite, arrows show where to insert the hook when working behind the petals made in previous rounds. Make a note of which loop each st should be worked into: you should be working into the unworked blo (see page 43).

WRITTEN PATTERN

Using yarn A, make 2 ch.

Round 1: work 8 sc in second chain from hook. Join rnd with sl st to top of first ch (8 sc). Fasten off yarn.
Attach yarn B to flo of any st from round 1.

Round 2: 1 ch, * (1 sc, 1 hdc, 1 dc, 1 hdc, 1 sc) in flo of each st around. Join rnd with sl st to top of first ch (8 petals). Fasten off yarn.
Attach yarn C to unworked blo of any dc from round 1.

Round 3: 3 ch (counts as 1 dc here and throughout), 2 dcblo in same st, 3 dcblo in each st around, working behind petals from round 2. Join rnd with sl st to top of first ch (24 dc).

Round 4: 1 ch, 1 scflo in same st, (1 hdc, 2 dc) in flo of next st, (2 dc, 1 hdc) in flo of next st, * 1 scflo in next st, (1 hdc, 2 dc) in flo of next st, (2 dc, 1 hdc) in flo of next st; rep from * around. Join rnd with sl st to top of first ch (8 petals). Fasten off yarn.
Attach yarn D to unworked blo of any st from round 3.

Round 5: 3 ch, (2 dcblo, 3 ch, 3 dcblo) in same st, * 1 ch, miss next 2 sts from round 3, 3 hdcblo in next st from round 3, 1 ch, miss next 2 sts from round 3, ** (3 dcblo, 3 ch, 3 dcblo) in next st from round 3; rep from * around, ending last rep at **. Join rnd with sl st to top of first 3 ch (36 dc and 12 ch sps). Fasten off yarn.
Attach yarn E to any 3 ch corner sp from round 5.

Round 6: 3 ch, (2 dc, 3 ch, 3 dc) in same 3 ch corner sp, * 1 ch, (3 dc in next 1 ch sp, 1 ch) twice, ** (3 dc, 3 ch, 3 dc) in next 3 ch corner ch sp; rep from * around, ending last rep at **. Join rnd with sl st to top of first 3 ch (48 dc and 16 ch sps).
Fasten off yarn.

CHART PATTERN

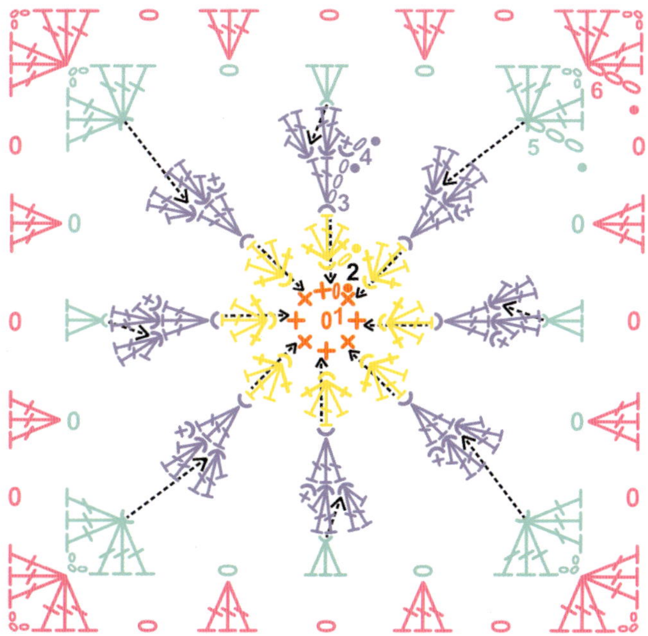

JOINING

Use the slip stitch method (see page 48) or join as you go (see pages 49–50).

80. DAISY

NOTE

In the chart opposite, arrows show where to insert the round 3 sts: work behind the round 2 petals into the unworked blo of the sts from round 1.

Make four of these small squares and join them together using the slip stitch method (see page 48) to achieve the size of the other motifs.

WRITTEN PATTERN

Using yarn A, make 4 ch, join with a sl st to form a ring.

Round 1: 1 ch (does not count as st), 8 sc in ring. Join rnd with sl st to top of first ch (8 sc).
Fasten off yarn.
Attach yarn B with a sl st to flo of any st from round 1.

Round 2: * 7 ch, sl st flo back into same st, sl st flo into next st; rep from * around (8 petals).
Fasten off yarn.
Attach yarn C with a sl st to unworked blo of any st from round 1, working behind petals from round 2.

Round 3: 2 ch (counts as 1 hdc), 2 hdcblo in same st, 3 ch, miss next st from round 1, * 3 hdcblo in blo of next st from round 1, 3 ch, miss next st from round 1; rep from * around. Join rnd with sl st to top of first 2 ch (12 hdc and 4 ch sps).

Round 4: sl st in each st to next 3 ch corner sp, 3 ch, (2 dc, 3 ch, 3 dc) in same ch sp, 1 ch, * (3 dc, 3 ch, 3 dc) in next 3 ch sp, 1 ch; rep from * around. Join rnd with sl st to top of first 3 ch (24 dc and 8 ch sps).
Fasten off yarn.

Make four of these small squares and join them together using the slip stitch method (page 48).

CHART PATTERN

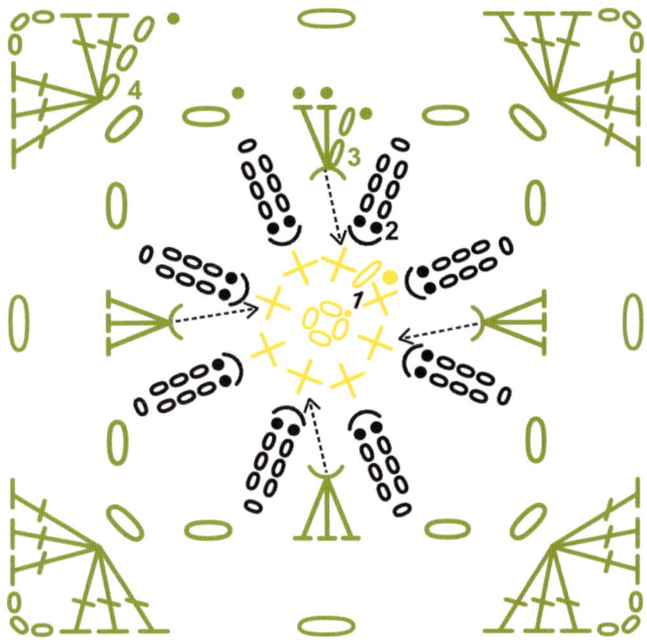

JOINING

Use the slip stitch method (see page 48).

81. ECHINACEA
(3D MOTIF)

SPECIAL STITCH

Sc2tog (see page 32).

NOTES

Petals are added to the unworked flo of round 3, working in front of round 4.

The four black sc stitches show where the flower should be attached to the background (see page 45).

WRITTEN PATTERN

Cone

NOTE: rounds 1–4 of Cone are worked in a spiral; do not join rounds but place marker to denote end of round.

Using yarn A, make 2 ch.

Round 1: work 6 sc in second chain from hook. Do not join round but place marker to work in a spiral (6 sc).

Round 2: 2 sc in each st around (12 sc).

Round 3: 1 sc in each st around (12 sc).

Round 4: (1 scblo, sc2togblo) around. Join rnd with sl st to top of first sc (8 scblo).
Fasten off yarn.

Petals

Join yarn B with a sl st to any unworked flo from round 3 of Cone, leaving round 4 unworked.

Round 5: * 8 ch, 1 sc in second ch from hook and each of next 6 ch (7 sc made), sl st back into flo of same st from round 3, sl st flo in next st from round 3 of Cone; rep from * around (12 petals).
Fasten off yarn.

Background

Attach yarn C to unworked blo of any indicated (black) stitch on round 4 of chart and work as for Solid Background Granny Square (page 47).

When working the first round of background, insert hook into marked stitches from round 4 of the Echinacea chart.

CHART PATTERN

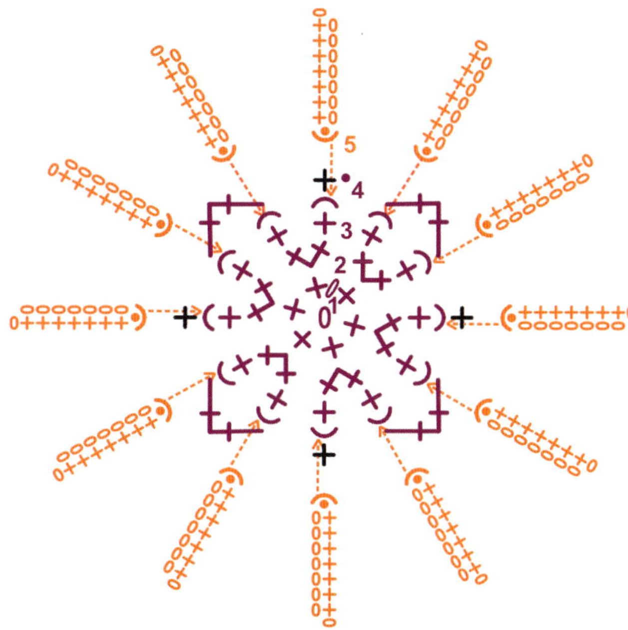

JOINING

Use the slip stitch method (see page 48).

82. CHRYSANTHEMUM
(3D MOTIF)

NOTE

The four black sc stitches indicate where the flower should be attached to the background granny square (see page 45).

Work 16 identical petals, as explained on page 44.

WRITTEN PATTERN

Using yarn A, make 4 ch, join with a sl st to form a ring.

Round 1: 1 ch (does not count as st here or throughout), 8 sc in ring. Join rnd with sl st to top of first ch (8 sc).

Round 2: 1 ch, 2 scflo in each st around. Join rnd with sl st to top of first ch (16 sc). Fasten off yarn.
Attach yarn B to any st from round 2.

Round 3: 2 ch (counts as 1 hdc here and throughout), 2 hdc in same st, 1 ch, (3 hdc, 1 ch) in each st around. Join rnd with sl st to top of first 2 ch (48 hdc and 16 ch sps).

Round 4: 2 ch, 1 hdc in same st, 2 hdc in each of next 2 sts, 1 ch, * 2 hdc in each of next 3 sts, 1 ch; rep from * around. Join rnd with sl st to top of first 2 ch (96 hdc and 16 ch sps).

Round 5: 2 ch, 1 hdc in same st, 2 hdc in each of next 5 sts, 1 ch, * 2 hdc in each of next 6 sts, 1 ch; rep from * around. Join rnd with sl st to top of first 2 ch (192 hdc and 16 ch sps).
Fasten off yarn.

Background

Attach yarn C to unworked blo of any indicated stitch on round 1 of chart and work as for Background Granny Square (page 46).

When working the first round of background, insert hook into marked stitches from round 1 of the Chrysanthemum chart.

CHART PATTERN

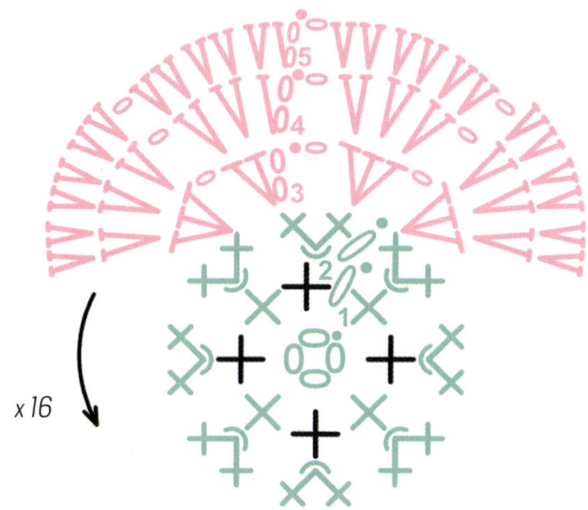

JOINING

Use the slip stitch method (see page 48) or join as you go (see pages 49–50).

83. HOLLYHOCK

SPECIAL STITCH

Split cluster (splcl) (see page 33).

WRITTEN PATTERN

Using yarn A, make 4 ch, join with a sl st to form a ring.

Round 1: 1 ch (does not count as st here or throughout), 12 sc in ring. Join rnd with sl st to top of first ch (12 sc). Fasten off yarn.
Attach yarn B to any st from round 1.

Round 2: 2 ch (does not count as st), * 1 splcl, 3 ch; rep from * five more times. Join rnd with sl st to top of first 2 ch (6 petals).
Fasten off yarn.
Attach yarn C to any ch sp from round 2.

Round 3: 1 ch, (1 sc, 1 hdc, 1 dc, 1 ch, 1 dc, 1 hdc, 1 sc, 1 ch) into each ch sp around. Join rnd with sl st to top of first ch (6 petals). Fasten off yarn.
Attach yarn D to any ch sp between petals from round 3.

Round 4: 1 ch, 1 sc in same ch sp, 4 ch, miss next ch sp, * 1 sc in next ch sp, 4 ch, miss next ch sp; rep from * around. Join rnd with sl st to top of first ch (6 sc and 6 ch sps).

Round 5: 3 ch (counts as 1 dc) 2 dc in same sc, 1 ch, 3 dc in next ch sp, 1 ch, * 3 dc in next sc, 1 ch, 3 dc in next ch sp, 1 ch; rep from * around. Join rnd with sl st to top of first 3 ch (36 dc and 12 ch sps). Fasten off yarn.
Attach yarn E to any ch sp from round 5.

Round 6: 2 ch (counts as hdc), 2 hdc in same ch sp, 1 ch, 3 hdc in next ch sp, 1 ch, (3 dc, 3 ch, 3 dc) in next sp, 1 ch, * (3 hdc in next ch sp, 1 ch) twice, (3 dc, 3 ch, 3 dc) in next ch sp, 1 ch; rep from * around. Join rnd with sl st to top of first 2 ch (48 sts and 16 ch sps).
Fasten off yarn.

CHART PATTERN

JOINING

Use the slip stitch method (see page 48) or join as you go (see pages 49–50).

84. APPLE BLOSSOM
(3D MOTIF)

SPECIAL STITCH

Picot (see page 33).

NOTES

The four black sc stitches show where the flower attaches to the background (see page 45).

Work five petals in the same way, as shown in the chart, opposite. Some are faded to show how they overlap.

WRITTEN PATTERN

Using yarn A, make 2 ch.

Round 1: work 8 sc in second chain from hook. Join rnd with sl st to top of first ch (8 sc).

Round 2: 1 ch, * 1 scflo, 1 sc in next st, 2 scflo in next st, 1 sc in next st, rep from * once more. Join rnd with sl st to top of first ch (10 scflo). Fasten off yarn.
Attach yarn B to any st from round 2.

Round 3: (3 ch, 1 dc, 3 tr, picot) in first st, (3 tr, 1 dc, 3 ch, sl st) in next st, * (sl st, 3 ch, 1 dc, 3 tr, picot) in next st, (3 tr, 1 dc, 3 ch, sl st) in next st; rep from * around (5 petals made). Fasten off yarn.

Background

Attach yarn C to unworked blo of any indicated (black) stitch on round 1 of chart and work as for Background Granny Square (page 46).

When working the first round of background, insert hook into marked stitches from round 1 of the Apple Blossom chart.

CHART PATTERN

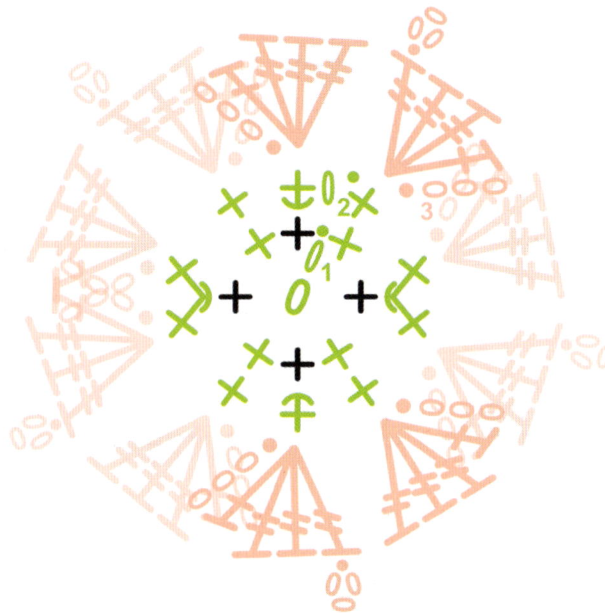

JOINING

Use the slip stitch method (see page 48) or join as you go (see pages 49–50).

85. BUTTERCUP

SPECIAL STITCH

Popcorn (pop) (see page 32).

NOTE

Make four of these small squares and join them together using the slip stitch method (see page 48) to achieve the size of the other motifs.

WRITTEN PATTERN

Using yarn A, make 4 ch, join with a sl st to form a ring.

Round 1: 1 ch (does not count as st), 8 sc in ring. Join rnd with sl st to top of first ch (8 sc).
Fasten off yarn.
Attach yarn B with a sl st to any st from round 1.
Note: 3 ch at beg of next round counts as first dc of pop.

Round 2: 3 ch (counts as 1 dc here and throughout), (pop, 2 ch) in each st around. Join rnd with sl st to top of first 3 ch (8 popcorns and 8 ch sps).
Fasten off yarn.
Attach yarn C with a sl st to any ch sp from round 2.

Round 3: 3 ch, (2 dc, 3 ch, 3 dc) in same ch sp, 1 ch, miss next ch sp, * (3 dc, 3 ch, 3 dc) in next ch sp, 1 ch; rep from * around. Join rnd with sl st to top of first 3 ch.
Fasten off yarn.

Make four of these small squares and join them together using the slip stitch method (page 48).

CHART PATTERN

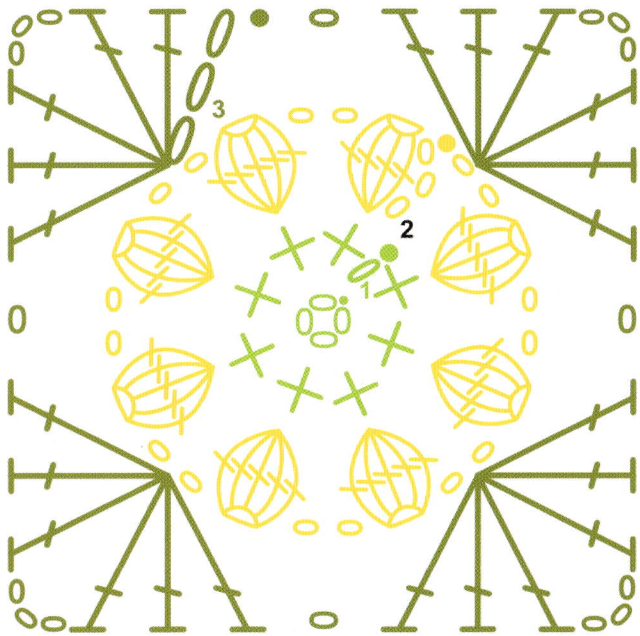

JOINING

Use the slip stitch method (see page 48).

86. DAFFODIL
(3D MOTIF)

SPECIAL STITCH

Picot (see page 33).

NOTES

The four black sc stitches indicate where the flower attaches to the background (see page 45). Work six petals into unworked blo of round 2 sts, behind the trumpet (see page 44).

WRITTEN PATTERN

Trumpet

Using yarn A, make 4 ch, join with a sl st to form a ring.

Round 1: 1 ch (does not count as st here or throughout), 8 sc in ring. Join rnd with sl st to top of first ch (8 sc).

Round 2: 1 ch, (1 scflo in next st, 2 scflo in next st) around. Join rnd with sl st to top of first ch (12 sc).

Round 3: 3 ch (counts as 1 dc), 1 dcflo in each st around. Join rnd with sl st to top of first 3 ch (12 dcflo).

Round 4: 1 ch, (1 sc, picot) in each st around.
Join rnd with sl st to top of first ch (12 sc and 12 picot).
Fasten off yarn.

Petals

Join yarn B with a sl st to any unworked blo from round 2 of Trumpet.

Round 5: * 6 ch, 1 sc in second ch from hook and each of next 4 ch (5 sc made), sl st back into blo of same st from round 2, sl st blo in each of next 2 sts from round 2 of Trumpet; rep from * around (6 petal spikes).

Round 6: 1 ch, * up side of next petal spike into the unworked bottom loops of spike, work 1 sc, 1 hdc, 1 dc, 1 hdc, then in fifth st work (1 hdc, 1 dc, 1 ch), now working down the other side of spike, into the sc sts, work (1 dc, 1 hdc) in first sc, then 1 hdc, 1 dc, 1 hdc and finally 1 sc, work 1 sc into next sl st; rep from * around. Join rnd with sl st to top of first ch (6 petals).
Fasten off yarn.

Background

Attach yarn C to unworked blo of any indicated (black) stitch on round 1 of chart and work as for Background Granny Square (page 46).

When working the first round of background, insert hook into marked stitches from round 1 of the Daffodil chart.

CHART PATTERN

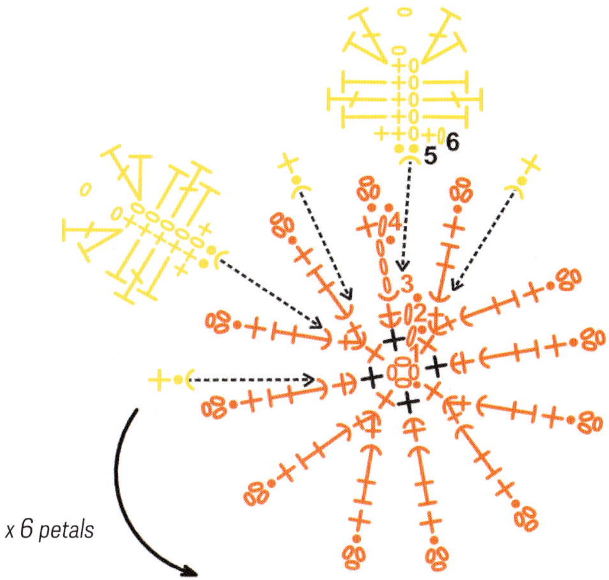

JOINING

Use the slip stitch method (see page 48) or join as you go (see pages 49–50).

87. COSMOS

SPECIAL STITCH

Spiked double crochet stitch (spdc) (see page 33).

NOTE

Stitches in round 4 are worked in front of round 3, working all stitches into unworked stitches from round 2. Stitches in round 5 are worked into stitches from round 3, working over the ch sps from round 4 and enclosing them. Stitches in round 6 are worked into stitches from round 4, working over the ch sps from round 5, enclosing them.

WRITTEN PATTERN

Using yarn A, make 4 ch, join with a sl st to form a ring

Round 1: 1 ch (does not count as st here or throughout), 8 sc in ring. Join rnd with sl st to top of first ch (8 sc). Fasten off yarn.
Attach yarn B to any st from round 1.

Round 2: 1 ch, 2 sc in each st around. Join rnd with sl st to top of first ch (16 sc). Fasten off yarn.
Attach yarn C to any st from round 2.

Round 3: 3 ch (counts as 1 dc), 2 dc in same st, 1 ch, miss next st, * 3 dc in next st, 1 ch, miss next st; rep from * around. Join rnd with sl st to top of first 3 ch (24 dc and 8 ch sps). Fasten off yarn.
Attach yarn B to any ch sp from round 3 and work all sts in round 4 in front of the ch sps from round 3.

Round 4: 1 ch (does not count as st), 1 spdc in missed st from round 2, 3 ch, * miss next 3 sts from round 3, 1 spdc in next missed st from round 2, 3 ch; rep from * around. Join rnd with sl st to top of first ch (8 spdc and 8 ch sps). Fasten off yarn.
Attach yarn C in first dc from any 3 dc group from round 3; when making sts, work over the ch sps made in round 4.

Round 5: 1 ch, (1 sc, 1 hdc) in same st, 3 dc in next dc from round 3, (1 hdc, 1 sc) in next dc from round 3, 1 ch, miss next spdc from round 4, * across next 3 dc from round 3 work (1 sc, 1 hdc) in next dc, 3 dc in next dc, (1 hdc, 1 sc) in next dc, 1 ch, miss next spdc from round 4; rep from * around. Join rnd with sl st to top of first ch (8 petals). Fasten off yarn.
Attach yarn B in any spdc from round 4, and work round 6 over any ch sps from round 5.

CHART PATTERN

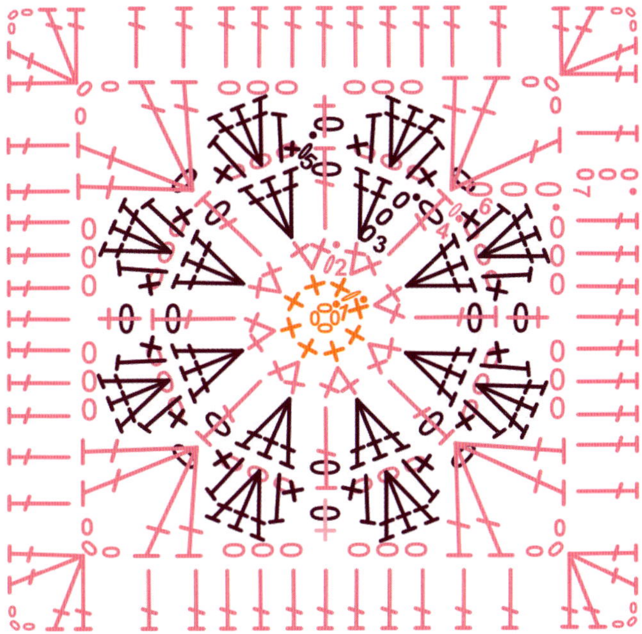

Round 6: 3 ch, (1 dc, 3 ch, 2 dc) in same st, * working behind petal made on round 5, make 3 ch, 1 sc in next spdc from round 4, enclosing the chain from round 5, 3 ch, ** (2 dc, 3 ch, 2 dc) in next spdc from round 4; rep from * around, ending last rep at **.
Join rnd with sl st to top of first 3 ch (8 petals).

Round 7: 3 ch, 1 dc in next st, * (2 dc, 3 ch, 2 dc) in next 3 ch corner sp, 2 dc, 3 dc in next 3 ch sp, 1 dc in next st, 3 dc in next 3 ch sp, ** 2 dc; rep from * around, ending last rep at **.
Join rnd with sl st to top of first 3 ch (60 dc and 4 ch sps).
Fasten off yarn.

JOINING

Use the slip stitch method (see page 48).

88. SCARLET PIMPERNEL

NOTE

In the chart opposite, arrows in round 4 show where to insert the hook when working behind the petals made in previous rounds. Make a note of which loop each st should be worked into: you should be working into the unworked blo (see page 43).

WRITTEN PATTERN

Using yarn A, make 4 ch.

Round 1: work 11 dc in fourth chain from hook (missed 3 ch counts as 1 dc). Join rnd with sl st to top of first 3 ch (12 dc).
Fasten off yarn.
Attach yarn B with a sl st to any st from round 1.

Round 2: 3 ch (counts as 1 dc), 2 dc in same st, 3 dc in next st, 2 dc in next st, * 3 dc in each of next 2 sts, 2 dc in next st; rep from * around. Join rnd with sl st to top of first 3 ch (32 dc).
Fasten off yarn.
Attach yarn C with a sl st to any central dc in a 3 dc group from round 2.

Round 3: 1 ch (does not count as st), 1 sc in same st, miss next st, 5 dc in next st, miss next st, * 1 sc in next st, miss next st, 5 dc in next st, miss next st; rep from * around. Join rnd with sl st to top of first ch (8 petals).
Fasten off yarn.
Attach yarn D with a sl st to any sc from round 3.
Note: next round is worked in blo.

Round 4: 2 ch (counts as 1 hdc), (1 hdcblo, 3 ch, 2 hdcblo) in same st, * 1 hdcblo in next st, 3 scblo, 3 hdcblo, 3 scblo, 1 hdcblo, ** (2 hdc, 3 ch, 2 hdc) in blo of next st; rep from * around, ending last rep at **. Join rnd with sl st to top of first 2 ch.
Fasten off yarn.

CHART PATTERN

JOINING

Use the slip stitch method (see page 48).

89. TEA ROSE

SPECIAL STITCH

3 dc cluster (cl3) (see page 32).

NOTE

Arrows show where to insert the round 4 sts: work into the ch sps from round 2 (see page 43).

WRITTEN PATTERN

Using yarn A, make 4 ch, join with a sl st to form a ring.

Round 1: 1 ch (does not count as st here or throughout), 8 sc in ring. Join rnd with sl st to top of first ch (8 sc).
Fasten off yarn.
Attach yarn B with a sl st to any st from round 1.

Round 2: 1 ch, 1 sc in same st, 4 ch, (1 sc in next st, 4 ch) around. Join rnd with sl st to top of first ch (8 sc and 8 ch sps).

Round 3: 1 ch, *(1 sc, 1 hdc, 7 dc, 1 hdc, 1 sc, 1 ch) in next ch sp, miss next ch sp; rep from * around. Join rnd with sl st to top of first ch (4 petals and 4 ch sps).
Fasten off yarn.
Working behind petals from round 3, reattach yarn B with a sl st to any unworked ch sp from round 2.

Round 4: 1 ch, * (1 sc, 1 hdc, 7 dc, 1 hdc, 1 sc, 3 ch) in next missed ch sp, ** miss next petal from round 3; rep from * around, ending last rep at **. Join rnd with sl st in first ch sp (4 petals and 4 ch sps).
Fasten off yarn.
Working behind petals from round 4, reattach yarn B with a sl st to any ch sp from round 4.

Round 5: 3 ch (counts as 1 dc here and throughout), (4 dc, 1 ch, 5 dc) in same ch sp, 2 ch, * (5 dc, 1 ch, 5 dc) in next 3 ch sp, 2 ch; rep from * around. Join rnd with sl st to top of first ch.
Fasten off yarn.
Attach yarn C with a sl st to any 2 ch sp from round 5.

Round 6: 3 ch, 2 dc in same 2 ch sp, (2 ch, cl3) three times all in next 1 ch sp, 2 ch, * 3 dc in next 2 ch sp, (2 ch, cl3) three times all in next 1 ch sp, 2 ch; rep from * around. Join rnd with sl st to top of first 3 ch. Fasten off yarn.
Attach yarn D with a sl st to any 2 ch sp after 3 dc group from round 6.

CHART PATTERN

Round 7: 3 ch, 2 dc in same ch sp, 1 ch, miss next cl (3 dc, 3 ch, 3 dc) in central cl at corner, 1 ch, miss next cl, * (3 dc in next 2 ch sp, 1 ch) twice, miss next cl (3 dc, 3 ch, 3 dc) in central cl at next corner, 1 ch, miss next cl; rep from * to end of last corner, 3 dc in next 2 ch sp, 1 ch. Join rnd with sl st to top of first 3 ch (48 dc and 16 ch sps).
Fasten off yarn.

JOINING

Use the slip stitch method (see page 48) or join as you go (see pages 49–50).

90. SAXIFRAGE

SPECIAL STITCH

Large puff (see page 32).

NOTE

Make four of these small squares and join them together using the slip stitch method (see page 48) to achieve the size of the other motifs.

WRITTEN PATTERN

Using yarn A, make 3 ch.

Round 1: work 11 hdc in fourth chain from hook (missed 2 ch counts as 1 hdc). Join rnd with sl st to top of first ch (12 hdc).
Fasten off yarn.
Attach yarn B with a sl st to any st from round 1.

Round 2: 1 ch (does not count as st here or throughout), 1 sc in same st, 2 ch, 1 large puff in next st, 2 ch, * 1 sc in next st, 2 ch, 1 large puff in next st, 2 ch; rep from * around. Join rnd with sl st to top of first ch (6 large puffs and 6 sc).
Fasten off yarn.
Attach yarn C with a sl st to any large puff from round 2.

Round 3: 1 ch, 1 sc in same st, * (2 dc, 3 ch, 1 dc) in next sc, 1 sc in next large puff, 1 hdc in next sc, 1 sc in next large puff, (1 dc, 3 ch, 2 dc) in next sc, ** 1 sc in next large puff; rep from * once more, ending last rep at **. Join rnd with sl st to top of first ch.
Fasten off yarn.

Make four of these small squares and join them together using the slip stitch method (page 48).

CHART PATTERN

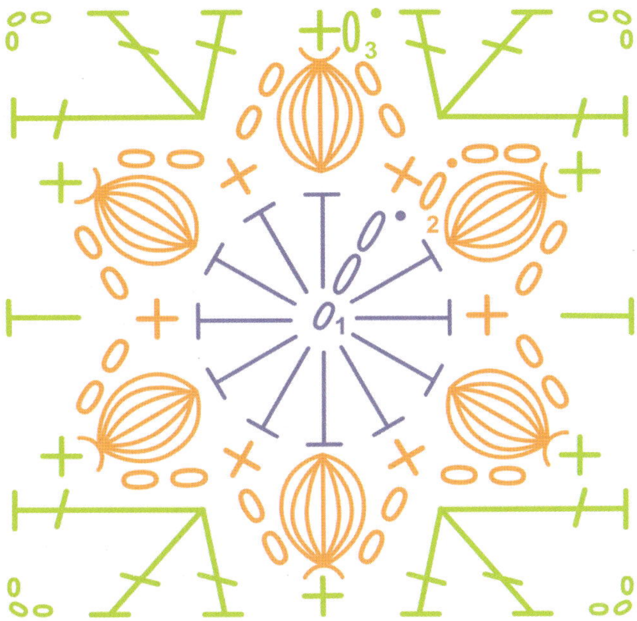

JOINING

Use the slip stitch method (see page 48).

91. STRAWBERRY LEAF
(3D MOTIF)

SPECIAL STITCH

Picot (see page 33).

NOTE

Work rounds 1–3 as a spiral: don't join rounds – place marker to denote end of round.

The four black sc stitches indicate where the leaf attaches to the background (see page 45).

WRITTEN PATTERN

Using yarn A, make 4 ch, join with a sl st to form a ring.

Round 1: 1 ch (does not count as st here or throughout), 8 sc in ring; do not join round but place marker to work in a spiral (8 sc).

Round 2: (2 scflo in next st) around (16 sc).

Round 3: 9 sc, (2 hdc in next st, 1 hdc in next st) three times, 2 hdc in next st. Join rnd with sl st to top of first st (20 sts).

Round 4: 2 ch (counts as 1 hdc), 1 hdc in same st, 7 sc, (2 hdc in next st, 1 hdc in next st) twice, 2 dc in each of next 2 sts, (1 tr, 2 ch, 1 tr) in next st, 2 dc in each of next 2 sts, 1 hdc, 2 hdc in next st, 1 hdc. Join rnd with sl st to top of first 2 ch (29 sts and 1 ch sp). Fasten off yarn A. Attach yarn B to 2 ch sp from round 4.

Round 5: 1 ch, (1 sc, picot) in 2 ch sp, (1 scblo in each of next 2 sts, picot) seven times, 1 scblo in next st, (1 scblo, picot) in next st, 5 ch, 1 sc in second ch from hook and each of next 3 ch, sl st back in scblo (1 scblo in next st, picot, 1 scblo in next st) to end of round.
Join rnd with sl st to top of first ch. Fasten off yarn.

Background

Attach yarn C to unworked blo of any indicated stitch on round 1 of chart and work as for Background Granny Square (page 46).

When working the first round of background, insert hook into marked stitches from round 1 of the Strawberry Leaf chart.

CHART PATTERN

JOINING

Use the slip stitch method (see page 48) or join as you go (see pages 49–50).

92. AZALEA

SPECIAL STITCHES

Popcorn (pop), spiked treble crochet (sptr) (see pages 32 and 33).

NOTE

Work the sptr in round 4 over the sc from round 3 and down into the ch sp from round 2.

WRITTEN PATTERN

Using yarn A, make 4 ch, join with a sl st to form a ring. Note 3 ch at beg of next round counts as first dc of pop.

Round 1: 3 ch (counts as 1 dc here and throughout), (1 pop, 2 ch) eight times into the ring. Join rnd with sl st to top of first 3 ch (8 pop and 8 ch sps).
Fasten off yarn.
Attach yarn B with a sl st to any ch sp from round 1.

Round 2: 3 ch, (2 dc, 3 ch, 3 dc) in ch same sp, 1 ch, miss next ch sp, * (3 dc, 3 ch, 3 dc) in next ch sp, 1 ch, miss next ch sp; rep from * around. Join rnd with sl st to top of first ch (24 dc and 8 ch sps).

Round 3: 1 ch, * (2 dc, 3 tr, 3 ch, 3 tr, 2 dc) all in next 3 ch sp, 1 sc in next 1 ch sp; rep from * around. Join rnd with sl st to top of first ch. Fasten off yarn.
Attach yarn C with a sl st to any 3 ch sp from round 3.

Round 4: 2 ch (counts as 1 hdc), (1 hdc, 3 ch, 2 hdc) in same ch sp, * 1 hdc in each of next 2 sts, 1 dc in each of next 3 sts, 1 sptr down into 1 ch sp from round 2, 1 dc in each of next 3 sts, 1 hdc in each of next 2 sts, **(2 hdc, 3 ch, 2 hdc) in next 3 ch sp; rep from * around, ending last rep at **. Join rnd with sl st to top of first 2 ch (60 sts and 4 ch sps). Fasten off yarn.

CHART PATTERN

JOINING

Use the slip stitch method (see page 48).

93. ASTRANTIA

NOTE

Each petal in round 2 is worked back along a length of 5 chain, sidewards, then slip stitched into place where indicated in round 1.
Each sc in round 3 is then inserted into the row end of each petal.

WRITTEN PATTERN

Using yarn A, make 4 ch.

Round 1: work 15 dc in fourth chain from hook (missed 3 ch counts as 1 dc). Join rnd with sl st to top of first 4 ch (16 dc).
Fasten off yarn.
Attach yarn B with a sl st to any st from round 1.

Round 2: * 5 ch, 1 sc in second ch from hook, 1 hdc in next ch, 1 dc in each of 2 rem ch, miss next dc from round 1, sl st in next dc; rep from * around (8 petals).
Fasten off yarn.
Attach yarn C with a sl st to tip of any petal around.

Round 3: 1 ch (does not count as st), 1 sc in same st, 6 ch, * 1 sc in point of next petal, 6 ch; rep from * around. Join rnd with sl st to top of first ch (8 sc and 8 ch sps).

Round 4: 3 ch (counts as 1 dc), * 5 dc in next ch sp, 1 dc in next sc, (4 dc, 3 ch, 4 dc) in next ch sp, ** 1 dc in next sc; rep from * around, ending last rep at **. Join rnd with sl st to top of first 3 ch.
Fasten off yarn.

CHART PATTERN

JOINING

Use the slip stitch method (see page 48).

94. URSINIA

SPECIAL STITCHES

3 dc cluster (cl3), spiked double crochet (spdc) (see pages 32 and 33).

NOTE

Work the spdc in round 5 over the ch sp from round 4 and down into the unworked sts from round 3.

WRITTEN PATTERN

Using yarn A, make 4 ch, join with a sl st to form a ring.

Round 1: 1 ch (does not count as st), 8 sc in ring.
Join rnd with sl st to top of first ch (8 sc).
Fasten off yarn.
Attach yarn B with a sl st to any st from round 1.

Round 2: 3 ch (counts as 1 dc here and throughout), 1 dc in same st, 2 ch, * (2 dc, 2 ch) in each st around.
Join rnd with sl st to top of first 3 ch (16 dc and 8 ch sps).
Fasten off yarn.
Attach yarn C with a sl st to any ch sp from round 2.

Round 3: 3 ch, 1 dc in same ch sp, 2 ch, (cl3, 3 ch, cl3) in next ch sp, 2 ch, * 2 dc in next ch sp, 2 ch, (cl3, 3 ch, cl3) in next ch sp, 2 ch; rep from * around. Join rnd with sl st to top of first 3 ch. Fasten off yarn.
Attach yarn D with a sl st to any corner 3 ch sp from round 3.

Round 4: 3 ch, (2 dc, 3 ch, 3 dc) in same ch sp, * 1 ch, 2 sc in next ch sp, 1 ch, 2 sc in next ch sp, 1 ch, ** (3 dc, 3 ch, 3 dc) in next 3 ch sp; rep from * around, ending last rep at **. Join rnd with sl st to top of first 3 ch.
Fasten off yarn.
Attach yarn E with a sl st to any corner 3 ch sp from round 4.

Round 5: 2 ch (counts as 1 hdc), (1 hdc, 3 ch, 2 hdc) in same ch sp, 1 ch, * 2 hdc in next ch sp, 1 ch, 1 spdc down into next dc from round 3, 1 dc in next ch sp, 1 spdc down into next dc from round 3, 1 ch, 2 hdc in next ch sp, 1 ch, ** (2 hdc, 3 ch, 2 hdc) in next 3 ch sp, 1 ch; rep from * around, ending last rep at **. Join rnd with sl st to top of first 2 ch.
Fasten off yarn.

CHART PATTERN

JOINING

Use the slip stitch method (see page 48) or join as you go (see pages 49–50).

95. CLOVER
(3D MOTIF)

SPECIAL STITCH

Picot (see page 33).

NOTE

The four black sc stitches indicate where the leaf should be attached to the background granny square (see page 45).

WRITTEN PATTERN

Using yarn A, make 4 ch, join with a sl st to form a ring.

Round 1: 1 ch, (2 sc, picot) four times into the ring. Join rnd with sl st to top of first ch (8 sc and 4 picot). Fasten off yarn. Attach yarn B to any sc without a picot from round 1.

Round 2: 1 ch, 1 scflo in same st, 5 ch, miss next picot, (1 scflo in next sc, 5 ch, miss next picot) around. Join rnd with sl st to top of first st (4 sc and 4 ch sps).

Round 3: 1 ch, *(1 sc, 1 hdc, 5 dc, 1 hdc, 1 sc) in next ch sp, sl st in next sc; rep from * three times more, 5 ch, 1 sc in second ch from hook and in each of next 3 ch. Join rnd with sl st to top of first ch (4 petals and one stem).
Fasten off yarn.

Background

Attach yarn C to unworked blo of any indicated stitch on round 1 of chart and work as for Background Solid Granny Square (page 47).

When working the first round of background, insert hook into marked stitches from round 1 of the Clover chart.

CHART PATTERN

JOINING

Use the slip stitch method (see page 48).

96. BEGONIA

SPECIAL STITCHES

Split cluster (splcl), 3 dc cluster (cl3) (see pages 32 and 33).

WRITTEN PATTERN

Using yarn A, make 4 ch.

Round 1: work 15 dc in fourth chain from hook (missed 3 ch counts as 1 dc). Join rnd with sl st to top of first 4 ch (16 dc).
Fasten off yarn.
Attach yarn B with a sl st to any st from round 1.

Round 2: 2 ch, yrh, insert in same st from round 1, draw loop through, yrh and pull through 2 loops, (yrh, insert into st, draw up a loop, yrh, pull through 2 loops) twice in next st, yrh and pull through all 4 loops on hook, 3 ch, (splcl, 3 ch) around. Join rnd with sl st to top of first 2 ch (8 splcl and 8 ch sps). Fasten off yarn. Attach yarn C with a sl st to any ch sp from round 2.

Round 3: 1 ch, 1 sc in same ch sp, * 5 ch, cl3 in next ch sp, (2 ch, cl3) twice more in same ch sp, 5 ch, ** 1 sc in next ch sp; rep from * around, ending last rep at **. Join rnd with sl st to top of first ch. Fasten off yarn.
Attach yarn D with a sl st to any 5 ch sp straight after a full cl3 group from round 3.

Round 4: 3 ch (counts as 1 dc), 2 dc in same ch sp, 1 ch, 3 dc in next 5 ch sp, 1 ch, 3 dc in next 2 ch sp, 3 ch, 3 dc in next 2 ch sp, 1 ch, * (3 dc in next 5 ch sp, 1 ch) twice, 3 dc in next 2 ch sp, 3 ch, 3 dc in next 2 ch sp, 1 ch; rep from * around. Join rnd with sl st to top of first 3 ch.
Fasten off yarn.

CHART PATTERN

JOINING

Use the slip stitch method (see page 48) or join as you go (see pages 49–50).

97. RANUNCULUS

SPECIAL STITCH

Puff2 (see page 32).

WRITTEN PATTERN

Using yarn A, make 4 ch.

Round 1: work 11 dc in fourth chain from hook (missed 3 ch counts as 1 dc). Join rnd with sl st to top of first 4 ch (12 dc). Fasten off yarn.

Attach yarn B with a sl st to any st from round 1.

Round 2: 2 ch (does not count as st here or throughout), 1 puff2 in same st, 2 ch, (1 puff2 in next st, 2 ch) around. Join rnd with sl st to top of first 2 ch (12 puffs and 12 ch sps). Fasten off yarn.

Attach yarn C with a sl st to any ch sp from round 2.

Round 3: 2 ch, (1 puff2, 1 ch) twice in same sp, (1 puff2, 1 ch) twice in each sp around. Join rnd with sl st to top of first 2 ch. Fasten off yarn.

Attach yarn D with a sl st to any ch sp from round 3.

Round 4: 2 ch, (1 puff2, 2 ch) twice in same sp, 1 puff2 into same sp, 1 hdc in each of next 5 ch sp, * (1 puff2, 2 ch) twice in next ch sp, 1 puff2 into same ch sp, 1 hdc in each of next 5 ch sp; rep from * around. Join rnd with sl st to top of first 2 ch. Fasten off yarn.

Attach yarn E with a sl st to central puff2 at any corner from round 4.

Round 5: 3 ch (counts as 1 dc), (2 dc, 3 ch, 3 dc) in same st, 1 dc in each sp and st across to central puff2 in next corner, * (3 dc, 3 ch, 3 dc) in central puff2, 1 dc in each sp and st across to central puff2 in next corner; rep from * around. Join rnd with sl st to top of first 3 ch (60 dc and 4 ch sps).

Fasten off yarn.

CHART PATTERN

JOINING

Use the slip stitch method (see page 48).

98. ZINNIA

SPECIAL STITCH

Spiked single crochet (spsc) (see page 33).

NOTE

Work the spsc in round 3 over the ch sp from round 2 and down into the next unworked stitch from round 1. In the chart opposite, arrows show where to insert round 5 stitches: work behind the round 4 petals into the stitches from round 3.

WRITTEN PATTERN

Using yarn A, make 4 ch, join with a sl st to form a ring.

Round 1: 1 ch (does not count as st here or throughout), 16 sc in ring. Join rnd with sl st to top of first ch (16 sc). Fasten off yarn.
Attach yarn B with a sl st to any st from round 1.

Round 2: 3 ch (counts as 1 dc here and throughout), 1 dc in same st, 1 ch, miss next st, * (2 dc, 1 ch) in next st, miss next st; rep from * around. Join rnd with sl st to top of first 3 ch (16 dc and 8 ch sps). Fasten off yarn.
Attach yarn C with a sl st to any ch sp from round 2.

Round 3: 1 ch, * 1 spsc back down into next missed st from round 1, directly below ch sp from round 2, 3 ch; rep from * around. Join rnd with sl st to top of first ch. Fasten off yarn.
Attach yarn D with a sl st to any ch sp from round 3.

Round 4: 1 ch, (1 sc, 1 hdc, 1 dc, 1 hdc, 1 sc, 1 ch) in each ch sp around. Join rnd with sl st to top of first ch.
Fasten off yarn.
Attach yarn E with a sl st to any unworked spsc from rnd 3.

Round 5: 1 ch, 1 sc in same st, 3 ch,* 1 sc in next spsc from round 3, 3 ch; rep from * around. Join rnd with sl st to top of first ch.

Round 6: sl st to next ch sp, 2 ch (counts as 1 hdc), 2 hdc in same ch sp, 1 ch, * (3 dc, 3 ch, 3 dc) in next ch sp, 1 ch, ** 3 hdc in next ch sp, 1 ch; rep from * around, ending last rep at **. Join rnd with sl st to top of first 3 ch.
Fasten off yarn.
Attach yarn F with a sl st to any corner 3 ch sp from round 6.

Round 7: 3 ch, (2 dc, 3 ch, 3 dc) in same corner 3 ch sp, 1 ch, * (3 dc in next 1 ch sp, 1 ch) twice, ** (3 dc, 3 ch, 3 dc) in next corner 3 ch sp; rep from * around, ending last rep at **. Join rnd with sl st to top of first 3 ch (48 dc and 16 ch sps).
Fasten off yarn.

CHART PATTERN

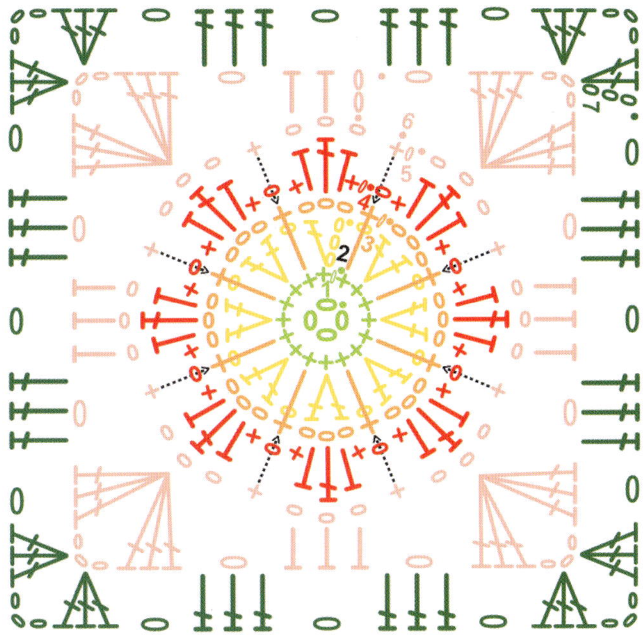

JOINING

Use the slip stitch method (see page 48) or join as you go (see pages 49–50).

99. CORNFLOWER
(3D MOTIF)

SPECIAL STITCH

Picot (see page 33).

NOTES

Rep round 3 petals eight times, inserting the hook as shown, working behind round 2 stamens, causing the round 2 stitches to become more 3D.

The four black sc stitches show where the flower attaches to the background (see page 45).

WRITTEN PATTERN

Using yarn A, make 4 ch, join with a sl st to form a ring.

Round 1: 1 ch (does not count as st here or throughout), 8 sc in ring. Join rnd with sl st to top of first ch (8 sc). Fasten off yarn.
Attach yarn B to flo of any st from round 1.

Round 2: 1 ch, 1 scflo in same st, 4 ch, 1 sc in second ch from hook, sl st in each of next 2 ch, 1 scflo back into original st from round 1, * 1 scflo in next st, 4 ch, 1 sc in second ch from hook, sl st in each of next 2 ch, 1 scflo back into original st from round 1; rep from * in flo of each st around. Join rnd with sl st to top of first ch (8 stamens). Fasten off yarn.
Attach yarn C to second scflo of any stamen from round 2.

Round 3: 1 ch, 1 sc in same st, 6 ch, [(1 dc, picot) three times, 3 ch, 1 sc] into fourth ch from hook, 1 sc in each of next 2 ch, 1 sc back into original st from round 2, 1 ch, * 1 sc in next st, 6 ch, [(1 dc, picot) three times, 3 ch, 1 sc] into fourth ch from hook, 1 sc in each of next 2 ch, 1 sc back into original st from round 2, 1 ch; rep from * around. Join rnd with sl st to top of first ch (8 petals). Fasten off yarn.

Background

Attach yarn D to unworked blo of any indicated (black) stitch on round 1 of chart and work as for Solid Background Granny Square (page 47).

When working the first round of background, insert hook into marked stitches from round 1 of the Cornflower chart.

CHART PATTERN

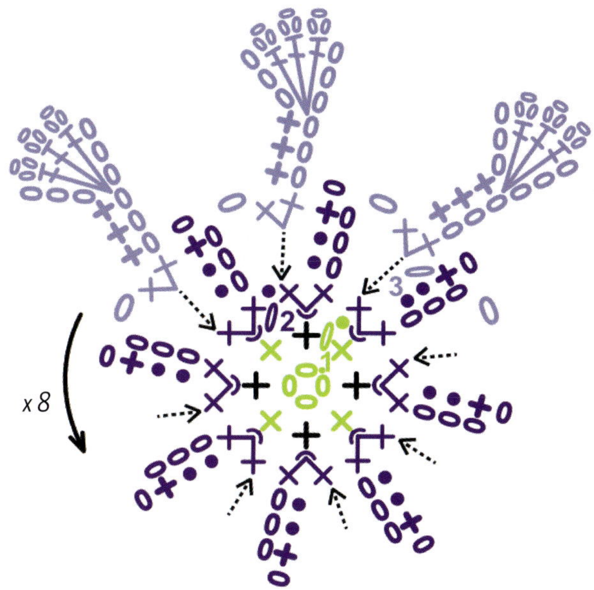

JOINING

Use the slip stitch method (see page 48).

100. IRISH ROSE
(3D MOTIF)

SPECIAL STITCHES

Raised single crochet back (RscB) and picot (see page 33).

NOTES

The four black sc stitches indicate where the flower should be attached to the background (see page 45). Work six identical petals, as indicated (see page 44).

WRITTEN PATTERN

Using yarn A, make 4 ch, join with a sl st to form a ring.

Round 1: 1 ch (does not count as st here or throughout), 12 sc in ring. Join rnd with sl st to top of first ch (12 sc).

Round 2: 1 ch, 1 scflo in same st, (3 ch, miss next st, * 1 scflo in next st, 3 ch, miss next st) around, ending last rep at *. Join rnd with sl st to top of first ch (6 ch sps and 6 scflo).

Round 3: sl st in next scflo, * (1 sc, 1 hdc, 3 dc, 1 hdc, 1 sc) in next ch sp, sl st in next scflo; rep from * around (6 petals). Fasten off yarn.
Attach yarn B with a sl st around post of any scflo from round 2.

Round 4: 1 ch, 1 RscB around same st, (4 ch, 1 RscB around next scflo from round 2) around. Join rnd with sl st to top of first ch (6 ch sps and 6 RscB).

Round 5: 1 ch, * (1 sc, 2 hdc, 5 dc, 2 hdc, 1 sc) in next ch sp, sl st in RscB; rep from * around (6 petals). Fasten off yarn.
Attach yarn C with a sl st around post of any RscB from round 4.

Round 6: 1 ch, 1 RscB around same st, (5 ch, * 1 RscB around next sc from round 4) around, ending last rep at *. Join rnd with sl st to top of first ch (6 ch sps and 6 RscB).

Round 7: 1 ch, * (1 sc, 2 hdc, 4 dc, 1 picot, 3 dc, 2 hdc, 1 sc) in next ch sp, sl st in RscB; rep from * around (6 petals). Fasten off yarn.

Background

Attach yarn D to unworked blo of any indicated (black) stitch on round 1 of chart and work as for Background Granny Square (page 46).

When working the first round of background, insert hook into marked stitches from round 1 of the Irish Rose chart, working blo.

CHART PATTERN

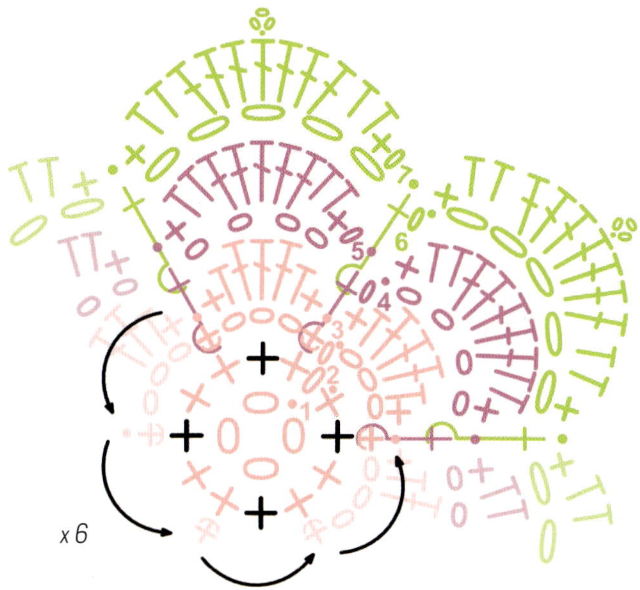

JOINING

Use the slip stitch method (see page 48) or join as you go (see pages 49–50).

THE PROJECTS

COLOR CONSTRUCTION

When it comes to choosing your color palette, go with your instinct and pick colors that you like and that you know you will be able to live with. Having said this, all your favorite hues might not look great together, and even one wrong color choice can make a piece feel discordant. It's a good idea to give your palette some thought before you begin, rather than when the project is complete!

FINDING INSPIRATION

You don't need to know about color theory to make these decisions. Use the following as inspiration: nature, your existing interior decor, a print or wallpaper, or even an existing blanket that you have admired from a book or social media. Helpfully, there are also apps and websites that can make color palettes out of the colors you see around you, which can be useful.

MAKING A YARN PALETTE

It is worth noting that the shades you see online can look very different in real life. The best way to create your palette is to actually place different yarns side by side to see how they complement each other. You can buy or make yarn pegs or twists of your favorite yarns so that you always have a 'real' palette to play with, then you can have fun arranging these into different groups of colors until you find the right combination. You can even play with different amounts of yarn so that you can experiment with stripes and proportions. A bold or dark shade can be too overwhelming in large quantities, but a small amount of it throughout your project might be just what the piece needs.

COLOR PROPORTIONS

Once you have decided your colors work harmoniously, you have a few options:

1. Freely pick up whatever color you fancy as you go.
2. Select a few colors to use less frequently; for example, use a mainly subdued palette with a few pops of a brighter tone, perhaps in the smaller, center rounds.
3. Use whatever color palette you like, but achieve harmony by making every last round of each block the same color and join the blocks with a neutral tone.

BLANKETS

A blanket is more or less the simplest project you can create with your granny squares, so I've included four projects that you can follow (pages 260–271), along with some general hints and inspirational tips for making up your own wonderful designs... Exact gauge (tension) is not needed for any of the blanket patterns.

GRANNY SQUARE ARRANGEMENT TIPS

1. Play with different arrangements. A random, patchwork-style blanket can look fabulous but, if you leave it entirely to fate, you might end up with color pooling in some areas, or too many similar squares together, which could look unbalanced.
2. Make patterns by placing certain squares next to each other. In the Bright Granny Blanket on pages 266–268, some squares are arranged in groups of four matching or similar squares to create the illusion of bigger squares, which draws the eye around the finished piece. Some of the more geometric squares, such as those that include triangles, can be arranged by matching like colors to like, therefore making the blocks of color seem larger or even turn into different shapes – a small triangle might turn into a large square or diamond.
3. Mix plain granny squares with the floral squares if you want to create a more sedate design. In the Granny Flowers Blanket on pages 269–271, a neutral cream shade has been used for the plain squares to tie all of the colors and patterns together in harmony, and as a foil to make the many hues pop.
4. Create a checkerboard pattern by interchanging two squares all over: a simple square and a more fussy one, perhaps.
5. Duplicate only one square all over. Depending on how you orient the blocks, a triangle might turn into a sawtooth or harlequin pattern, or even a check. Each square could be arranged to make stripes or zigzags of color – the mitered squares are very striking when alternated and worked in zigzags for instance.
6. Place the same block or group of blocks in each corner of the blanket or make a frame with one square repeated all around the edge.

The most important thing is to have fun and create a design that makes you smile!

1

RAINBOW ZIGZAG BLANKET

Use a simple Mitered granny square (see pages 74–75) to create this fabulously colorful blanket. You can follow the zigzag design in bright shades as here, or switch it up for a different look using pastel shades and an alternative granny square design (see pages 264–265).

YARN & HOOK

Scheepjes Merino Soft: light worsted (8-ply/DK) 115yd/105m/1¾oz/50g (50% merino, 25% microfiber, 25% acrylic)

Yarn A: violet (Carney 636) x 1 ball

Yarn B: turquoise (Botticelli 628) x 2 balls

Yarn C: spring green (Constable 629) x 3 balls

Yarn D: bright yellow (Dürer 644) x 2 balls

Yarn E: orange (Munch 620) x 2 balls

Yarn F: bright pink (Matisse 635) x 3 balls

Note: I used Yarn C for the edging and Yarn F for joining blocks.

4mm (US G/6, UK 8) hook

MEASUREMENTS

Motif: 4 x 4in (10 x 10cm)

Blanket: 41 x 41in (104 x 104cm)

PATTERN NOTES

3 ch at beg of row counts as 1 dc throughout.

Row 1 of the Mitered motif is joined into a round, but after that the piece is not worked in rounds but in unturned rows, with each new color added at the beginning of the last unturned row.

PATTERN

Mitered motif (see pages 74–75).

Make 100.

JOINING THE SQUARES

Block all squares neatly to shape.

Arrange your squares as in the sample shown below to create zigzags, with 10 squares across and 10 squares high. You will slip stitch join all the squares together using Yarn F.

Begin from the top right square, and join in diagonal rows, along the zigzag. This helps you to make sure that the blocks are turned the right way each time, ensuring that the pattern remains correct.

Arrange adjoining pieces with right sides facing each other, as if you were to sew them together, then attach yarn to the right-hand end of the edge to be joined and work a row of sl sts all along the edge, through both motifs at the same time.

To work a slip stitch, insert hook into first set of adjoining stitches from front and back pieces. When working along an edge with the top of the stitches facing, then just take the outside loops of the stitch (the ones that do not touch). If working along the side of a stitch, take the adjoining loops from the stitch as close to the edge as possible and as neatly as possible. Now work a yarn over hook and draw through all the loops on your hook to complete a slip stitch.

Repeat along the zigzag seam, working into every set of stitches evenly.

Work along one side of the first block, joining to the first motif next to it along that side, then turn the corner and join the next of two blocks that join to the first corner motif along the next side.

Repeat this throughout the blanket, working in diagonal rows, joining the motifs with a zigzag line of slip stitch crochet.

The slip stitch seam will be visible on the reverse of the work but should be almost impossible to see on the front.

EDGING

Join yarn C with a slip stitch to any corner space.

Edging Rnd: 3 ch, (2 dc, 3 ch, 2 dc) in same space, * 1 ch, (3 dc, 1 ch) in each ch sp along edge to next corner of blanket, (3 dc, 3 ch, 3 dc) in next corner space; rep from * twice more, 1 ch, (3 dc, 1 ch) in each ch sp to end of round, join round with sl st in top of first 3 ch.

Fasten off yarn and weave in all ends neatly.

Block the blanket lightly to shape.

Here you can see how the repeating pattern is constructed across the blanket.

2

PASTEL ZIGZAG BLANKET

By simply swapping the design and color palette, you can create a completely different look! For this sugar-sweet variation, use 100 Mitered Solid granny squares (see pages 76–77) in pastel shades (the measurements and joining instructions are the same as on pages 260–263).

YARN & HOOK

Scheepjes Merino Soft: light worsted (8-ply/DK) 115yd/105m/1¾oz/50g (50% merino, 25% microfiber, 25% acrylic)

Yarn A: purple (Chagall 655) x 1 ball

Yarn B: light teal (Ernst 653) x 2 balls

Yarn C: lemon (de Goya 648) x 2 balls

Yarn D: green (Constable 629) x 3 balls

Yarn E: peach (Caravaggio 642) x 3 balls

Yarn F: lilac (Monet 639) x 4 balls

Note: I used Yarn D for the edging and Yarn F for joining the blocks.

4mm (US G/6, UK 8) hook

PATTERN NOTES

3 ch at beg of row counts as 1 dc throughout. When working the edging, you will work evenly in double crochet stitches, working across some stitches and some ends of rows. Work 1 dc into top of each regular stitch and 2 dc into the side of each end of row.

EDGING & FINISHING

Join yarn D with a slip stitch to any corner space.

Edging Rnd: 3 ch, (1 dc, 3 ch, 2 dc) in same space, *work in double crochet stitches evenly to next corner space of blanket, ** (2 dc, 3 ch, 2 dc) in next corner space; rep from * around, ending at **, join round with sl st in top of first 3 ch. Fasten off yarn and weave in all ends neatly.

Block the blanket lightly to shape.

Here you can see how the repeating pattern is constructed across the blanket.

3

BRIGHT GRANNY BLANKET

This blanket uses an assortment of squares to create a patchwork effect, with some of the motifs arranged to give the illusion of larger squares, adding extra interest to the final pattern.

MATERIALS

Scheepjes Merino Soft: light worsted (8-ply/DK), 115yd/105m/1¾oz/50g (50% wool, 25% acrylic, 25% microfiber)

Yarn A: violet (Carney 636) x 2 balls

Yarn B: turquoise (Botticelli 628) x 2 balls

Yarn C: green (Constable 629) x 2 balls

Yarn D: yellow (Dürer 644) x 2 balls

Yarn E: orange (Munch 620) x 2 balls

Yarn F: pink (Matisse 635) x 2 balls

Yarn G: purple (Chagall 655) x 1 ball

Yarn H: lilac (Monet 639) x 1 ball

Yarn I: pale pink (Waterhouse 649) x 1 ball

Yarn J: cream (Raphael 602) x 1 ball

Yarn K: lemon (de Goya 648) x 1 ball

Yarn L: peach (Caravaggio 642) x 1 ball

Yarn M: light teal (Ernst 653) x 1 ball

4mm (US G/6, UK 8) hook

MEASUREMENTS

Motif: 4 x 4in (10 x 10cm)

Blanket: approximately 41 x 41in (104 x 104cm)

PATTERN

Make 100 motifs in desired colors.
Alternatively, hook the suggested motifs:

- **Solid Striped** (page 58) x 4 in yarns CFBD
- **Solid** (page 60) x 10 in yarn C
- **Two-Color** (page 62) x 5 in yarns AJ
- **Quartered** (page 68) x 5 in yarns BCEH
- **Half and Half Solid** (page 70) x 8 in yarns EF
- **Mitered** (page 74) x 10 in yarns ABCDEF
- **Block Stitch** (page 84) x 4 in yarns FDACE
- **Lace Holes** (page 86) x 8 in yarn A
- **Circle to Square** (page 88) x 4 in yarns GCIFA
- **Granny Circle to Square** (page 90) x 4 in yarns EFCG
- **Starburst** (page 92) x 4 in yarns DLEF
- **Popcorn Center** (page 100) x 4 in yarns FDCB
- **Popcorn Flower** (page 104) x 4 in yarns EGBD
- **Cluster Flower** (page 110) x 4 in yarns DAEDG
- **Rosette** (page 124) x 4 in yarns BEDF
- **Flower Power** (page 126) x 4 in yarns LHGD
- **Scallop Center** (page 128) x 4 in yarns AMLE
- **Diamond** (page 132) x 2 in yarns DKBCF
- **Popcorn** (page 138) x 4 in yarns GBDE
- **3D Flower** (page 144) x 4 in yarns DFBC

JOINING SQUARES

Block all squares neatly to shape.

Join all of the 100 squares together in a 10 x 10 grid using a slip stitch join. Use whichever colors you have left to join. You can follow the same arrangement as me (see page 266) or make up your own.

Arrange adjoining motifs with right sides facing each other, as if you were to sew them together, then attach yarn to the right-hand end of the edge to be joined and work a row of sl sts all along the edge, through both motifs at the same time (see page 48).

Repeat along the join, working into every set of stitches evenly.

When joining, work in straight seams, joining the first two rows of ten motifs along the horizontal seam in one long seam, then when they are secured, join the next row of ten and so on until all 100 are joined.

Now close the remaining 9 vertical seams in 9 long seams to reduce the amount of tail ends.

EDGING

Join yarn D with a slip stitch to any corner space.

Edging Rnd: 3 ch, (1 dc, 3 ch, 2 dc) in same space, * work in double crochet stitches evenly to next corner space of blanket, ** (2 dc, 3 ch, 2 dc) in next corner space; rep from * around, ending at **, join round with sl st in top of first 3 ch.

Fasten off yarn and weave in all ends neatly.

Block the blanket lightly to shape.

4

GRANNY FLOWERS BLANKET

This blanket uses squares 51–100 plus square 2, a regular plain granny, to create a blooming beautiful blanket!

MATERIALS

Scheepjes Merino Soft: light worsted (8-ply/DK) 115yd/105m/1¾oz/50g (50% merino, 25% microfiber, 25% acrylic)

Yarn A: cream (Raphael 602) x 8 balls

Yarn B: spring green (Constable 629) x 1 ball

Yarn C: moss green (Manet 627) x 1 ball

Yarn D: purple (Hockney 638) x 1 ball

Yarn E: lilac (Copley 634) x 1 ball

Yarn F: burgundy (Modigliani 652) x 1 ball

Yarn G: bright red (Picasso 621) x 1 ball

Yarn H: pale pink (Titian 647) x 1 ball

Yarn I: coral pink (Degas 632) x 1 ball

Yarn J: peach (Caravaggio 642) x 1 ball

Yarn K: orange (van Eyck 645) x 1 ball

Yarn L: bright yellow (Dürer 644) x 1 ball

Yarn M: turquoise (Botticelli 628) x 1 ball

Yarn N: mid-blue (Vermeer 612) x 1 ball

Yarn O: violet (Carney 636) x 1 ball

4mm (US G/6, UK 8) hook

MEASUREMENTS

Motif: 4½ x 4½in (11.5 x 11.5cm)

Blanket: approximately 45¼ x 45¼in (115 x 115cm)

PATTERN NOTES

Work one each of motifs 51–100 (pages 154–253).

You will join these motifs as-you-go to 50 Single Color squares, as shown in the pattern on page 270. Arrange each motif so that you have alternate floral and plain squares as shown in the picture.

PATTERN

Make 50 floral motifs in your chosen colors – finish these squares completely and block them.

Make only one Single Color granny square (page 56) in Yarn A, but hook it with an extra round – so that it has 5 rounds in total. This is the only plain square you need to make now. You will make the remaining 49 Single Color squares as you join the blanket together.

Joining as you go

To join each of the floral squares to the plain squares, you will need to work one extra round in Yarn A around each floral square, joining the square to the motif(s) before it as you go. To do this, see the instructions below, depending on what type of motif you are working with. Follow my layout (shown right) if you like, or choose your own arrangement.

For joining a floral motif with a regular granny last round:

Join Yarn A to any corner space, then simply work an extra granny round, joining to the square(s) before as in the join-as-you-go instructions (see pages 49–50).

For joining a floral motif with a solid last round:

Join Yarn A to any corner space, then simply work an extra granny round, placing your three double crochet groups by missing 3 dc and placing 3 dc into the next st all across the side.

At the same time, join to the square(s) before as for the regular granny join-as-you-go method (see pages 49–50).

For the plain squares:

Make a Single Color granny square (page 56) to round 4 but do not fasten off. Work one further round on this square in Yarn A, joining to the square(s) before as per the join-as-you-go instructions.

Weave in all ends neatly.

Block the blanket lightly to shape.

5

GEUM PILLOW

Use a pretty floral motif to decorate a plain cushion cover – if you prefer a different flower, just swap in a different granny-square design.

MATERIALS

Scheepjes Merino Soft: light worsted (8-ply/DK) 115yd/105m/1¾oz/50g (50% merino, 25% microfiber, 25% acrylic)

Yarn A: turquoise (Botticelli 628) x 1 ball

Yarn B: bright yellow (Dürer 644) x 1 ball

Yarn C: peach (Caravaggio 642) x 1 ball

Yarn D: spring green (Constable 629) x 1 ball

Yarn E: lilac (Copley 634) x 2 balls

4mm (US G/6, UK 8) hook

Pillow cover and pad, 15¾ x 15¾in (40 x 40cm) – I chose a pillow cover in a color to blend in with the crochet colors

GAUGE (TENSION)

Exact gauge is not essential for this design.

MEASUREMENTS

Motif: 4 x 4in (10 x 10cm)

Pillow: 15¾ x 15¾in (40 x 40cm)

PATTERN NOTES

3 ch at beg of row counts as 1 dc throughout.

PATTERN

Geum motif (see pages 158–159): make 16.

JOINING SQUARES

Block all squares neatly to shape.

With yarn E, slip stitch to join all the squares together in a four by four square as follows:

Arrange adjoining pieces with right sides facing each other, as if you were to sew them together, then attach yarn to the right-hand end of the edge to be joined and work a row of sl sts all along the edge, through both motifs at the same time (see page 48).

Repeat along entire seam.

The slip stitch seam will be visible on the reverse of the work but should be almost invisible from the front.

EDGING THE PILLOW

Once all squares are joined neatly, join yarn E with a slip stitch to any corner space.

Edging Rnd: 3 ch, (2 dc, 3 ch, 3 dc) in same space, * 1 ch, (3 dc, 1 ch) in each space along edge to next corner, (3 dc, 3 ch, 3 dc) in next corner space; rep from * twice more, 1 ch, (3 dc, 1 ch) in each space to end of round, join round with sl st in top of first 3 ch.

Fasten off yarn and weave in all ends neatly.

Block the pillow piece lightly to shape.

Stitch neatly to the front of the pillow cover using a coordinating sewing thread.

6

SCARF

In this bright, bold project I used a super bulky wool and a 10mm hook to create a striking, snuggly scarf that will work up in a flash. As the motifs turn out so large, you only need to join them one square wide to create a substantial and head-turning scarf.

MATERIALS

Any bulky to super bulky weight yarn will work here to recreate this project. Or play with the weight to make a scarf of differing size. I used: Rowan Big Wool: super bulky (super chunky) 87yd/80m/3½oz/100g (100% wool)

Yarn A: denim blue (Steel Blue 052) x 1 ball

Yarn B: orange-yellow (Yoke 078) x 1 ball

Yarn C: fuchsia (Pantomime 079) x 1 ball

Yarn D: red-pink (Cerise 089) x 1 ball

Yarn E: lime green (Citron 091) x 1 ball

Yarn F: mid-green (Midori 093) x 1 ball

Yarn G: peach (Melon 094) x 1 ball

Yarn H: baby pink (Nougat 095) x 1 ball

Yarn I: cream (Linen 048) x 1 ball

10mm (US N/15, UK 000) hook

You will also need small amounts of yarn for joining your squares: you can use the same bulky yarn used to make the scarf, but it can be hard to sew with. Therefore, I used a finer weight yarn in matching colors to sew the motifs together. Choose something similar in make up (fiber content) to the bulky yarn you use, but keep the weight of the yarn to light worsted (DK/8-ply) or worsted (aran/10-ply) weight so that it is easier to use and the stitches will be less visible.

GAUGE (TENSION)

Exact gauge is not essential for this design.

MEASUREMENTS

Motif: approximately 8¾ x 8¾in (22 x 22cm)

Scarf: approximately 89 x 11in (226 x 28cm)

EXTRA SKILLS NEEDED

Invisible sewn join (see page 278).

PATTERN

Make one of each of the following motifs, using the yarn shades given here, or using your own palette:

- **Traditional** (page 54) in yarns FBDG.
- **Quartered** (page 68) in yarns DHEG.
- **Mixed** (page 82) in yarns AGFC.
- **Block Stitch** (page 84) in yarns GFBCH.
- **Circle to Square** (page 88) in yarns CEHBF.
- **Granny Star Circle** (page 106) in yarns FGDA.
- **In A Muddle** (page 114) in yarns DAHB.
- **Rudbeckia** (page 160) in yarns BCHE (I used an additional color for round 3).
- **Gerbera** (page 164) in yarns EFGC.
- **Geranium** (page 180) in yarns EHBD.

FINISHING THE SQUARES

Weave in all ends and block lightly to shape.

JOINING THE SQUARES

To sew the motifs together, use an invisible seam, much like a mattress stitch in knitting.

Place the pieces next to each other with RS facing upwards. Using a blunt tapestry needle, attach the yarn to one of the motifs at the end of the seam, starting at the center of a corner.

Insert the needle down into the center corner in the middle of the stitch, between the two loops, then take up one stitch, coming back up again in the middle of the next st. Repeat this action in the corresponding stitch on the other motif.

Now insert the needle back into the stitch you exited from on the first motif, down into the middle of the stitch then back and up out of the middle of the next stitch, then repeat this on the adjoining motif. Continue in the same way along the entire seam.

Fasten off neatly.

EDGING THE SCARF

Using your hook, attach Yarn I to any corner of the scarf.

Edging rnd: 3 ch, (1 dc, 2 ch, 2 dc) in same corner sp, * then work evenly in double crochet stitches all down the side of the scarf to the next corner, work (2 dc, 2 ch, 2 dc) in next corner, then rep from * twice more, work evenly in dc to end of round, join rnd with sl st to top of first 3 ch.

Note: as a general rule, try to put roughly 15 dc across the side of each square to avoid ruffling up the edges and to ensure you have enough yarn to complete the edge with one ball of yarn.

Fasten off the yarn and weave in all remaining ends.

7

CARDIGAN

I have chosen some of the most flowery squares for this pastel confection of a cardigan, so that it almost feels like wearing a bouquet of flowers! However, it would look just as striking in bright, bold shades and some of the more two-dimensional squares.

MATERIALS

Any DK (8-ply/light worsted) weight yarn will substitute here to create a similar top. You could try other fibres too. I used: Cascade 220 Superwash: (8-ply/light worsted) 219yd/200m/3½oz/100g (100% wool)

Yarn A: cream (Ecru/Aran 817) x 2 (2, 3, 3, 4, 4) balls

Yarn B: lilac (Iris 840) x 2 (2, 2, 2, 3, 3) balls

Yarn C: pale green (Laurel Green 250) x 2 (2, 2, 2, 3, 3) balls

Yarn D: salmon pink (Salmon 1941) x 2 balls

Yarn E: pale yellow (Yellow 824) x 2 balls

Yarn F: blue (Caribbean 847) x 1 ball

Yarn G: mid-green (Green Spruce 288) x 1 ball

4mm (US G/6, UK 8) hook

GAUGE (TENSION)

Each square measures 4 x 4in (10 x 10cm)

MEASUREMENTS

This top is designed to be worn with a positive ease, meaning that it shouldn't be tight, but you can adapt the fit to suit your style. It is designed to be a short summer cardigan, so check the length measurements in the box below and, if you wish, add an extra row of squares to the bottom edge or make a deeper bottom edging.

PATTERN NOTES

3 ch at beg of row counts as 1 dc throughout.

There are six sizes to choose from, with suggested ease given, but you can wear with whatever fit you wish.
The model is wearing size XS.

	XS	S	M	L	XL	XXL
To fit bust	33½–37½in 85–95cm	38–41½in 97–105cm	41¾–45¼in 106–115cm	45½–49¼in 116–124cm	49½–53¼in 125–135cm	54–59in 137–150cm
Actual bust	41in (104cm)	44in (112cm)	47¼in (120cm)	50½in (128cm)	56¾in (144cm)	60in (152cm)
Length	16½in (41.5cm)	16½in (41.5cm)	17½in (44cm)	17¾in (45cm)	18½in (46.5cm)	18¾in (47.5cm)

PATTERN

Make 60 (60, 60, 60, 76, 76) assorted motifs in an assortment of the shades as shown, or in your own colorway. I used five of each of the following squares for sizes XS to L; for sizes XL and XXL, I used six of each granny design plus six extras:

- **Granny Circle to Square** (page 90) in yarns EDCB.
- **Granny Star Circle** (page 106) in yarns FEDC.
- **Petals** (page 108) in yarns FEBGD.
- **Scallop Center** (page 128) in yarns FDAC.
- **Medallion** (page 142) in yarns FCBEA.
- **Dianthus** (page 170) in yarns CBFED.
- **Camellia** (page 174) in yarns EGBGDC.
- **Forget-Me-Not** (page 200) in yarns EFCD.
- **Daisy** (page 212) in yarns EBA.
- **Buttercup** (page 222) in yarns FCADEB – I worked the four buttercups in different colors.
- **Tea Rose** (page 230) in yarns GEFA.
- **Azalea** (page 236) in yarns DGCB.

FRONT AND BACK

Arrange the squares for the front and back of the body. For the back, lay out one 5 wide x 4 tall panel for sizes XS, S, M and L, or one 7 wide x 4 tall panel for sizes XL and XXL.

For the front, lay out two 2 wide x 4 tall panels for the front pieces of sizes XS, S, M and L; lay out two 3 wide x 4 tall panels for sizes XL and XXL.

Join the squares together, using slip stitch joined through the outside loops (see page 48 for join). Join the front and back pieces together at the shoulder seams using slip stitch.

SLEEVES

Arrange 12 squares for each of the sleeves in a 4 x 3 grid (the sleeves are 3 squares long and 4 squares in circumference); join using slip stitch.

For sizes XS and S, use sleeves as they are without the following edging.

For all other sizes, work along each short (3-square) edge as follows:

Using your hook and with RS facing, join Yarn A to one corner of a short (3-square) edge.

Row 1: 3 ch, work evenly in double crochet across edge, turn.

Size M fasten off yarn.

All other sizes:

Row 2: 3 ch, 1 dc in each st across, turn.

Rep row 2 a further - (-, -, 1, 2, 3) times (or work number of rows to create the desired circumference of sleeves).

Fasten off yarn.

Rep along each short edge of the other sleeve piece.

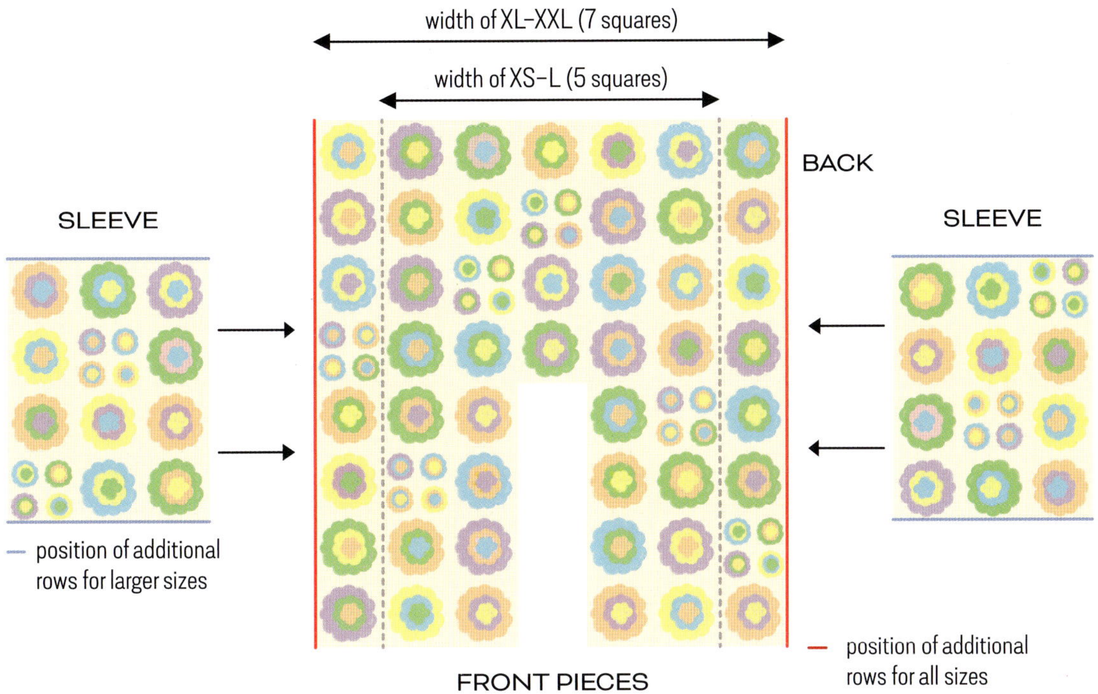

SIDES

Using your hook and with RS facing, join Yarn A to bottom corner of side edge.

Row 1: 3 ch, work evenly in dc across the entire side edge of the joined front and back pieces, turn.

Size XS and XL fasten off yarn.

All other sizes:

Row 2: 3 ch, 1 dc in each st across, turn.

Rep row 2 a further - (1, 3, 5, -, 1) times.

Fasten off yarn.

Rep on other side.

ATTACHING THE SLEEVES

Lay the joined front and back pieces out flat in front of you. Position the sleeve pieces so that the central seams align with the shoulder seams. Pin or clip in place. Using your hook and with RS facing, join sleeve to body with a slip stitch seam through outside loops as worked before to join the motifs.

Fold the cardigan and sleeves RS together, then pin or clip the underarm and side edges.

Now complete the side seam and underarm in one long seam using a sl st join.

Repeat for the other side/sleeve.

CUFFS

Using your hook and with RS facing, attach yarn A to any stitch around the cuff edge. If you wish to make your sleeves slightly longer before you make the cuffs, you can add a round or rounds of trebles evenly around the edge here before working round 1.

Round 1: 3 ch, inserting hook into each stitch, chain space and join around, work dc2tog all around edge, join round with sl st to top of first 3 ch.

Round 2: 3 ch, (1 RdcF, 1 RdcB) around, join rnd with sl st to top of first 3 ch.

Fasten off yarn.

NECKLINE

Using your hook and with RS facing, join Yarn A to bottom of the right-front edge if right-handed or bottom of left-front edge if left-handed.

Row 1: 3 ch, work evenly in dc up the front edge, to one stitch before the turn for the neck, dc3tog, inserting in next st, join between squares and following neck edge st, work evenly in dc across neck to one stitch before turn for opposite front, dc3tog, inserting hook as before, then work evenly in dc down remaining front edge. Make sure when working the edge that there are not too many or too few stitches, to avoid a ruffled edge. Fasten off Yarn A, do NOT turn work.

Attach Yarn B back at the beginning of the row.

Row 2: 3 ch, 1 dc in each st across edge, Fasten off Yarn B, do NOT turn work.

Attach Yarn C back at the beginning of the row.

Row 3: 3 ch, 1 dc in each st across edge, Fasten off Yarn C.

BOTTOM EDGING

Using your hook and with RS facing, join Yarn A to bottom edge of the cardigan at corner of left front if right-handed or right front if left-handed.

Row 1: 3 ch, work evenly in dc across the bottom edge.

Size XS and S fasten off yarn.

All other sizes:

Row 2: 3 ch, 1 dc in each st across, turn.

Rep row 2 a further - (-, 1, 2, 3, 4) times.

Fasten off yarn.

Weave in all ends and block lightly to shape.

8

GRANNY BAG

You only need a few squares joined together to make a really simple yet elegant clutch bag or purse. This project uses a chunky purse frame to really make a statement but you could simply add a zip or magnetic snap to the top of the bag and attach the strap to the bag itself.

MATERIALS

Any sport (4-ply) to lightweight light worsted (DK/8-ply) yarn will work here. I used: Rico Creative Ricorumi light worsted (DK/8-ply) 62yd/57m/¾oz/25g (100% cotton)

Yarn A: pink (Smokey Rose 010) x 1 ball

Yarn B: pale peach (Peach 023) x 1 ball

Yarn C: mustard yellow (Mustard 064) x 1 ball

Yarn D: purple (Lavender 072) x 1 ball

Yarn E: blue (Aqua 074) x 1 ball

Yarn F: pale grey (Reed 075) x 1 ball

Yarn G: green (Pea 077) x 1 ball

3mm (US C/2 or D/3, UK 11) hook

Bag frame: 4 x 8in (10 x 20cm)

Fabric lining: 23½ x 18in (60 x 46cm)

GAUGE (TENSION)

Exact gauge is not essential for this design.

MEASUREMENTS

Motif: 3½ x 3½in (8.5 x 8.5cm)

Approximately 11in tall x 8¼in wide (28 x 21cm)

PATTERN

Make 12 assorted motifs in an assortment of the shades as shown, or in your own colorway.

Make one of each of the following squares:

- **Popcorn Daisy** (page 102) in yarns CBFE.
- **Popcorn Flower** (page 104) in yarns ABEG.
- **Flower Power** (page 126) in yarns BDAC.
- **Rudbeckia** (page 160) in yarns AGD.
- **Mallow** (page 162) in yarns FCEGD.
- **Chamomile** (page 166) in yarns ADG.
- **Fleabane** (page 168) in yarns CAE.
- **Coreopsis** (page 178) in yarns BADCE.
- **Peony** (page 184) in yarns EBAG.
- **Cosmos** (page 226) in yarns BEC.

Make two:

- **Calendula** (page 154) in yarns BFC and EAG.

Make twelve:

- **Traditional** granny squares (page 54) using whatever shades you have left; fasten off after working round 2.

FINISHING

Join the 12 large motifs together into two blocks of six squares, in the layout of 2 x 3 squares. Use a slip stitch through outside loops to join them (see below and page 48).

Arrange adjoining motifs with right sides facing each other, as if you were to sew them together, then attach yarn to the right-hand end of the edge to be joined and work a row of sl sts all along the edge, through both motifs at the same time.

Repeat along the join, working into every set of stitches evenly.

Now join the 12 small motifs into one long strip using the same slip stitch joining method. (This will be the bag gusset.)

Once these three pieces are complete, lay them onto the fabric and cut out the pieces for the lining fabric: cut each piece (front, back and gusset) using your crocheted pieces as your patterns but adding a ¼in (5mm) seam allowance all round.

Join the crochet pieces together with a slip stitch join, with one of the blocks made from six squares as the front of the bag, one as the back, and the long strip as the bottom and sides of the bag (the gusset). The strip won't quite make it up to the top on each side, but make sure that it comes up to the same height on each side. Weave in all the ends and block neatly to shape.

Press under ¼in (5mm) hems along the short ends of the fabric gusset strip. Fold the gusset strip in half to find the center of the strip and finger crease to mark it. Fold the front and back bag lining pieces lengthwise and finger press the crease at the bottom end of each one as well. Matching the crease on the gusset and bag front lining pieces, pin the gusset lining to the front lining, RS together. Compare this to the crocheted bag to check the fit. You can make the hems at the ends of the gusset deeper if needed for a good fit. Sew the gusset lining to the front lining, taking a ¼in (5mm) seam allowance. Attach the gusset lining to the back lining in the same way. Tuck the bag lining into the bag, WS together. Depending on whether you are using a bag frame or not, you may wish to turn the top seam allowance of the lining to the inside, pin in place.

Fit the finished bag into a bag frame, or add in a zip to the top of the bag to finish. If you wish to use as a clutch bag or pouch, your bag is complete!

Alternatively, add on a bag strap as long as desired by working your desired length of chain, then work as many rows of single crochet into the chain as you wish for the strap. I made a strap 43½in (110cm) long.

First published in 2027

This book uses material previously published as *The Granny Square Card Deck™* and *The Granny Square Flowers Card Deck™*

Search Press Limited
Wellwood, North Farm Road,
Tunbridge Wells, Kent TN2 3DR

1 2 3 4 5 6 7 8 9 10

Photographs by:
Stacy Grant (pages 9, 10–11, 15, 17, 19, 51, 254–255, 257, 258, 261, 263, 265, 267, 271, 273, 275, 277, 279, 285, 287)
Leanne Jade (pages 281–282)
All other photographs by Mark Davison

Crochet chart illustrations by Sean Miles
Stitch illustrations by Bess Harding

ISBN: 978-1-80092-483-3
ebook ISBN: 978-1-80093-416-0

US crochet terms are used throughout this book. For a US to UK conversion chart please refer to pages 30–31 and the fold-out flaps.

For errata, please visit the Search Press website (www.searchpress.com) or the Bookmarked Hub (www.bookmarkedhub.com).

GPSR information can be found at www.searchpress.com

Printed in China, TT062026

Find Claire Montgomerie:

- online at www.clairemontgomerie.com
- on Instagram via @clairemontgomerie

MIX
Paper | Supporting responsible forestry
FSC® C016973

Acknowledgments

Working on the *Granny Square Card Decks* these past few years has been an utter pleasure and there are so many wonderful people that, without whom, writing them wouldn't have been possible. Firstly, a huge thank you to all the wonderful team at Search Press who trusted me with writing the decks and designed such beautiful products, with special thanks to my incredible and ever patient editor Becky Robbins.

Thanks, of course, to all my amazing hook wielding friends, Jenny M, Jenny S and Lilly at The Wool Gallery who helped with the crocheting of seemingly endless motifs. (Thanks too for all the crochet evenings in the pub!) To my mum, Mary, for hooking hundreds of squares for me over the years and for introducing me to crochet in the first place. The decks would just not be the same without the painstaking illustration of numerous crochet charts, so thank you to Sean for translating my terrible scribbles and vague descriptions into handsome and, crucially, legible charts.

Thank you to Cascade Yarns (www.cascadeyarns.com), Rowan Yarns (knitrowan.com) and Scheepjes (www.scheepjes.com) for providing such glorious yarns for me to play with.

Finally, I am so grateful to all the readers and crochet card deck enthusiasts from all over the world. I love to see how you have used the decks as a crochet tool so please don't forget to let me know what you make!